MAXIMIZE YOUR READING

3

Maximize Your Reading 3

Copyright © 2017 by Pearson Education, Inc.

Pearson Education, Inc., 221 River Street, Hoboken, NJ 07030 USA

Staff credits: The people who made up the *Maximize Your Reading* team are Pietro Alongi, Rhea Banker, Tracey Munz Cataldo, Mindy DePalma, Gina DiLillo, Niki Lee, Amy McCormick, Lindsay Richman, and Paula Van Ells.

Text composition: MPS North America LLC

Design: EMC Design Ltd

Photo credits: Cover: Moodboard/Getty Images. Page 16: Studio49/Fotolia; 28: Ihsan Gercelman/Fotolia; 28: Rcaucino/Fotolia; 46: Miguel Garcia Saaved/Fotolia; 47: Fabianohugen/Fotolia.

ISBN-13: 978-0-13-466136-0   ISBN-10: 0-13-466136-2

Printed in the United States of America

3   17

pearsonelt.com/maximizeyourreading

CONTENTS

Reading Level 3 – Intermediate to High Intermediate

PRE-TEST

Part 1 Comprehension Skills

Preview and skim the passage quickly. Then circle the letter of the best answer for each question.

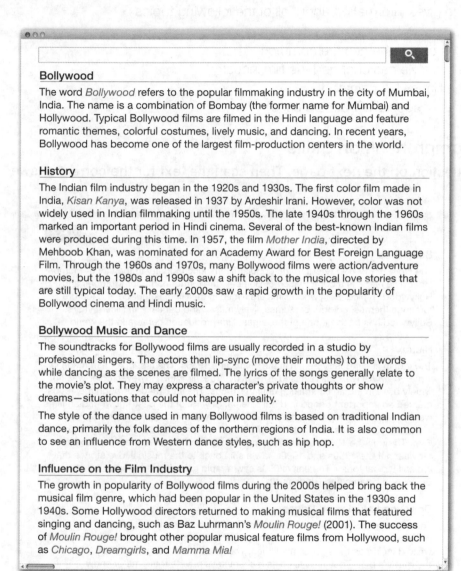

Bollywood

The word *Bollywood* refers to the popular filmmaking industry in the city of Mumbai, India. The name is a combination of Bombay (the former name for Mumbai) and Hollywood. Typical Bollywood films are filmed in the Hindi language and feature romantic themes, colorful costumes, lively music, and dancing. In recent years, Bollywood has become one of the largest film-production centers in the world.

History

The Indian film industry began in the 1920s and 1930s. The first color film made in India, *Kisan Kanya*, was released in 1937 by Ardeshir Irani. However, color was not widely used in Indian filmmaking until the 1950s. The late 1940s through the 1960s marked an important period in Hindi cinema. Several of the best-known Indian films were produced during this time. In 1957, the film *Mother India*, directed by Mehboob Khan, was nominated for an Academy Award for Best Foreign Language Film. Through the 1960s and 1970s, many Bollywood films were action/adventure movies, but the 1980s and 1990s saw a shift back to the musical love stories that are still typical today. The early 2000s saw a rapid growth in the popularity of Bollywood cinema and Hindi music.

Bollywood Music and Dance

The soundtracks for Bollywood films are usually recorded in a studio by professional singers. The actors then lip-sync (move their mouths) to the words while dancing as the scenes are filmed. The lyrics of the songs generally relate to the movie's plot. They may express a character's private thoughts or show dreams—situations that could not happen in reality.

The style of the dance used in many Bollywood films is based on traditional Indian dance, primarily the folk dances of the northern regions of India. It is also common to see an influence from Western dance styles, such as hip hop.

Influence on the Film Industry

The growth in popularity of Bollywood films during the 2000s helped bring back the musical film genre, which had been popular in the United States in the 1930s and 1940s. Some Hollywood directors returned to making musical films that featured singing and dancing, such as Baz Luhrmann's *Moulin Rouge!* (2001). The success of *Moulin Rouge!* brought other popular musical feature films from Hollywood, such as *Chicago*, *Dreamgirls*, and *Mamma Mia!*

---

1 This passage is from _____ .

   a a newspaper article

   b a history textbook

   c an online encyclopedia

   d a business e-mail

2 The author of this passage intends to _____ .

   a inform people about the topic

   b give an opinion about the topic

   c teach people how to do something

   d persuade people to take some action

3 The purpose of this passage is to _____ .

   a compare two different film styles

   b introduce a particular style of film

   c explain the history of music in film

   d list the most popular Indian films

4 This passage gives information about all of the following topics
EXCEPT _____ .

   a what types of plot themes are common

   b how the film style has changed the film industry

   c where the film style originated

   d what types of special effects are used

Part 2   Comprehension Skills

Read each question on the next page. Then scan the text for the correct answer.

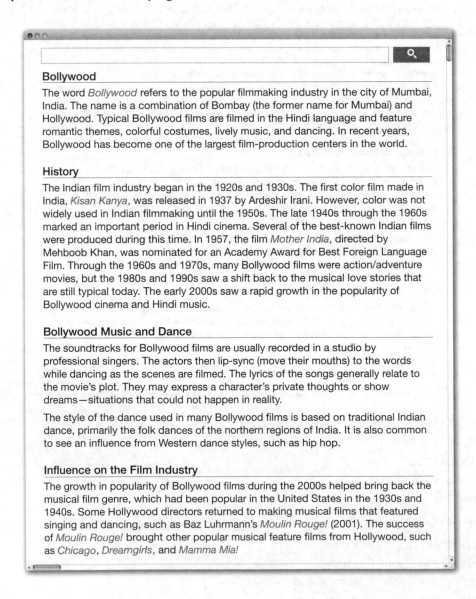

Bollywood

The word *Bollywood* refers to the popular filmmaking industry in the city of Mumbai, India. The name is a combination of Bombay (the former name for Mumbai) and Hollywood. Typical Bollywood films are filmed in the Hindi language and feature romantic themes, colorful costumes, lively music, and dancing. In recent years, Bollywood has become one of the largest film-production centers in the world.

History

The Indian film industry began in the 1920s and 1930s. The first color film made in India, *Kisan Kanya*, was released in 1937 by Ardeshir Irani. However, color was not widely used in Indian filmmaking until the 1950s. The late 1940s through the 1960s marked an important period in Hindi cinema. Several of the best-known Indian films were produced during this time. In 1957, the film *Mother India*, directed by Mehboob Khan, was nominated for an Academy Award for Best Foreign Language Film. Through the 1960s and 1970s, many Bollywood films were action/adventure movies, but the 1980s and 1990s saw a shift back to the musical love stories that are still typical today. The early 2000s saw a rapid growth in the popularity of Bollywood cinema and Hindi music.

Bollywood Music and Dance

The soundtracks for Bollywood films are usually recorded in a studio by professional singers. The actors then lip-sync (move their mouths) to the words while dancing as the scenes are filmed. The lyrics of the songs generally relate to the movie's plot. They may express a character's private thoughts or show dreams—situations that could not happen in reality.

The style of the dance used in many Bollywood films is based on traditional Indian dance, primarily the folk dances of the northern regions of India. It is also common to see an influence from Western dance styles, such as hip hop.

Influence on the Film Industry

The growth in popularity of Bollywood films during the 2000s helped bring back the musical film genre, which had been popular in the United States in the 1930s and 1940s. Some Hollywood directors returned to making musical films that featured singing and dancing, such as Baz Luhrmann's *Moulin Rouge!* (2001). The success of *Moulin Rouge!* brought other popular musical feature films from Hollywood, such as *Chicago*, *Dreamgirls*, and *Mamma Mia!*

1 What are the most common features of Bollywood films?

    a action and adventure

    b traditional music and dancing

    c Western music and hip hop

    d English and Hindi dialogue

2 Which Indian film was nominated for an Academy Award in 1957?

    a Ardeshir Irani

    b *Mother India*

    c Mehboob Khan

    d *Kisan Kanya*

3 What type of Indian films became common in the 1960s and 1970s?

    a color

    b musicals

    c romance

    d action

4 How did Bollywood films influence the U.S. film industry in the 2000s?

    a Hollywood directors began making musicals again.

    b Indian actors began starring in Hollywood films.

    c Hollywood action films started including more romance.

    d Hollywood films began including Hindi dialogue.

Part 3 Comprehension Skills

Read the passage and answer the questions.

HEALTH TODAY

Do you want to eat healthier, more nutritious foods? Would you like to feel better and have more energy? Then add more fermented foods to your diet.

Fermentation is a natural chemical process in which bacteria and yeast feed on the sugars in food. This process creates lactic acid, which makes the food easier to digest, improves its flavor, and increases its nutritional value. It's what gives cheese and yogurt their tart flavor, what makes bread rise, and what turns grapes into wine. Some of the world's healthiest cultures, particularly in Asian countries such as Japan, have diets that are rich in traditional fermented foods. Examples include miso, soy sauce, and rice vinegar. This may be one reason why many people in those countries live so long.

We are usually told that we should avoid bacteria in our food, but fermentation increases the levels of bacteria that are actually beneficial to the body. In addition, fermentation reduces the level of sugar in food, so it can help you maintain a healthy weight. Thus, increasing the amount of fermented food you eat can improve your immunity and make you feel better and live longer.

Fermenting foods is easy and inexpensive to do yourself. You don't have to spend a lot of time in the kitchen or buy expensive equipment. Find out how fermentation can change your life and how easy it can be! Order our 40-hour *Fermentation for Health* course, with 20 how-to videos and 10 e-books full of recipe ideas, nutritional information, and a helpful list of frequently asked questions.

1 What is the topic of this passage?

    a fermentation saves money

    b fermentation procedures

    c the process of fermentation

    d the benefits of fermented foods

2 What is the main idea of the passage?

   a Fermenting your own food can be costly, but the health benefits are worth it.

   b People should make and eat their own fermented foods to improve their health.

   c Buying fermented products in a store is more convenient than making them yourself.

   d People from Asian cultures enjoy the taste of fermented foods more than Westerners do.

3 What can be inferred from the passage?

   a The author has never tried fermented foods.

   b The author is an online business owner.

   c The author thinks fermented food may be dangerous.

   d The author has lived in an Asian country.

Part 4   Comprehension Skills

Read each question. Then scan the text for the answer.

 HEALTH TODAY

Do you want to eat healthier, more nutritious foods? Would you like to feel better and have more energy? Then add more fermented foods to your diet.

Fermentation is a natural chemical process in which bacteria and yeast feed on the sugars in food. This process creates lactic acid, which makes the food easier to digest, improves its flavor, and increases its nutritional value. It's what gives cheese and yogurt their tart flavor, what makes bread rise, and what turns grapes into wine. Some of the world's healthiest cultures, particularly in Asian countries such as Japan, have diets that are rich in traditional fermented foods. Examples include miso, soy sauce, and rice vinegar. This may be one reason why many people in those countries live so long.

We are usually told that we should avoid bacteria in our food, but fermentation increases the levels of bacteria that are actually beneficial to the body. In addition, fermentation reduces the level of sugar in food, so it can help you maintain a healthy weight. Thus, increasing the amount of fermented food you eat can improve your immunity and make you feel better and live longer.

Fermenting foods is easy and inexpensive to do yourself. You don't have to spend a lot of time in the kitchen or buy expensive equipment. Find out how fermentation can change your life and how easy it can be! Order our 40-hour *Fermentation for Health* course, with 20 how-to videos and 10 e-books full of recipe ideas, nutritional information, and a helpful list of frequently asked questions.

1 What happens during the process of fermentation?

   a Bacteria become yeast and sugar.

   b Yeast turns sugar and bacteria into food.

   c Bacteria and yeast feed on sugar in food.

   d Sugar and bacteria feed on yeast.

2 According to the author, which of the following is NOT a result of eating fermented foods?

  a better digestion

  b a longer life

  c greater intelligence

  d a healthy weight

3 How many videos does the course include?

  a 10

  b 20

  c 40

  d 0

Part 5 Comprehension Skills

Read the passage and answer each question.

124

Buck lived at a big house in the sun-kissed Santa Clara Valley. Judge Miller's place, it was called. It stood back from the road, half hidden among the trees, through which glimpses could be caught of the wide cool veranda that ran around its four sides. The house was approached by graveled driveways, which wound about through wide-spreading lawns and under the interlacing boughs of tall poplars.

At the rear, things were on even a more spacious scale than at the front. There were great stables, where a dozen grooms and boys held forth, rows of vine-clad servants' cottages, an endless and orderly array of outhouses, long grape arbors, green pastures, orchards, and berry patches.

And over this great domain Buck ruled. Here he was born, and here he had lived the four years of his life. It was true, there were other dogs. There could not but be other dogs on so vast a place, but they did not count. They came and went, resided in the populous kennels, or lived obscurely in the recesses of the house after the fashion of Toots, the Japanese pug, or Ysabel, the Mexican hairless—strange creatures that rarely put nose out of doors or set foot to ground. On the other hand, there were the fox terriers, a score of them at least, who yelped fearful promises at Toots and Ysabel looking out of the windows at them and protected by a legion of housemaids armed with brooms and mops.

1 The main purpose of this passage is _____ .

  a to explain the location of the Santa Clara Valley

  b to introduce the character of Judge Miller

  c to describe the character of Buck

  d to describe the setting where Buck lives

2 From this passage, we can infer that Buck is Judge Miller's _____ .

    a son

    b neighbor

    c dog

    d servant

3 From this passage, we can infer that Judge Miller is _____ .

    a very wealthy

    b a kind man

    c rarely at home

    d in the hospital

Part 6 Comprehension Skills

Read the paragraph. Then circle the letter of the correct answer.

The Indian film industry began in the 1920s and 1930s. The first color film made in India, *Kisan Kanya*, was released in 1937 by Ardeshir Irani. However, color was not widely used in Indian filmmaking until the 1950s. The late 1940s through the 1960s marked an important period in Hindi cinema. Several of the best-known Indian films were produced during this time. In 1957, the film *Mother India*, directed by Mehboob Khan, was nominated for an Academy Award for Best Foreign Language Film. Through the 1960s and 1970s, many Bollywood films were action/adventure movies, but the 1980s and 1990s saw a shift back to the musical love stories that are still typical today. The early 2000s saw a rapid growth in the popularity of Bollywood cinema and Hindi music.

1 This paragraph describes _____ .

    a the steps in a process

    b a sequence of events over time

    c a comparison between two people or things

    d different causes and effects

Part 7 Comprehension Skills

Read the paragraph. Then circle the letter of the correct answer.

Although Tom Fredrickson and Carol Newman agree on some issues, the two candidates running for mayor of Springfield differ in a number of key areas. First, Fredrickson has been called the "green candidate" and has said he plans to assemble a committee of citizen volunteers to research ways the city can use energy more efficiently. He has also proposed spending $1,000,000 on a new transportation center designed to encourage greater use of the city's public transportation system. On the other hand, Carol Newman has focused more on education reform. She says she wants to renovate and modernize the city's high school, which was built more than forty years ago. Her proposed project would cost about $500,000. Fredrickson and Newman agree that property taxes should be lowered. However, Newman would like to impose a higher fee on cars traveling on Highway 97. Fredrickson has not proposed raising any taxes so far. The main point of disagreement between the two candidates is the idea of installing cameras on the city's street corners. Although Fredrickson says that the cameras will save money because the city will need fewer police officers, Newman opposes the idea because she says the cameras and their maintenance will cost just as much as—or more than—hiring a few more officers.

1 This paragraph describes _____ .
- **a** the steps in a process
- **b** a sequence of events over time
- **c** a comparison between two people or things
- **d** different causes and effects

Part 8   Comprehension Skills
Read the paragraph. Then circle the letter of the correct answer.

Fermentation is a natural chemical process in which bacteria and yeast feed on the sugars in food. This process creates lactic acid, which makes the food easier to digest, improves its flavor, and increases its nutritional value. It's what gives cheese and yogurt their tart flavor, what makes bread rise, and what turns grapes into wine. Some of the world's healthiest cultures, particularly in Asian countries such as Japan, have diets that are rich in traditional fermented foods. Examples include miso, soy sauce, and rice vinegar. This may be one reason why many people in those countries live so long.

1 This paragraph describes _____ .
- **a** the steps in a process
- **b** a sequence of events over time
- **c** a comparison between two people or things
- **d** different causes and effects

Part 9   Vocabulary Building
Read the list of words. Then answer the question.

disqualified	insincere	irregular	misunderstand
imperfect	illegal	nonfat	unpopular

1 What is the meaning of the prefix in each word?
- **a** out
- **b** very
- **c** not
- **d** around

joy	care	respect
hope	cheer	faith

2 Which suffix can be added to each word to make it an adjective?
- **a** able
- **b** ful
- **c** ly
- **d** ous

Part 10   Vocabulary Building

Circle the letter of the word form that correctly completes each sentence.

1 There are some very _____ homes in this neighborhood.
  a attraction
  b attractive

2 If you want to get a good job, you need to stop being so _____ .
  a irresponsible
  b responsibility

3 This has been a very _____ day. I finished all of the tasks on my list.
  a productive
  b productively

Part 11   Vocabulary Building

Read the text with the missing words. Then answer the questions.

By Elaine Sanderson, *Boston Globe*
April 9, 2014

_____

Home Again is Beth Naven's new ████████ that takes place in a small town in rural Vermont. The ████████ is a creepy ████████ about two ████████ searching for answers about their family's dark and ████████ past. *Home Again* isn't quite as spine-chilling as Naven's first novel, *Blackbird*, but it's nearly as scary because of the strange, dark atmosphere she creates with her rich descriptions of the ████████.

Naven ████████ about the innermost feelings of the ████████, allowing the ████████ to look into their hearts and truly feel their fear.

The ████████ tells the story of the Davis ████████, Marie and Dahlia. Marie, a ████████ who lives in Los Angeles, has just learned that she has ████████. After her first round of treatment, her doctor recommends that she go home to Vermont, to ████████ and spend time with family.

Her older ████████, Dahlia, who moved back to Vermont several years before, now lives alone in the large old ████████ family farmhouse. When Marie arrives, the two begin sharing ████████ from their dark past. Family secrets ████████, and the two ████████ that they must find answers—answers they aren't sure they want to know. Their journey ends when they ████████ something they shouldn't have.

1 What type of text is this?
  a a movie review
  b a course review
  c a book review
  d a research review

2 What type of story is *Home Again*?
  a romance
  b horror
  c historical fiction
  d biography

3 Who are the main characters of the story?

   a sisters

   b mother and daughter

   c friends

   d teacher and student

4 What does the term *spine-chilling* mean in the first paragraph?

   a boring

   b painful

   c confusing

   d frightening

Part 12 Vocabulary Building

Circle the letter of the preposition that correctly completes each sentence.

1 You're very tall. Do you take _____ your father or your mother?

   a. over   **b.** after

2 Please check your papers carefully before handing them _____ .

   a. in   **b.** on

3 You won't have a chance to do the project _____ , so please do a good job the first time.

   a. over   **b.** out

4 Once you've become accustomed to having a smartphone, it's very difficult to do _____ one.

   a. with   **b.** without

Part 13 Vocabulary Building

Underline the subject of a sentence.

1 My English professor has traveled all over the world.

Part 14 Vocabulary Building

Underline the verb in the sentence.

1 Emily and Steven have been living in Costa Rica for seven years.

Part 15 Vocabulary Building

Circle the letter of the correct signal word or phrase to complete the sentence.

1 Stephen would like to study Japanese; _____ , he is already busy studying Russian and Spanish.

   a also

   b finally

   c in addition

   d however

2 We'll need to invite all of the members of the Smith family, _____ their husbands, wives, and children, to the wedding.

   a as well as

   b therefore

   c although

   d however

3 There are many reasons why the company should expand overseas. _____ , our largest competitor just opened an office in Beijing.

    a As a result

    b First

    c Moreover

    d Finally

Part 16   Vocabulary Building

Circle the letter of the word that correctly completes the sentence.

1 Many people don't take full advantage of _____ health insurance plans.

    a their

    b they

    c them

    d there

2 That building looks dangerous. Half of _____ windows are broken.

    a its

    b it

    c it's

    d its'

3 Don't worry about giving _____ a ride to the game tonight. We'll take our own car.

    a our

    b us

    c we

    d ours

4 Something about that man makes me uncomfortable. I don't trust _____ .

    a her

    b his

    c he

    d him

Part 17   Vocabulary Building

Circle the letter of the demonstrative pronoun that correctly completes each sentence.

1 My computer crashed for the third time since I bought it. _____ is one reason why it's a good idea to buy a service plan.

    a That

    b These

    c Those

    d There

2 The university president announced the new campus safety policies saying, " _____ rules will be strictly enforced."

    a This

    b These

    c Those

    d That's

3 The elderly woman looked at the line of men in the police station. Suddenly, she pointed to one of them and shouted, "_____ him! He's the one who stole my purse!"

   a That's

   b This is

   c It is

   d Those are

Part 18 Vocabulary Building

For each group of sentences, circle the letter of the referent for the underlined word or phrase.

1 Luddites are a group of people who do not use electronics or other types of technology, such as computers or cell phones. These individuals believe that technology is unnecessary or even harmful.

   a electronics

   b Luddites

   c computers or cell phones

   d group

2 Gardening experts recommend several types of flowering bushes that grow well in colder climates. These include lilacs, hydrangeas, and rose of Sharon.

   a gardening experts

   b colder climates

   c lilacs and hydrangeas

   d flowering bushes

3 The dramatic use of light and shadow, called *chiaroscuro*, is common in some later Renaissance artwork. This technique was used often by painters such as Caravaggio and Rembrandt.

   a artwork

   b Renaissance

   c chiaroscuro

   d light

Part 19 Vocabulary Building

Circle the letter of the correct pronoun to complete the sentence.

1 The growth in popularity of Bollywood films during the 2000s helped bring back the musical film genre, _____ had been popular in the United States in the 1930s and 1940s.

   a who

   b which

   c whom

   d when

2 Her older sister Dahlia, _____ moved back to Vermont several years before, now lives alone in the old run-down family farmhouse.

   a who

   b that

   c whom

   d which

COMPREHENSION SKILLS

Previewing, Scanning, and Skimming

PREVIEWING

Titles and Previewing Questions

Previewing a passage before you read can help you understand it better, and it can save time. When you preview, you look very quickly at a passage to get an idea of what it is about and how to read it. Previewing is very helpful for course assignments and for reading comprehension sections on tests or exams.

To preview, read the title of the passage before you begin reading. Very often, the title gives the topic or main idea of the passage. Then think of a few previewing questions based on the title. Begin with question words such as *Who? When? Where?* and *How?* These questions will help you focus on the topic while reading.

Practice 1

Read the titles from news articles. Write the number of each previewing question under the correct title.

1 What caused the damage to the homes?

2 What sport does the person play?

3 What kind of work did the woman do?

4 Why did the athlete need an operation?

5 Whom did the woman help?

6 How did the animal help the person?

7 How long was the person lost?

8 Where was the person hiking?

9 Where are the people staying now?

10 When can the person play sports again?

11 Who is giving the prize?

12 Where did the dangerous weather happen?

Hundreds Left Homeless after Storm	Woman Wins Award for Charity Project

Operation Slows Down Athlete	Hunter's Dog Rescues Missing Hiker

Titles and First Sentences

Before you begin reading a passage, preview the title and think of previewing questions.

Then read the first sentence or two of the text and ask yourself, "What is this passage about?"

Practice 2

Read these first sentences from news articles. Then write the number of the correct title to each. There is one extra title.

1. International Education on the Rise
2. Operation Slows Down Athlete
3. Woman Wins Award for Charity Project
4. Dog Rescues Missing Hiker
5. New Traffic Light Causes New Problems
6. Hundreds Left Homeless after Storm

1 _____ A massive hurricane swept through the state yesterday, destroying property and leaving many people without power.

2 _____ A new study shows that the number of university students getting their degrees in other countries has increased.

3 _____ A lucky New Jersey man was saved from spending a cold night in the woods when he was found by a furry, four-footed friend.

4 _____ Anita Caldwell grew up believing that it was her duty to help others.

5 _____ Washington High School track star Crispin Matthews will have to sit out the spring season as he recovers from ankle surgery.

Skimming with Previewing Questions

Before you begin reading a passage, preview the title and think of previewing questions. Then skim the passage (read it quickly) to get the main idea.

When you skim, think about your previewing questions as you quickly look for the answers. This will help you find the most important information.

Later, when you read the passage carefully, you will already know the main ideas and be able to focus on the details.

Practice 3

Read the previewing questions. Then skim the passage and circle the letters of the two previewing questions that are answered in the passage.

1

Hundreds Left Homeless after Storm

A massive hurricane swept through the state yesterday, destroying property and leaving many people without power. The storm, which hit land at approximately 2:00 P.M. on Friday, ripped through the area, causing large-scale damage to homes. The towns of Millport, New Bradbury, and Belmont were hardest hit, leaving hundreds of homes without electricity by Friday evening. The local governments estimate that about 350 people have been left homeless by the storm. High winds and flood waters were responsible for most of the destruction.

a Where are the people staying now?

b Where did the dangerous weather happen?

c What can people do to help?

d What caused the damage to the homes?

2

Woman Wins Award for Charity Project

Anita Caldwell grew up believing that it was her duty to help others. Even as a young girl in elementary school, she was an active member of her community. Her mother recalls a time when Anita was eight years old and an elderly neighbor was sick. Anita visited the woman every day, bringing her food and helping with the housework and gardening. "She was always doing something to help other people," says Anita's mom proudly. Now that she is in her 40s, Anita hasn't changed much. She is the founder of Health-Wise, a program that collects fresh vegetables and fruits donated from local farms and delivers them to the elderly in nursing homes.

a What kind of work does the woman do?

b Whom does the woman help?

c Where is the woman from?

d Who is giving the award?

3

Hunter's Dog Rescues Missing Hiker

A lucky New Jersey man was saved from spending a cold night in the woods when he was found by a furry, four-footed friend. Tom Fahner was hiking on Mount Gilmore last Saturday. He reached the top of the mountain and noticed that the sun was setting. "I knew I had to hurry to get down before dark," he said. On the way down, Tom took a wrong turn and found himself lost in the deep forest. "It was getting dark fast. I looked down and couldn't see the trail anymore," said the hiker. Tom called for help, but no one came, so he made a shelter with tree branches and decided to camp for the night. "It was too cold to sleep; I just tried to stay warm." Sometime during the night, Tom heard something running through the woods. It stopped in front of the shelter and started to bark loudly. It was Bruce Edwards's hunting dog, Rosco. The two were night hunting. Rosco called his owner, who came to Tom's rescue and guided him back to the trail and down the mountain to safety.

a Where was the person hiking?
b How did the animal help the person?
c Was the person hurt?
d How long was the person lost?

4

Operation Slows Down Athlete

Washington High School track star Crispin Matthews will have to sit out the spring season as he recovers from ankle surgery. Matthews, a senior this year, says he is disappointed he'll miss this last season at Washington, but he understands that it's for the best. Matthews's ankle was injured during the high-jump event last year. The injury did not heal properly, requiring surgery to repair the bone. Matthews had hoped to join the track team at Holden University, where he will be a student next year, but he says he isn't sure that will be possible. "I'll do whatever the doctors tell me to do," he says. "I want to start running again as soon as possible." Well-wishers may send cards and flowers to Howard Medical Center.

a What sport does the person play?
b When can the person play sports again?
c Why did the athlete need an operation?
d When will the operation take place?

Previewing Longer Passages

Previewing longer passages helps you prepare for how easy or difficult the reading will be, what type of information will be most important, and which details to look for.

Follow these steps for previewing longer passages:

- Read the title and any bold headings. Look at any pictures. Form previewing questions based on these.
- Think about the genre of the writing—for example, is it an e-mail, a news article, or a story?
- Read the first few lines of the passage. What do they tell you about the title?
- Skim the passage. (Read it quickly.) Notice the language and content. Is it formal, informal, or technical? Are there lots of names, numbers, or difficult words?

Practice 4

Preview and skim the text. Then read the question and circle the letter of the correct answer.

Unit 7 Earth's Atmosphere

Geographic Location

The *aurora borealis*—also known as the northern lights—is a natural phenomenon that occurs at Earth's northernmost points. These amazing light displays are most commonly seen in the sky in areas near the North Pole, such as northern

Canada, the U.S. state of Alaska, Greenland, and the countries of Scandinavia. It was the astronomer Galileo who first named the phenomenon in 1616. In Latin, aurora means "dawn," and borealis means "north." The name translates to "northern dawn."

Appearance of Auroras

Auroras may occur at any time of the year. However, because the North Pole has daylight for 24 hours a day for several months of the year, they can only be seen from about October through April. Depending on the exact location and atmospheric conditions, they may look very different. They may range in color from blue or violet to green, red, or orange. They can look like a faint glow on the horizon—like a sunrise or sunset—or they can appear as moving beams or rays of brightly colored light. They are also sometimes described as looking like curtains or ribbons waving in the sky.

Causes and Formation

Auroras are caused when the sun creates high-energy gas called solar wind. When this solar wind approaches our planet, it hits Earth's magnetic field, which creates an electrical current. The electricity begins to travel along the surface of Earth's atmosphere and gathers more energy until it reaches the poles. The light of the aurora is created when these high-energy electrical particles mix with other gases, such as oxygen and nitrogen. The different colors depend on the amounts and types of gases that are present in the atmosphere at the time the aurora occurs.

117

1 What type of passage is this?

   a a news article

   b a textbook entry

   c an e-mail message

   d a blog post

2 What is the main topic of this passage?

   a business

   b health

   c science

   d history

3 Which topic is probably NOT discussed in this passage?

   a where auroras appear

   b what auroras look like

   c how auroras are formed

   d how auroras were discovered

4 Which best describes this passage?

   a a general introduction to auroras

   b an explanation of the different types of auroras

   c an example of how auroras are used in literature

   d a discussion of how auroras affect the environment

SCANNING

Scanning for Information

You scan a text when you need to find specific information. For example, you may scan a movie listing, a list of part-time jobs, or a schedule of exercise classes.

How to Scan

When you scan, move your eyes across the text quickly, looking only for the information you need. Do not read all of the words. Just keep your eyes moving and looking for specific information.

Practice 1

Read each question and then scan the events calendar for the answer. Write a short answer to each question on the next page.

— December 2016 —

Ongoing
Until January 14, 2017: South American Pottery, Clinton Gallery
Until February 27, 2017: New Student Exhibits, Brent Library

Saturday, November 30, 2016
3:00 P.M.–5:00 P.M.: Donald Liebow, Piano
5:00 P.M.–7:00 P.M.: Mark Santolo, Trumpet
7:30 P.M.–8:30 P.M.: Carol Noonan reads from her book, *Voices of Home*
8:30 P.M.–9:30 P.M.: *Walking on Snow*, Theater Club Holiday Show

Sunday, December 1, 2016
1:00 P.M.–2:15 P.M.: Lecture: "Beyond Digital Media," Professor Hal Smith
4:00 P.M.–5:30 P.M.: Yoga Class, Fielding Fitness Center
7:30 P.M.–9:00 P.M.: Wendy Moses, Violin

Monday, December 2, 2016
11:45 A.M.–1:00 P.M.: Foreign Language Study Groups Lunch Meetings:
                       (Mandarin, Russian, German), Greenway Cafeteria
7:00 P.M.–10:00 P.M.: Russian Film: *Is It Easy to Be Young?*

Tuesday, December 3, 2016
11:30 A.M.–1:30 P.M.: Career Fair, Main Hall
4:30 P.M.–5:45 P.M.: Women's Book Club Meeting, Reynolds Room
6:15 P.M.–7:45 P.M.: Writing Workshop, *The Effective Academic Essay*,
                      Brent Library
7:00 P.M.–8:00 P.M.: ~~Study Abroad Meeting~~ CANCELLED

Wednesday, December 4, 2016
11:45 A.M.–1:00 P.M.: Foreign Language Study Groups Lunch Meetings:
                       (Japanese, French, Spanish), Greenway Cafeteria
12:00 P.M.–1:00 P.M.: Math Study Group, Reynolds Room
7:00 P.M.–9:00 P.M.: ArtBeat Coffeehouse, College Café—Poetry Open Mic
                      open to everyone!

1 What is the date of the career fair?

December _____ , 2016

2 Who wrote the book *Voices of Home?*

_____

3 Which two days of the week do language study groups meet?

_____

4 What time does the movie start on Monday evening?

_____ P.M.

5 Which event was canceled?

_____

6 For how many hours does the math study group meet?

_____

7 What is the title of the theater club's holiday show?

_____

8 Where are the New Student Exhibits located?

_____

Practice 2

Read each question and then scan the list of websites for the answer. Circle the letter of the correct answer to each question on the next page.

Brazilian Carnival - Wimikedia, your online information source
www.wimikedia.org/Brazil_Carnival
Brazilian Carnival is a cultural festival held forty days before the beginning of Lent, usually in February . . .
history, locations, music, parade

OFFICIAL RIO CARNIVAL 2013 GUIDE: Programs, Schedules, Venues, Samba Parade Tickets . . .
www.rio-carniv.org
In Brazil, Carnival (Carnaval in Portuguese) is celebrated throughout the country ...The 2013 festivities begin Friday, February 8. Rio de Janeiro has long been the site of the largest celebrations . . .
program details, photos, ticket sales, 2013 parade schedule

How to Samba: Brazilian Dance Lesson: Video Series | iHow-to.net
www.ihow-to.net/samba
Heat up the dance floor! With these free video *dance lessons featuring famous Samba dancer Luiza Brunet*, learn how to dance the Brazilian Samba with music, costumes, and dance steps.

All About Brazil Carnival | Brazil Carnival 2013 | BrazilBook.com
www.brazilbook.com/brazil-carnival/ -2013.asp
Brazil Carnival Information and Guide including history, culture, music, photos, Samba dance lesson videos, Portuguese lessons and much more! . . .

From Samba to carnival: Brazil's thriving African culture - CBNews.com
www.cbnews.com/2012/10/23/world/africa/ . . . brazil/ind.html
Oct 23, 2012 – From samba and carnival to food, music, and religion, African culture is everywhere in Brazil.

Brazil's 10 most popular celebrations – travel tips and articles – Global Loner
www.globalloner.com/brazil/travel-tips-and-articles/6123
Aug 3, 2012 – Read Brazil's top 10 festivals for travel tips, tourist advice, news and articles from all around the world by Global Loner.

Learn the Language of Brazil – Portuguese Language – Brazilian Portuguese
www.portuguese-today.net/index
Learn Portuguese for FREE – Portuguese lessons, Brazilian Pronunciation, Portuguese Phrases and FREE eBooks
lessons, 365 Portuguese words. useful phrases

1 Which two sites offer Portuguese lessons?
  a brazilbook.com and globalloner.com
  b wimikedia.org and ihow-to.net
  c portuguese-today.net and brazilbook.com

2 Which two sites offer dance lessons?
  a globalloner.com and brazilbook.com
  b ihow-to.net and brazilbook.com
  c rio-carniv.org and ihow-to.net

3 Which site gives information about different Brazilian festivals besides Carnival?
  a globalloner.com
  b rio-carniv.org
  c wimikedia.org

4 Which site offers 365 useful words?
  a CBnews.com
  b portuguese-today.net
  c brazilbook.com

5 On what date did the 2013 Brazilian Carnival begin?
  a Aug. 3
  b Feb. 8
  c Oct. 23

6 What site offers free eBooks?
  a wimikedia.org
  b ihow-to.net
  c portuguese-today.net

7 What site offers parade tickets?
  a rio-carniv.org
  b brazilbook.com
  c globalloner.com

8 Which site features videos of a famous samba dancer?
  a globalloner.com
  b ihow-to.net
  c brazilbook.com

Scanning for Key Words

These exercises will help you learn to move your eyes over a passage quickly and look for important words. This skill, called scanning, is useful when you need to find the answers to questions quickly, for example when you take a test.

Scanning means looking for specific information. You do not need to read every word or line, and you do not need to understand the whole text.

Practice 3

Read the key words in the box. Scan the paragraph for one word at a time and underline that word every time you find it.

1

dangerous	kill/kills	disease/diseases

What creature kills the largest number of humans every year? If you're thinking about large animals such as sharks, lions, or tigers, then think again. The tiny insect known as the mosquito kills millions of people around the world annually. These annoying insects are especially frightening because they spread many types of dangerous diseases, such as yellow fever, dengue fever, West Nile virus, and malaria, which can kill humans. What makes mosquitoes so dangerous to humans is that they travel from person to person, biting many different people and spreading the deadly diseases quickly and efficiently among them. Mosquitoes are scary insects.

2

insect/insects	tree/trees	problem/problems

Certain types of insects, such as the Asian long-horned beetle, have become a major problem as global trade has expanded. When goods and products are transported between countries by plane or ship, insects or their eggs often come along for the ride and are transported from their native habitats. The population of these insects can then grow too quickly. This can have a terrible effect on the environment, causing major damage to trees and food crops. The Asian long-horned beetle is an insect that is native to Japan, China, and Korea. The beetle makes holes in trees and eats the wood on the inside, eventually killing the tree. In Asia, the beetles are eaten by various birds and other insects, so most trees are safe. However, when the beetle was transported to North America on ships from China, it caused big problems. Since 1996, when it was first identified in New York City, the beetle has destroyed thousands of trees. Teams of environmentalists and scientists have been working hard to find ways to deal with the problem.

3

bee/bees	disappear/disappeared	reason/reasons

Sometime during the fall of 2006, something strange began to happen across North America. Beekeepers—farmers who raise bees in order to make honey—began to notice that large numbers of bees had simply disappeared. Some farmers reported losing up to 90 percent of their bees.

Even stranger, the bees disappeared very suddenly. The mystery of the vanishing bees is known as Colony Collapse Disorder, or CCD. Studies have been conducted and the results have been analyzed; however, no single reason has been found. There are a number of theories. The first is that the pesticides used for farming are causing the bees to become weak and die. Second, some researchers think a virus may be attacking the bees. Others blame a combination of reasons, such as problems caused by new farming techniques or even radiation from cell phone towers.

Practice 4

Read the title and the key words in the box. Scan the text for one word at a time and underline that word every time you find it.

business	success	principle/principles

Principles of Business Success

(1) What makes a business succeed? The answer is always changing because the world is always changing. Along with it, customers' interests and needs are also changing. These days, factors such as globalization and the rapidly developing world of technology determine the chances that a business will succeed.

(2) There are certain basic principles that guarantee long-lasting success in business if companies apply them consistently. These principles come from experts in the business world who have observed and analyzed what good managers and CEOs do to ensure the success of their organizations.

(3) The first principle for success in business is *Always try to be the best*. This may sound overly simple, but anyone involved in business will tell you that it's not easy. It takes more than just offering a high-quality product. It's also essential to understand the needs of the customers and work hard to meet them. Companies must continue to do market research to find out what customers really want and need.

(4) Another principle is *Be open to new ideas*. Good companies continue doing what works, but great companies also make changes when it's necessary. Of course, it's important to think through any changes in order to make sure they are correct. The point is that companies shouldn't be afraid of change. Making the right changes at the right time is an important key to success.

(5) The third principle is *Be responsible, both economically and socially*. This means cutting back on unnecessary spending and finding ways to reduce harmful effects on the environment by recycling, reducing waste, and using natural materials. Being socially responsible means contributing something positive to the community and the world. For example, companies could support local or global charities.

(6) Finally, *Learn from mistakes*. If mistakes are made, move on, but make all the necessary changes to avoid doing the same thing again in the future.

(7) If companies follow these principles, they'll be well on their way to success.

SKIMMING

Presentation

Skimming a News Article

When you skim a news article, you read the passage quickly to get the general idea. Skimming involves reading some parts of the text and skipping other parts. When you skim, follow these steps:

- Look at the title.
- Think about the type of passage it is (e.g., a news article, an opinion essay, a review) and what information might be important.
- Look at parts of the text that usually include important ideas and information. These include the first paragraph, the first sentence of each paragraph, and the last paragraph.
- Ask yourself questions as you look through the text, such as "What/Who is the article about?" and "What happened?"

Practice 1

Look at the title of the news article. You have 45 seconds to skim the text for the most important information. Then circle the letters of the three true statements on the next page.

Sixty-day Bread Could Help Reduce Waste

A company in the United Kingdom says it has found a way to keep bread fresh and mold-free for sixty days. The new technique uses microwave technology to kill the mold spores in bread before they can begin to grow and cause the bread to spoil.

A Wasteful World

Food waste is a big problem, especially in developed countries such as the United States and United Kingdom. Some studies estimate that a typical American family throws away 40 percent of the food it buys. Nationally, this amounts to $165 billion dollars a year wasted.

Bread is one of the most commonly wasted foods. Because bread is wrapped in plastic to keep it from becoming dry, the water that evaporates inside of the bag creates a perfect environment for mold to grow. A survey conducted in the UK showed that 32 percent of bread purchased grew moldy and was thrown out before people had eaten it.

The company hopes that its new technology will help to reduce the amount of wasted bread by as much as one-third. It also plans to use the system on other types of foods, such as fresh meats and some vegetables and fruits.

Microwave Technology

Under normal conditions, it takes about ten days for mold to grow on fresh bread. However, representatives of Microzap, the company that developed the new microwave procedure, claim their process keeps mold away for two months.

The technique uses the same type of waves as a small home microwave oven. However, the company says the Microzap system distributes the rays more evenly, so there are no hot and cold spots as with a home microwave.

Personal Taste

The company says that its microwave method is safer and healthier than adding chemicals to preserve the bread. In addition, because the microwaves are very low strength, the taste and texture of the bread remain the same.

Will people want to eat bread that's two months old? That will be the real test in the coming years when microwave-fresh products become available on the market.

a The article is about the opening of a new food company.

b The company hopes its idea will help solve a problem.

c The new technology will be used mainly on bread.

d The article explains how different types of bread are made.

e The article explains why bread spoils quickly.

Presentation

Skimming a Review

People write reviews to express opinions and make recommendations. A review may be about a movie, book, new computer, restaurant, hotel, school, and so on. You can find reviews online or in magazines and newspapers.

When you skim a review, follow these steps:

- Read the first and last sentences.
- Look for descriptive words and phrases that explain the writer's opinion. Examples include *excellent*, *high-quality*, *convenient*, *terrible*, *boring*, *enjoyed*, *loved*, and *didn't like*.
- Ask yourself, "What is this person's opinion?"

Practice 2

You have 20 seconds to skim each review. Then circle the letter of the correct answer to complete the sentence.

1 I just finished reading *Young Philby* by Robert Littell. Spy novels are my favorite books to read, and after this book, Littell is definitely one of my favorite spy novelists. I read his book *Legends* last year, which was OK, but some parts were a little boring, and I found the plot a little confusing. However, I loved *Young Philby*. The book is about Kim Philby, a British spy during World War II. He was caught passing secret information to the Soviet government. Littell does a fantastic job of describing Philby's character. The story was easy to follow, even with a lot of historical details. Littell's writing style kept me interested the whole way through. In fact, I couldn't put the book down! If you like spy novels, this is a great one.

The reviewer's opinion of the book is _____ .

   a mainly negative   **b** very positive   **c** negative and positive

2 The new PC laptop from Greenline computers has some good features. It's thin and light, so it's easy to carry between classes. It has a touch screen, which I didn't like at first, but I'm getting used to it. Compared to similar laptops, it has a lot of storage. I use it mostly for writing papers, so it's perfect for me. It's also priced reasonably for college students at $349. On the other hand, there are some things I don't like about this computer. For one thing, it's very noisy because the fan is always running. The processor is also too slow, so the computer crashes when I try to watch videos online, and the picture quality is terrible. It's a good computer for me while I'm in school, but after I graduate, I'll spend a little more and get something faster.

The reviewer _____ .

   a recommends the computer for students

   b thinks the computer is good for watching videos online

   c wishes he had spent more on a better computer

3 There are a lot of gyms to choose from in the city, and each one has different features and classes to offer. If you live in the Park Center area, StrongLife Health Club has a convenient location and is one of the area's newer gyms, so the equipment is in good shape. Unfortunately, StrongLife doesn't have a pool, so if you like to swim, choose someplace else. Most of the instructors are excellent, and the class schedule is convenient for anyone. The only class I don't recommend is kickboxing. I think it's too hard, and the instructor doesn't explain things well. In my opinion, the best class is yoga. Linda is a fantastic teacher! I don't think StrongLife is the perfect gym, but it still has a lot of good things to offer.

The reviewer's opinion of the gym is _____ .

   a positive

   b negative

   c mixed

Presentation

Skimming Reading Passages on Tests

When you skim, you read a passage quickly to get the general idea. Skimming involves reading some parts of the text and skipping other parts.

When you skim, follow these steps:

- Look at the title.
- Think about the type of passage it is (e.g., a news article, an opinion essay, a review) and what information might be important.
- Look at parts of the text that usually include important ideas and information.

These include the first paragraph, the first sentence of each paragraph, and the last paragraph.

Skimming is a useful skill for saving time on tests. Always read the test questions carefully first. Then skim a passage to find the answers to questions such as these:

What is the main idea of the passage?

What is the writer's opinion of the topic?

What is the purpose of the article?

Practice 3

Read the question first. Then skim the passage and circle the letter of the correct answer.

1 What is the purpose of the text?

   a to introduce different types of birds

   b to explain the results of a study

   c to show that birds are similar to humans

Hatching order affects birds' behavior later in life. Researchers studied several families of zebra finches. The study found that the order in which baby birds in the same nest hatched from their eggs affected the birds' behavior later. When the birds could fly, the younger birds—those that hatched later—were more adventurous than their older brothers and sisters. Researchers believe this helps the younger birds survive by making them able to travel farther from the nest to find their own food.

2 What is the main idea of the passage?

   a Roman people's attitudes changed when the economy weakened.

   b During the 500-year period of ancient Rome, most people had pride in their society.

   c Ancient Rome failed as a result of changes in Roman people's attitudes.

Experts agree that the main reason for the fall of ancient Rome was a change in attitude of the Roman people and in the culture of Rome. During the first part of the 500-year empire, most Roman people led happy lives, worked hard, and felt pride in their society, government, and culture. However, records from much later show that over time, many people began to disapprove of the emperors. The economy weakened, and people became lazy and unsatisfied. The result was a variety of social problems, which led the government to fail.

3 Which opinion does the writer express about photojournalists?

   a They should not go into difficult or dangerous situations.

   b They should take photos even when people are in trouble.

   c They should only take photos that show hunger or violence.

Photojournalists take photos of people, events, and situations for newspapers, magazines, websites, and other sources that publish the news. These specialized photographers sometimes find themselves in difficult or dangerous situations. For example, they may see people in trouble or in pain. They may be on the scene of accidents or travel into battle with the military during a war. In these situations, many people—even the photographers themselves—wonder whether they should help . . . or just take photos?

Photojournalists have been criticized for taking photos of people in trouble rather than stopping to help. However, in many cases, their photos help solve big problems, such as hunger and violence. When the public sees the photos, many people may take action and make a difference. By showing the "real picture" of what's happening in faraway places, photojournalists have the power to change the world. It is their job to be the eyes of the public and show the world the truth.

COMBINED SKILLS: PREVIEWING, SCANNING, AND SKIMMING

> **Presentation**
>
> Combined Skills: Previewing, Scanning, and Skimming
>
> When you read longer texts, you can combine different reading strategies to help you read faster and understand better.
>
> - Preview the text before you begin reading. Look at any pictures or bold headings, and think about the type of writing it is.
> - Skim the text quickly to get the main ideas.
> - Think about the important information you need to know, and then scan the text quickly to find that information.

Practice 1

Read the Practice 1 Presentation instructions for previewing, scanning, and skimming the following passage. Then read each question on the next page, follow the instructions, and circle the letter of the correct answer.

The Fall of Ancient Rome

The Colosseum

How did 500 Years of Power Come to an End?

Ancient Rome was one of the most powerful civilizations in history. The Roman Empire lasted about 500 years, from 27 BCE to 476 CE. The emperors of ancient Rome, famous rulers such as Augustus and Nero, were both respected and feared. The large Roman army traveled far, spreading the emperors' power throughout Europe, the Near East, and North Africa. Most Roman people were wealthy and lived well. Why then didn't the empire continue? What caused such a strong government and society to become weak and ultimately fail?

Romans' Changing Attitudes

Experts agree that the main reason for the fall of ancient Rome was a change in the attitude of the Roman people and in the culture of Rome. During the first part of the empire, people worked hard and felt pride in their society, government, and culture. However, later records show that, eventually, the people began to disapprove of the emperors. The economy became weak, and people became lazy and unsatisfied. The next section explains possible reasons for these changes.

Reasons for a Weakened Society

The change in Roman culture and society was probably not caused by just one factor but by a combination of reasons. Historians point to three main reasons:

- A decreasing belief in religion caused the Roman people to think less about honesty and ethical behavior, which resulted in increased crime and social problems.
- The use of the poisonous metal lead in water pipes and cosmetics created health problems and mental illness in much of the population.
- Climate change affected the environment and resulted in cooler summers. This had a negative effect on agriculture. There simply was not enough food for the people of Rome.

1 Based on the pictures, title, and bold headings, which statement best describes the topic of this excerpt?

   a It is about tourism in modern-day Rome.

   b It is about ancient Roman architectural styles.

   c It is about reasons for the end of the Roman Empire.

2 Scan the text quickly. When did the Roman Empire end?

   a 27 BCE

   b 476 CE

   c 500 CE

3 Scan the text quickly. Which two emperors are mentioned by name?

   a Augustus and Nero

   b Nero and Julius Caesar

   c Augustus and Julius Caesar

4 Scan the text quickly. According to experts, what was the main reason for the fall of ancient Rome?

   a weak rulers and a small army

   b not enough food to feed the people

   c people's changing attitudes

5 Skim the excerpt very quickly. Which statement best describes the main idea of the text?

   a The fall of ancient Rome was caused by changes in society due to religious, health, and environmental factors.

   b Historians agree that ancient Rome is one of the most interesting periods in Western history.

   c In early Rome, most people worked hard and were wealthy, but that changed over time.

Understanding Paragraphs

UNDERSTANDING PARAGRAPHS

Practice 1

Read each group of sentences. Decide if they form a unified paragraph. Circle the letter of the correct answer.

1 The government of South Korea is trying something new in the nation's classrooms: English-teaching robots. Last February, schools around the country began trying out Engkey. That's the name of an English-speaking robot that can take attendance, read stories, sing songs, and have conversations in English. The robots were designed especially for teaching children. South Korea's Education Ministry says it plans to have Engkey in every one of its 8,400 kindergarten classrooms.

   a unified paragraph   **b** not a unified paragraph

2 Financial cuts in the city of Manchester, New Hampshire, have resulted in the loss of 95 full-time teaching jobs in the schools. The state of New Hampshire has a population of about 1,300,000, and it borders the Atlantic Ocean. Ken Burns is a well-known documentary filmmaker who has a home in New Hampshire. His best-known works are *Jazz* and *The Civil War*.

   a unified paragraph   **b** not a unified paragraph

3 A MOOC is a new option for people who enjoy learning online. MOOC is an acronym that stands for "massive open online course." A MOOC is different from a traditional online course in several ways. First of all, in a MOOC, there's no limit to how many students can join. Some popular courses may have over a hundred thousand students. Secondly, most MOOCs don't carry official university credits. Finally, MOOCs are supported by grants and other public and private funding sources, so they are free.

   a unified paragraph   **b** not a unified paragraph

4 British university students are still angered by the government's decision to allow universities to raise tuition fees by as much as 200 percent. Student groups such as the National Union of Students (NUS) have held numerous protests in cities, some of which have drawn up to 50,000 people. In the United States, tuition costs vary widely from one university to another. Tuition costs are different around the world. In some countries, university education is paid for by the government.

   a unified paragraph   **b** not a unified paragraph

5 Cheating on university entrance exams has been a major problem in China recently. Every year, millions of students across the country gather in large halls to take the test. Authorities have created new systems to try to stop students from cheating. At most test sites across China, students must pass through airport-style metal detectors to make sure they are not bringing in any electronic devices, including watches. Cameras have also been installed at test locations, broadcasting the testing to the offices of top local education officials. In some areas, hundreds of police are called in to patrol the testing.

    a unified paragraph   **b** not a unified paragraph

Presentation

Topic Sentences

The topic sentence is usually the first sentence of a paragraph. It gives the topic of the paragraph—what the paragraph is about. It also includes the main idea—what the sentences in the paragraph say or explain about the topic.

Practice 2

Read each paragraph. Write the number of the correct topic sentence to complete the paragraph. You will not use all of the topic sentences.

1. The aurora borealis, or northern lights, may look very different depending on the atmospheric conditions.
2. Mosquitos pose a threat to millions of people all over the world.
3. At the North Pole, the aurora borealis can only be seen between October and April.
4. A study showed that most people preferred white bread to wheat bread.
5. Hatching order affects birds' behavior later in life.
6. Ancient Rome was one of the most powerful civilizations in history.
7. A soldier in the army was one of the most common professions in ancient Rome.
8. Researchers have found that some birds hatch more quickly than others.
9. Bread is one of the most commonly wasted foods.
10. Mosquitoes, ants, and spiders are the most common biting insects.

1 __ These annoying insects spread many types of dangerous diseases, such as yellow fever, dengue fever, West Nile virus, and malaria. What makes mosquitoes so dangerous to humans is that they travel from person to person, biting many different people and spreading deadly diseases quickly and efficiently. Mosquitoes kill thousands of people around the world every year.

2 __ They may range in color from blue or violet to green, red, or orange. They can simply look like a faint glow on the horizon—like a sunrise or sunset—or they can appear as moving beams or rays of brightly colored light. They are also sometimes described as looking like curtains or ribbons waving in the sky.

3 ___ Because bread is wrapped in plastic to keep it from becoming dry, the water that evaporates inside of the bag creates a perfect environment for mold to grow. A survey conducted in the United Kingdom showed that 32 percent of bread purchased grew moldy and was thrown out before people had eaten it.

4 ___ The Roman Empire lasted about 500 years, from 27 BCE to 476 CE. The emperors of ancient Rome, famous rulers such as Augustus and Nero, were both respected and feared. The large Roman army traveled far, spreading the emperors' power throughout Europe, the Near East, and North Africa.

5 ___ Researchers studied several families of zebra finches. The order in which baby birds in the same nest hatched from their eggs affected the birds' behavior later. When the birds could fly, the younger birds—those that hatched later—were more adventurous than their older brothers and sisters. Researchers believe this adventurousness helps the younger birds survive by enabling them to travel farther from the nest to find food.

Presentation

Irrelevant Sentences

All of the sentences in a paragraph should relate to both the topic and the main idea. They should also all relate to one another. If a sentence does not do these things, it is called irrelevant.

Practice 3

Read each paragraph. Underline the irrelevant sentence.

1 Experts agree that the main reason for the fall of ancient Rome was a change in attitude of the Roman people and in the culture of Rome. During the first part of the 500-year empire, most Roman people worked hard and felt pride in their society, government, and culture. The most common jobs for average Roman people were in agriculture and education, as well as in the military. However, records from much later show that over time, many people began to disapprove of the emperors. The economy weakened, and people became lazy and dissatisfied.

2 Sometime during the fall of 2006, something strange began to happen across North America. Beekeepers—farmers who raise bees in order to make honey—began to notice that large numbers of bees had simply disappeared. Some farmers reported losing up to 90 percent of their bees. Small family farms have been declining for years because larger farms are taking over. Even stranger, the bees disappeared very suddenly. The mystery of the vanishing bees is known as Colony Collapse Disorder, or CCD. The reason for the disorder is still unknown.

3 The first principle for success in business is *Always try to be the best*. This may seem overly simple, but anyone involved in business will tell you that it's not easy. It takes more than just offering a high-quality product. Most people looking for a job these days use Internet job boards to search for opportunities. It's also essential to understand the needs of the customers and work hard to meet them. Companies must continue to do market research to find out what customers really want and need.

IDENTIFYING THE TOPIC OF A PARAGRAPH

Presentation

Identifying the Topic of a Paragraph

Knowing the topic of a text you are reading is important. When you know the topic, you can make connections to what you already know about it. This helps you make sense of the passage.

The topic sentence usually includes the first mention of the topic. The topic is often repeated several times in a passage.

A topic should not be too general or too specific. It should be just broad enough to cover all of the information in a passage.

Practice 1

Read each paragraph. Circle the letter of the correct topic.

1 It took many years of searching before Pluto was discovered in 1930. Long before that, in the late 1800s, an astronomer named Percival Lowell noticed that two planets, Uranus and Neptune, did not go around the sun in a perfect circle as expected. This discovery meant that something else—another large body—must be pulling on the two planets. The search for a ninth planet began. On February 18, 1930, a young astronomer named Clyde Tombaugh found an object among the stars. After several colleagues confirmed his observations, Tombaugh's discovery was finally named the ninth planet. It was called Pluto after the Roman god of the underworld.

   a the astronomer who found Pluto

   b the discovery of Pluto

   c the name Pluto

2 Pluto was considered a planet for 76 years. Then, in 2006, another discovery caused some astronomers to question whether Pluto was a planet or something else. Astronomers found a group of huge floating rocks—asteroids—near the same area as Pluto. One of these asteroids was actually bigger than Pluto. Some astronomers began to say that Pluto was actually just part of this group of asteroids and not really a planet. However, others disagreed and said Pluto should be considered a planet. The debate over the status of Pluto continues to this day.

   a the definition of an asteroid

   b the reasons why astronomers disagree

   c the debate about Pluto's status as a planet

3 As a result of the Pluto debate, astronomers realized that there was no clear definition of the word *planet*. There were many ideas about what a planet was and was not. Consequently, a group of astronomers from the International Astronomical Union got together and created a definition on which they could all agree. The definition states that a planet is a body that 1) moves around the sun, 2) is large enough for its own gravity to make it round, and 3) has "cleared [the] neighborhood" around its orbit of smaller objects. Under this new definition, the scientists decided that Pluto was too small to be a planet, and they changed its status to "dwarf planet."

   a the International Astronomical Union

   b the definition of a planet

   c types of astronomical objects

4 Today, there are still varying opinions about Pluto's status. Some astronomers agree that Pluto's size makes it unworthy of the "planet" title. They are satisfied with its new designation as a dwarf planet. However, many others disagree with the new classification and think Pluto should again be counted as the ninth planet. There are respected scientists on both sides of the issue. The only thing that seems clear is that the debate will continue.

   a the size of Pluto

   b changing the definition of a planet

   c different ideas about the status of Pluto

Practice 2

Read each paragraph. Circle the letter of the best topic.

1 Autism is a complex developmental disorder that begins in childhood, usually before the age of three, and lasts throughout a person's lifetime. It is common, affecting approximately one in ninety children born in the United States. In particular, autism affects the parts of the brain that control social interaction and communication. Autism affects people in a wide range of ways. In other words, a person may be affected very mildly or quite severely, and the symptoms may be different from person to person.

   a the symptoms of autism

   b an explanation of autism

   c autism and communication

2 Autism affects children in a variety of ways. Children may have trouble expressing their thoughts and ideas in words, and they may have trouble understanding ideas. They may also be extremely sensitive to certain sounds, or they may be bothered by physical contact. Symptoms may be mild or severe, depending on the child.

   a the symptoms of autism

   b adults with autism

   c treatment of autism

3 Autism can take some time to diagnose. An autistic child's parents are usually the first to notice something different about their son or daughter. They may notice that their child behaves differently from other children the same age, for example, in the way he or she communicates with others. When unusual behavior continues, parents often consult a doctor. This is the beginning of a complex process of diagnosis. There are no medical tests for autism, and a child with autism very often has normal physical tests; consequently, it may take months or even years to diagnose the disorder. If autism is suspected, both the parents and the doctors begin a period of observation. Over time, through the use of interviews, questionnaires, and consultations with specialists, it may be determined that the child has autism.

   a parents of autistic children

   b treatment of autism

   c how autism is diagnosed

4 After a diagnosis of autism is made, a number of things can be done to help the child and his or her family cope with the disorder. As there are no medicines to cure or treat autism, treatment usually focuses on helping the child learn to communicate and interact with others. Therapists may use music, computer software programs, and other types of sensory experiences to try to help the child feel more comfortable when interacting with the surrounding world.

   a how autism is treated

   b autism therapists

   c computer programs for autism

IDENTIFYING THE MAIN IDEA

Presentation

Identifying the Main Idea

A well-written paragraph has one topic and one main idea. The main idea is a statement that gives more information about the topic. It indicates what the paragraph says or explains about the topic. (Often—but not always—the main idea is the same as the topic sentence.)

A writer can develop different main ideas about the same topic. For example:

   Topic: the effects of stress

Main ideas:

- Stress helps people perform their work better.
- People experience stress differently.
- Stress is dangerous and shortens people's lives.

As with topics, a main idea should not be too general or too specific. It should be broad enough to cover all of the information in the paragraph.

Practice 1

Read each paragraph. Then circle the letter of the sentence that states the main idea.

1 There are varying opinions about the status of Pluto. Some astronomers agree that Pluto's size makes it unworthy of the "planet" title. They are satisfied with its new designation as a dwarf planet. However, many others disagree with the new classification and think Pluto should again be counted as the ninth planet. There are respected scientists on both sides of the issue. The only thing that seems clear is that the debate will continue.

   a Astronomers cannot agree about Pluto.

   b Pluto should be renamed the ninth planet.

   c The debate about Pluto will never end.

2 Photojournalists have been criticized for taking photos of people in trouble rather than stopping to help. However, in many cases, their photos help solve big problems, such as hunger and violence. When the public sees the photos, many people may take action and make a difference. By showing the "real picture" of what's happening in faraway places, photojournalists have the power to change the world. It is their job to be the eyes of the public and show the world the truth.

   a Photojournalism is an exciting career choice.

   b Photojournalists can help solve world problems.

   c Photojournalists show the public faraway places.

3 Another principle of business success is *Be responsible, both economically and socially*. This means cutting back on unnecessary spending and finding ways to reduce harmful effects on the environment by recycling, reducing waste, and using natural materials. Being socially responsible means contributing something positive to the community and the world. For example, companies could support local or global charities.

   a Many business owners are not responsible and waste money.

   b Global business is causing harmful effects on the environment.

   c Good businesses care about how they affect the world.

Practice 2

Read each paragraph. Then circle the letter of the sentence that states the main idea.

1 Autism can take some time to diagnose. An autistic child's parents are usually the first to notice something different about their son or daughter. They may notice that their child behaves differently from other children the same age, for example, in the way he or she communicates with others. When unusual behavior continues, parents often consult a doctor. This is the beginning of a complex process of diagnosis. There are no medical tests for autism, and a child with autism very often has normal physical tests; consequently, it may take months or even years to diagnose the disorder. If autism is suspected, both the parents and the doctors begin a period of observation. Over time, through the use of interviews, questionnaires, and consultations with specialists, it may be determined that the child has autism.

   a Interviews are not an effective way to diagnose autism.

   b There should be medical tests for autism.

   c Autism takes a long time to diagnose.

2 Cheating on university entrance exams has been a major problem in China recently, so authorities have created new systems to try to stop students from cheating. Every year, millions of students across the country gather in large halls to take the test. At most test sites across China, students must pass through airport-style metal detectors to make sure they are not bringing in any electronic devices, including watches. Cameras have also been installed at test locations, broadcasting the testing to the offices of top local education officials. In some areas, hundreds of police are called in to patrol the testing.

   a Chinese students must pass difficult exams to go to college.

   b China has increased security to stop cheating during exams.

   c Entrance exam halls in China are dangerously crowded.

3 Certain types of insects, such as the Asian long-horned beetle, have become a major problem as global trade has expanded. When goods and products are transported between countries by plane or ship, insects or their eggs often come along for the ride and are transported from their native habitats. The population of these insects can then grow too quickly. This can have a terrible effect on the environment, causing major damage to trees and food crops. The Asian long-horned beetle is an insect that is native to Japan, China, and Korea. The beetle makes holes in trees and eats the wood on the inside, eventually killing the tree. In Asia, the beetles are eaten by various birds and other insects, so most trees are safe. However, when the beetle was transported to North America on ships from China, it caused big problems. Since 1996, when it was first identified in New York City, the beetle has destroyed thousands of trees. Teams of environmentalists and scientists have been working hard to find ways to deal with the problem.

a Asian long-horned beetles cause major environmental problems outside of Asia.

b Scientists do not know how to solve the problem of Asian long-horned beetles.

c Some types of insects travel between countries more easily than others.

Practice 3

Read the passage. Then circle the letter of the sentence that states the main idea.

1

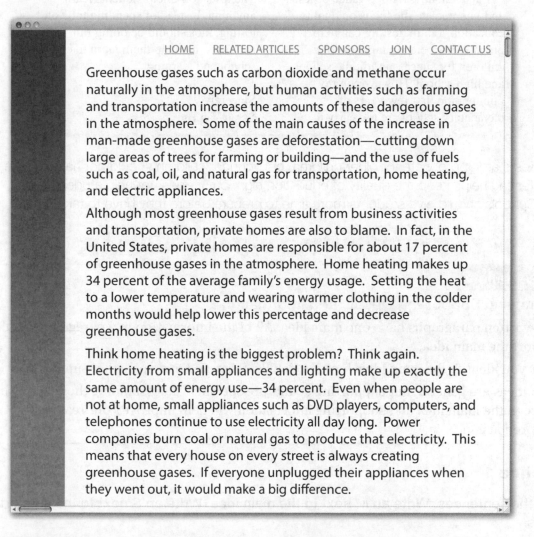

HOME   RELATED ARTICLES   SPONSORS   JOIN   CONTACT US

Greenhouse gases such as carbon dioxide and methane occur naturally in the atmosphere, but human activities such as farming and transportation increase the amounts of these dangerous gases in the atmosphere. Some of the main causes of the increase in man-made greenhouse gases are deforestation—cutting down large areas of trees for farming or building—and the use of fuels such as coal, oil, and natural gas for transportation, home heating, and electric appliances.

Although most greenhouse gases result from business activities and transportation, private homes are also to blame. In fact, in the United States, private homes are responsible for about 17 percent of greenhouse gases in the atmosphere. Home heating makes up 34 percent of the average family's energy usage. Setting the heat to a lower temperature and wearing warmer clothing in the colder months would help lower this percentage and decrease greenhouse gases.

Think home heating is the biggest problem? Think again. Electricity from small appliances and lighting make up exactly the same amount of energy use—34 percent. Even when people are not at home, small appliances such as DVD players, computers, and telephones continue to use electricity all day long. Power companies burn coal or natural gas to produce that electricity. This means that every house on every street is always creating greenhouse gases. If everyone unplugged their appliances when they went out, it would make a big difference.

a In addition to business and transportation, private homes are a major source of greenhouse gases.

b The problem of greenhouse gases will not be solved easily.

c People should unplug their appliances to reduce greenhouse gases.

Dear Editor,

I am writing to share my opinion on testing in our elementary schools. In our city, all elementary school students, including the youngest children, must now take standard reading and math tests twice a year. The test scores are used to decide whether students will move on to the next grade and to rate teacher performance.

I understand the importance of tests, and I appreciate the focus on quality education. I think testing can help prepare older elementary school children for success in middle school and high school. However, in my opinion, the first few years of elementary school are too early to start testing. Very young children learn best by playing and exploring the world. It's useless to start giving them tests at such an early age.

In addition, I have heard that some schools are even cutting time for art, music, and physical education to make more time for test preparation. This is the wrong thing to do. Those subjects teach children important skills for life. The tests don't help students learn anything. Instead of spending time on testing, kids should be doing fun activities that help them learn to enjoy school and learning.

Sincerely,
Sarah Van Buren

a Tests are appropriate for older children, but younger children should not have to take tests.

b Testing helps keep the quality of education high, but it does not help students learn.

c Schools should give students more time to prepare before they have to take a test.

IDENTIFYING SUPPORTING DETAILS AND INFORMATION

> **Presentation**
>
> Identifying Supporting Details and Information
>
> Well-written paragraphs have one main idea. All of the information in a paragraph should support the main idea.
>
> After you identify the main idea, look for details, facts, and examples that support it.
>
> Main ideas are general, but supporting details are specific. Understanding the relationship between the main idea and supporting information will help improve your reading comprehension.

Practice 1

Read the sentences. Write an _M_ next to the main idea. Write an _S_ next to the supporting details.

1 __ One of the main causes for the increase in man-made greenhouse gases is deforestation—cutting down large areas of trees for farming or building.

__ Although greenhouse gases occur in nature, humans are also responsible.

__ Human activities such as farming and transportation increase the amounts of these dangerous gases in the atmosphere.

__ In addition, humans burn fuels such as coal, oil, and natural gas for transportation, home heating, and electric appliances.

2 ___ Home heating makes up 34 percent of the average family's energy usage.

___ Setting the heat to a lower temperature and wearing warmer clothing in the colder months would help lower this percentage and decrease greenhouse gases.

___ In the United States, private homes are responsible for about 17 percent of greenhouse gases in the atmosphere.

___ Private homes create a large amount of greenhouse gas, especially from home heating.

3 ___ Even when people are not at home, small appliances such as DVD players, computers, and telephones continue to use electricity all day long.

___ Power companies burn coal or natural gas to produce that electricity.

___ Electricity use creates a large amount of greenhouse gas.

___ This means that every house on every street is always creating greenhouse gases.

Practice 2

Read the main idea sentence. Then circle the letters of all the sentences that support it.

1 Main idea: Poaching—the illegal killing of protected animals for their skins and other parts—is increasing around the world.
  a A new study found an increase in wildlife crime in several African countries.
  b About 30,000 elephants are killed every year for their ivory.
  c The Japanese consume approximately 12 percent of the world's fish.
  d In Malaysia, officials captured 20 tons of elephant ivory last month.
  e Demand is high in Asian countries, such as China, where parts of tigers, elephants, and rhinos are used in medicine.

2 Main idea: A student in Colombia has uncovered the shell of an ancient giant turtle.
  a The 60-million-year-old shell is about the size of a small car, and it was found inside a coal mine.
  b Columbia is the world's fourth largest exporter of coal.
  c The student worked for four days to remove the shell from the earth.
  d This type of giant turtle lived about five million years after the end of the dinosaurs.
  e Experts believe that more living space, a good food supply, and fewer dinosaurs allowed the turtles to survive and grow to their large size.

3 Main idea: A type of European catfish surprised scientists by catching and eating pigeons.
  a The fish jump out of the water, bite the bird, and then roll back into the water, still holding the bird.
  b Pigeons do not eat fish.
  c A French biologist observed the fish and saw fifty-four attacks on pigeons.
  d One catfish can lay up to 4,000 eggs a year per pound of body weight.

Making Inferences

MAKING INFERENCES FROM DIALOGUE

Presentation

Making Inferences from Dialogue

An inference is a kind of guess. When you make an inference, you use information you already know about a topic or situation along with clues from the passage to guess more about it.

To make an inference about a dialogue:

Think about what you know about the topic or situation from your own experience or from learning about it in school.

Look for clues in the passage, such as questions and answers, descriptive words, or punctuation that tell what people are saying, how they are feeling, or what they are thinking.

Practice 1

Read the conversation. Then circle the letter of the correct answer to complete each sentence.

MAN: Look at this job. I'll bet I could do this.

WOMAN: Hm. Are you sure you have the right qualifications?

MAN: Sure. How hard can it be?

WOMAN: Well, for one thing you have to enjoy being around little children. Do you like that sort of thing?

MAN: I guess so. I have some experience working at a high school.

WOMAN: Younger kids are different. Why don't we look at some of these other links up here? Click on "Office Jobs."

1 The people are looking at jobs _____ .
 a in the newspaper
 b on a website

2 The man thinks the job would be _____ .
 a easy
 b difficult

3 The job is probably at _____ .
 a an elementary school
 b a high school

4 The man probably _____ the right experience for the job.
 a has
 b does not have

5 The woman thinks the man _____ apply for the job.
 a should
 b should not

Practice 2

Read the conversation. Then circle the letter of the correct answer to complete each sentence.

MAN: Hello.

WOMAN: Hello, Jim?

MAN: Yes.

WOMAN: This is Ann Smith from the Orson City High School parents' committee.

MAN: It's nice to hear from you, Ann. What can I do for you?

WOMAN: Well, we're raising money for a new gymnasium for Orson City High School. I wondered if you'd like to make a donation.

MAN: I used to give money to the high school when my son went there. That was a several years ago, though.

WOMAN: Yes, Tim's in college now, right?

MAN: Yes, at Franklin University. In fact, I've been donating to them the past few years.

WOMAN: I see. I completely understand. Well, thanks for your time.

MAN: Wait a minute . . . I think I can support kids here in Orson City this year, too.

1 The people are speaking _____ .
   a in person
   b on the phone

2 The people _____ each other.
   a know
   b don't know

3 The man lives in _____ .
   a Orson City
   b a different city

4 The woman thinks the man _____ to make a donation.
   a wants
   b does not want

5 The man's next question will probably be _____ .
   a "Where should I send the donation?"
   b "Where does your daughter go to college?"

Practice 3

Read the conversation. Then circle the letter of the correct answer to complete each sentence.

MAN: Looks like you're studying hard. Do you have a test coming up?

WOMAN: No. I just got this letter from the Career Center. It lists the part-time jobs available next semester.

MAN: You're thinking of getting a job? On top of your school work, basketball team, and volunteering?

WOMAN: Yes, I know. I've thought about that. I would have to quit volunteering at the senior center.

MAN: You told me you love working there! And I'm sure the seniors appreciate you.

WOMAN: The people there are wonderful. Some of them have become my good friends. It would be really hard to say goodbye after all this time.

MAN: It's too bad you have to give that up. Why don't you ask if they have any part-time jobs at the senior center?

WOMAN: You know, that's a really good idea. Thank you.

1 The people are university _____ .
   a professors
   b students

2 The man thinks the woman _____ to get a job.
   a is too busy
   b is not qualified

3 The woman has been volunteering at the senior center for a _____ time.
   a short
   b long

4 The man thinks the senior center might _____ .
   a help the woman find a job
   b pay the woman for her work

5 The woman will probably _____ working at the senior center.
   a continue
   b stop

MAKING INFERENCES IN FICTION

Presentation

Making Inferences in Fiction

An inference is a kind of guess. Fiction writers often use dialogue or descriptions to help readers draw inferences about a situation or about a character's motives or feelings.

To make inferences about fiction, use information you know along with clues from the text, such as dialogue, descriptive words, and punctuation.

Practice 1

Read the passage from *The Curious Case of Benjamin Button* by F. Scott Fitzgerald. Then circle the letter of the correct answer to each question.

"Is the child born?" begged Mr. Button.

Doctor Keene frowned. "Why, yes, I suppose so—after a fashion." Again he threw a curious glance at Mr. Button.

"Is my wife all right?"

"Yes."

"Is it a boy or a girl?"

"Here now!" cried Doctor Keene in a perfect passion of irritation, "I'll ask you to go and see for yourself. Outrageous!" He snapped the last word out in almost one syllable, then he turned away muttering: "Do you imagine a case like this will help my professional reputation? One more would ruin me—ruin anybody."

"What's the matter?" demanded Mr. Button appalled. "Triplets?"

"No, not triplets!" answered the doctor cuttingly. "What's more, you can go and see for yourself. And get another doctor. I brought you into the world, young man, and I've been physician to your family for forty years, but I'm through with you! I don't want to see you or any of your relatives ever again! Good-bye!"

Then he turned sharply, and without another word climbed into his phaeton, which was waiting at the curbstone, and drove severely away.

Mr. Button stood there upon the sidewalk, stupefied and trembling from head to foot. What horrible mishap had occurred?

1 What event are the two people talking about?
   a a car accident
   b the start of a new job
   c a baby's birth
   d a birthday party

2 How does Mr. Button feel?
   a worried
   b happy
   c calm
   d sad

3 How does Doctor Keene feel?
   a joyful
   b excited
   c satisfied
   d upset

4 What might have happened?
   a Mr. Button's wife was hurt.
   b Something was wrong with the baby.
   c Doctor Keene was fired from his job.
   d The babies were triplets.

Practice 2

Read the passage from *The Lords of the Wild* by Joseph A. Altsheler. Then circle the letter of the correct answer to each question.

The tall youth, turning to the right, went down a gentle slope until he came to a little stream, where he knelt and drank. Despite his weariness, his thirst and his danger, he noticed the silvery color of the water, and its soft sighing sound, as it flowed over its pebbly bed, made a pleasant murmur in his ear. Robert Lennox always had an eye for the beautiful, and the flashing brook, in its setting of deep, intense forest green, soothed his senses, speaking to him of comfort and hope.

He drank again and then sat back among the bushes, still breathing heavily, but with much more freedom. The sharp pain left his chest, new strength began to flow into his muscles, and, as the body was renewed, so the spirit soared up and became sanguine once more. He put his ear to the earth and listened long, but heard nothing, save sounds natural to the wilderness, the rustling of leaves before the light wind, the whisper of the tiny current, and the occasional sweet note of a bird in brilliant dress, pluming itself on a bough in its pride. He drew fresh courage from the peace of the woods, and resolved to remain longer there by the stream. Settling himself into the bushes and tall grass, until he was hidden from all but a trained gaze, he waited, body and soul alike growing steadily in vigor.

1 Where is the man?
a in the countryside
b at the beach
c in a small town
d on a boat

2 The man might be _____ .
a a hiker
b a soldier
c a farmer
d a scientist

3 Which phrase best describes the man's feelings?
a relaxed and peaceful
b happy and excited
c relieved but cautious
d calm but lonely

4 What is the man probably doing?
a hiding from enemies
b searching for a friend
c preparing to camp
d hunting for food

5 What probably happened to the man before this scene?
a He was lost in the forest.
b He was bitten by a snake.
c He was hurt in a battle.
d He was found by his friends.

MAKING INFERENCES IN NONFICTION

Presentation

Making Inferences in Nonfiction

An inference is a kind of guess. Making inferences helps you understand a text more deeply. With nonfiction, you need to use your own knowledge about a topic along with clues from the text to infer information about the topic or about the writer's opinions or feelings.

Practice 1

Read the passage. Circle the letter of the sentences that are inferences you can make.

1   Some authors write many books only to have just one or two become popular. Charles Dickens is definitely not one of those authors. One of his best-known works is *David Copperfield*, which was written in 1849. In the book, the main character, David, tells the story of his own life. Many parts of the story are sad. David's parents die when he is a boy, and he has to go to work in a factory. A master of comedy, Dickens somehow tells David's tragic story with amazing humor. Of all of Dickens's books, David Copperfield's story is the closest to the author's own life.

   a Many of Charles Dickens's books became famous.
   b The writer has read all of Dickens's books.
   c David Copperfield was Dickens's favorite character.
   d Dickens had a difficult childhood.
   e The writer enjoys reading Charles Dickens's books.

2   Even if you're not a Harry Potter fan, you probably know a lot about the young glasses-wearing wizard and his adventures at Hogwarts School. With millions spent over the past fifteen years on advertising and promotion for the seven books in the series—each book also having been made into a movie—the story has been impossible to avoid. Surprisingly, some have even called author J. K. Rowling "the most imaginative writer of all time." Where does that kind of inspiration come from? As it turns out, you don't need to have a wildly exciting life in order to create one in your imagination. In fact, an average childhood with an average amount of boredom allowed J. K. Rowling to escape to the excitement of her own mind. Her first story was written for her younger sister. In the story, her sister fell into a rabbit hole and was fed strawberries by the rabbit.

   a The writer is a big Harry Potter fan.
   b The writer disagrees with the opinion that J.K. Rowling is one of the most imaginative writers of all time.
   c J.K. Rowling did not have a very exciting childhood.
   d J.K. Rowling began writing stories as a child.
   e The writer thinks J.K. Rowling should write more books.

Practice 2

Part 1

Read the blog entry. Then circle the letter of the correct answer to complete each statement.

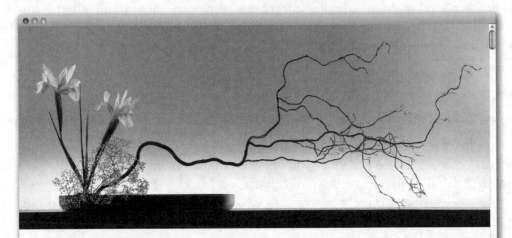

I recently took a class in *ikebana*, the traditional Japanese art of flower arranging. Ikebana is similar to Western-style flower arranging in that both styles use a variety of seasonal flowers and greens arranged in an attractive way. However, they differ in several important ways. First, in ikebana, the act of arranging the flowers should be peaceful and calming. The artist is completely silent while creating the arrangement. It is a time to remember our connection to the natural world and appreciate the beauty around us. For me, practicing ikebana has become a wonderful way to forget about the troubles of daily life. Second, in contrast to crowded Western-style arrangements, which use many types of flowers of different colors and can look "busy," ikebana features open, pleasing designs of mainly stems and leaves and just a few flowers (or even none at all). Another important aspect of ikebana is the idea that the individual arranger should express his or her own character or emotions through the arrangement. In this way, the ikebana arrangement is more than flowers in a vase. It is a form of human communication. Although I still love making traditional Western bouquets, ikebana has given me a new way to relax and appreciate the beauty of nature.

1 The writer has tried _____ of flower arranging.
   a one style
   b two styles

2 The writer thinks Western-style arrangements _____ colors.
   a use too many
   b don't use enough

3 Overall, the writer prefers _____ flower arranging.

  a ikebana

  b Western-style

4 For the writer, flower arranging is mostly a way to _____ .

  a express her emotions

  b relieve her stress

5 In the future, the writer will probably _____ .

  a practice only Western-style flower arranging

  b practice both ikebana and Western-style flower arranging

Part 2

Read the blog entry. Then circle the letter of the correct answer to complete each statement.

If you're planning a trip to Brazil, it's worth making a stop in the city of Curitiba. The weather is good, and there are many interesting sites to see (but here's a tip from me: bring a coat if you go during the winter months).

In addition, Curitiba is an excellent model of green urban design. Last year, it won an international award for its environment-conscious city planning. I think we can learn a lot from Curitiba about how to reduce waste and protect the planet. If we tried just one or two of its programs here, our city would be so much better off.

To begin with, Curitiba has over 1,000 public parks, so residents have plenty of natural surroundings to enjoy. Imagine a park in our downtown area instead of abandoned buildings and that ugly old parking garage.

Also, about 70 percent of the residents of Curitiba use public transportation, so there aren't any traffic jams, and there's hardly any pollution. The buses run often and on time, and the bus stops are also comfortable and attractive. So different from here!

Here's my favorite aspect of Curitiba's plan: the city has an exchange program in which residents can exchange bags of trash for bus tickets, food, school supplies, chocolate, or even movie tickets! As a result of these and other programs, the city is able to recycle 70 percent of its waste. That's double the rate of our city! I know we can do better than that. I believe that, with time, Curitiba's programs are achievable here. It just takes commitment and a few people to get things started!

Interested? E-mail me at jack_redman1977@pearson.net to find out more.

1 The writer _____ visited Curitiba.

  a has

  b has not

2 The writer thinks Curitiba's systems could be _____ for his city.

   a possible

   b unrealistic

3 The writer thinks the old buildings in his city's downtown should _____ .

   a be rebuilt

   b become a park

4 The buses in the writer's city _____ .

   a are often late

   b usually run on time

5 The writer wants people to e-mail him to _____ .

   a discuss moving to Curitiba

   b help improve their city

FOLLOWING IDEAS IN PARAGRAPHS

Presentation

Following Ideas in Paragraphs

Use your reading skills to follow a writer's ideas through a paragraph. Keep the main idea in mind, and pay attention to the supporting sentences the writer includes.

Practice 1

Read the paragraph. Then circle the letter of the correct phrase to complete the paragraph.

1 Even if you're not a Harry Potter fan, you probably know a lot about the young glasses-wearing wizard and his adventures at Hogwarts School. With millions spent over the past fifteen years on advertising and promotion for the seven books in the series—each book also having been made into a movie—the story has been _____ .

   a impossible to avoid

   b easy to forget

   c difficult to understand

   d hard to find

2 Surprisingly, some have even called Harry Potter author J. K. Rowling "the most imaginative writer of all time." Where does that kind of inspiration come from? As it turns out, you don't need to have a wildly exciting life in order to create one in your imagination. In fact, an average childhood with an average amount of boredom allowed J. K. Rowling to escape to the excitement of her _____ .

   a own mind

   b mother's arms

   c living room

   d backyard

3 J. K. Rowling was born in England on July 31, 1965. Her first name is Joanne, but she prefers to be called Jo. She began writing stories when she was a very young child, and when she was growing up, she loved reading her stories to her younger sister, Dianne. In fact, the main character in Rowling's very first story—an adventure story about a girl who falls into a rabbit's hole—was _____ .

   a her sister

   b named Jo

   c her mother

   d a rabbit

4 Rowling got the idea for Harry Potter in 1990 at age 25 when she was returning to London by train after a trip to northern England. The idea came to her suddenly and mysteriously. In a newspaper interview, the author said, "I really don't know where the idea came from. It started with Harry, and then all these characters and situations came flooding into my head." When she got home that evening, Rowling sat down and began writing the book that _____ .

   a no one would read

   b ended her career

   c she would never complete

   d would make her famous

5 Today, there are seven novels in the Harry Potter series, and they have been translated into sixty-five languages. The seventh and final book, *Harry Potter and the Deathly Hallows*, was the fastest-selling book of all time. The Harry Potter series may be finished, but J. K. Rowling continues to write books for children and adults. When asked if she planned to write any more books about Harry Potter in the future, Rowling said, "I can't say I'll never write another book about that world, but I think _____ ."

   a I'll give up writing

   b it's unlikely

   c it's unfortunate

   d it's certain

Practice 2

Read the paragraph. Then circle the letter of the correct phrase to complete the paragraph.

1 Ecotourism, also known as "ecological" or "green" tourism, has become a popular way to travel in recent years. Ecotourism refers to a travel experience with the aim of learning about the local people and having a positive effect on the environment. Supporters of ecotourism say it's both _____ .

   a expensive and dangerous

   b good and bad

   c fun and educational

   d convenient and popular

2 An ecotour may include opportunities to study local plants and animals, do volunteer work such as planting trees or teaching in schools, or learn about local culture and heritage. An important feature is the idea that visitors should not disturb the local environment and culture; rather, their presence and actions should have _____ .

    a a positive impact

    b a lot of energy

    c a beginning and an end

    d a focus on food

3 Ecotourism can be good for developing countries. For many nations—such as Costa Rica, Kenya, Madagascar, and Nepal—income from ecotourism makes up a large portion of the economy. Ecotourism helps educate visitors and local people about the need to conserve and protect the _____ .

    a land and natural resources

    b tourists from crime

    c banks and city offices

    d tourists during emergencies

4 However, not all of the effects of ecotourism are positive. There are often no limits on the number of visitors to a location. Over time, the constant presence of large numbers of people has an effect on the natural surroundings and wildlife. Hotels, restaurants, and shops are built near protected natural areas to accommodate more visitors. In addition, animals become accustomed to human presence and change _____ .

    a the way they look

    b their names and addresses

    c their behavior and eating habits

    d the color of their fur

5 Some countries are trying to address the issues and challenges presented by ecotourism. However, if this travel trend continues to gain popularity, much more will have to be done to ensure that it leads to positive effects rather than _____ .

    a negative ones

    b government ones

    c natural ones

    d popular ones

Recognizing Patterns

SEQUENCE PATTERN

Presentation

Sequence Pattern: Steps in a Process

A sequence pattern is one way of organizing information in a text. Writers use a sequence pattern to list steps in a process, for example in instructions or recipes. The steps are written in the order that they should be done.

This pattern uses many words and phrases to signal the order of the steps. Examples include *first, first of all, second, next, then, after, before, finally, once, when, now, while,* and *at the same time.*

Practice 1

Read each paragraph. Underline the words and phrases that indicate a sequence.

1. How to Change a Flat Tire

Imagine that you are driving down the highway. It's a nice day, and you are listening to music on your car radio. Suddenly, you feel a bump, and the car starts to slide back and forth unevenly. You have a flat tire! Fortunately, it isn't very difficult to change a tire yourself as long as you have the right tools. Here's how. First, you need to get the car off the road. Before you stop, be sure to find a straight part of the road where other cars can see you. When you have found a safe place to stop, pull over and turn on your flashing hazard lights. Exit the car and open the trunk. Remove the spare tire and all of the necessary tools, and place them near the flat tire. After that, carefully loosen the bolts in the flat tire. Then use the jack—a special tool for lifting—to raise the car up. When the car is about six inches off the ground, remove the bolts and take off the flat tire. You are now ready to put on the spare tire and reattach the bolts. Once you have securely tightened them, you can lower the car. Finally, put your tools away and continue driving.

2. How to Get the Best Price for a Product Online

There are several things you can do to make sure you get the best deal before you make a purchase on the Internet. First of all, you should decide whether you need to buy a new or used product. Many websites offer both new and used versions of the same product. Second, look for websites that offer sales on the product you're looking for. Do a general search using the product name and the phrase on sale. When you have located several sites that carry the product you want, click the links to open three or four different sites. Open the product page on all of the sites at the same time. Look at each site and compare the price as well as any services offered, such as warranties or repair agreements. Once you have found the site with the best deal, bookmark the store's site and close the other ones. Next, open your browser again, and do a search using your selected store's name and the phrase promotion code. You will be amazed to find coupons and codes you can enter for extra savings or free shipping on your product. Now you are ready to purchase your product.

Sequence Pattern: Order of Events

A sequence pattern is one way of organizing information in a text. Writers use a sequence pattern to describe a series of events that happened in a particular order or at a particular time. This pattern uses many words and phrases to signal the order of the events. Examples include the following:

Specific dates or time periods: *in 1968, June 3rd, at 6:00 P.M., in the 1950s, during World War II*

Time words and expressions: *today, soon, at that time, in the morning, last week, yesterday*

Words and phrases that tell the order of events: *in the beginning, first, next, then, later, after that, finally, before, after, when, while*

Practice 2

Read the sentences from an article about the artist Andy Warhol. Number the sentences in the correct order so that they form a paragraph.

1

_____ During this time, Warhol began drawing. He listened to the radio and surrounded his bed with pictures of movie stars.

_____ Later in life, he described this as an important time for his development as an artist.

_____ When he was in third grade, he suffered from a serious illness, which forced him to stay in bed and miss school for many months.

_____ Andy Warhol was born in Pittsburgh, Pennsylvania in 1928.

2

_____ After he graduated in 1949, he went to New York and began working as an illustrator for magazines such as *Vogue* and *The New Yorker*.

_____ In college, Warhol studied commercial art at the Carnegie Institute of Technology in Pittsburgh.

_____ During this time, he became known for his colorful drawings of shoes, which appeared in those magazines.

3

_____ Later in the 1960s, Warhol began to work from a New York studio, which he called The Factory.

_____ In the 1960s, Warhol began painting objects such as bananas, soup cans, and Coca-Cola® bottles.

_____ During his time at The Factory, Warhol made over 300 films.

_____ Soon, he became famous around the world for these paintings of everyday objects.

_____ His first movie, entitled _Sleep_, was filmed in 1964 and showed nothing but a man sleeping for six hours.

4

_____ After Warhol recovered, his lifestyle and his artwork changed.

_____ In the summer of 1968, Andy Warhol was shot in the stomach by a woman who had worked for him at The Factory.

_____ During this time, he began painting portraits of famous celebrities, such as Elvis Presley and Marilyn Monroe.

_____ The next day, when the woman was arrested, she said, "He had too much control over my life."

5

_____ In his later years, Warhol spent much of his time promoting younger artists, such as Keith Haring.

_____ More than 2,000 people attended his funeral, which was held at St. Patrick's Cathedral in New York City.

_____ He died in 1987 after suffering complications following surgery.

COMPARISON AND CONTRAST PATTERN

Presentation

Compare-and-Contrast Pattern

Comparing and contrasting are ways of organizing information in a text. Writers use this pattern to discuss the similarities and differences between two or more things. Signal words for comparing and contrasting include the following:

	To compare	**To contrast**
Coordinating conjunctions and paired conjunctions	and, as well as, both . . . and . . .	but, yet
Transition signals	similarly, too, also	in contrast, on the other hand, however, instead,
Subordinators		though, although, even though, while
Others (adjectives, prepositions, verbs)	be similar to, be like, be alike, be the same, have X in common	differ, be different from, be unlike, rather than

Practice 1

Read the paragraph. Then write the number of each phrase in the correct box.

Thai and Korean food are two types of Asian cuisine that are popular in Western countries. Both types of food feature delicious main dishes. They are also alike in their use of spicy, hot peppers, and both styles of cooking include rice and noodles. Thai cuisine uses sweet tropical flavors, such as coconut and fruit. Korean food, however, tends to use mainly savory seasonings, such as sesame oil and green onions. Thai dishes feature a lot of seafood, but the focus of Korean food is more on meat—especially beef. In fact, Korean cooking may be best known for its barbecued beef dishes. As far as presentation is concerned, Thai food can be very colorful, often using carved fruit and vegetables as decorations. By contrast, Korean dishes tend to be simpler and less decorative.

1. a lot of seafood
2. spicy hot peppers
3. simpler and less decorative
4. mainly savory seasonings
5. popular in Western countries

6. fruit and vegetable decorations
7. known for barbecue dishes
8. rice and noodles
9. sweet tropical flavors
10. delicious main dishes

Thai Food	Both Thai and Korean Food	Korean Food

Practice 2

Read the paragraph. Then write the number of each phrase or sentence in the correct box.

The anthropologist Edward T. Hall first introduced the idea of "high-context" and "low-context" cultures to explain cultural differences in communication. According to Hall, high-context cultures are more common in Eastern countries such as Japan and China, whereas most Western countries are low-context cultures. Of course, communication is important in both high- and low-context cultures; it is just the communication style that differs.

According to Hall, both types of culture use nonverbal cues to communicate. High-context conversation involves greater use of nonverbal features such as voice, tone, and gestures. By contrast, people in low-context cultures, such as the United States and Germany, rely more on words to convey meaning. They tend to speak directly, but people from high-context cultures, such as Japan or China, often communicate indirectly.

Conversation is used to begin personal relationships in both high- and low-context cultures. People from high-context cultures share a lot of detailed personal information with friends and coworkers. By contrast, people in low-context cultures generally share only necessary information with smaller, select groups of people.

1. People communicate indirectly.

2. Conversation begins personal relationships.

3. common in Eastern countries

4. People communicate directly.

5. Communication is important.

6. People share only necessary information.

7. common in Western countries

8. Nonverbal cues are used to communicate.

9. People share detailed personal information.

High-Context Cultures	Both High- and Low-Context Cultures	Low-Context Cultures

CAUSE AND EFFECT PATTERN

Cause and Effect Pattern

Cause/effect is a way of organizing information in a text. Writers use this pattern to discuss the reasons (causes) and the results (effects) of an action, event, or decision.

Words and phrases that signal causes or effects include the following:

	To signal a cause	To signal an effect
Coordinating conjunctions and paired conjunctions	for	so
Transition signals		therefore, as a result, consequently, thus
Subordinators	because, since, as	
Others (adjectives, prepositions, verbs)	because of, due to, (as) a result of, result from, be caused by	the cause of, the reason for, to cause, produce, help, make, create, affect, lead to, result in, be responsible for

Practice 1

Read each paragraph. Then underline the words and phrases that signal a cause or an effect.

1. Auroras are caused when the sun creates high-energy gas called solar wind. When this solar wind hits Earth's magnetic field, it creates an electrical current. The electricity begins to travel along the surface of Earth's atmosphere and gathers more energy until it reaches the poles. The light of an aurora is a result of these high-energy electrical particles mixing with other gases, such as oxygen and nitrogen.

2. Although most greenhouse gases result from business activities and transportation, private homes also cause problems. In fact, private homes in the United States are responsible for about 17 percent of greenhouse gases in the atmosphere. Home heating makes up 34 percent of the average family's energy usage. Setting the heat to a lower temperature and wearing warmer clothing in the colder months would help lower this percentage and produce fewer greenhouse gases.

Practice 2

Part 1

Read each paragraph. Then circle the letter of the correct word or phrase to complete each sentence.

Historians point to three main reasons for the fall of ancient Rome:

A decreasing belief in religion caused the Roman people to care less about honesty and ethical behavior. This resulted in increased crime and social problems.

The use of the poisonous metal lead in water pipes and cosmetics created health problems and mental illness in much of the population.

Climate change affected the environment and resulted in cooler summers. This had a negative effect on agriculture. There was simply not enough food for the people of Rome.

1 The change in people's behavior _____ decreasing religious beliefs.
   a was caused by   **b** resulted in

2 Crime and social problems were _____ people caring less about honesty.
   a the cause of   **b** the result of

3 The use of lead _____ health problems and mental illness.
   a produced   **b** was a result of

4 Climate change _____ cooler summers.
   a was due to   **b** caused

5 Food shortages _____ cooler weather.
   a were caused by   **b** created

Part 2

Read each paragraph. Then choose the correct word or phrase to complete each sentence.

Not all of the effects of ecotourism have been positive. There are often no limits on the number of visitors to a location. over time, the constant presence of large numbers of people has a negative effect on the natural surroundings of wildlife. More hotels, restaurants, and shops are built near protected natural areas to accommodate more visitors. In addition, animals become accustomed to human presence and change their behavior and eating habits.

1. Ecotourism _____ some negative effects.
   a. has been caused by   **b.** has caused

2. Large numbers of visitors _____ negative effects on wildlife.
   a. lead to   **b.** are created by

3. Hotels, restaurants, and shops are built _____ the need to accommodate more visitors.
   a. to create   **b.** because of

4. Animal behavior has changed _____ human presence.
   a. due to   **b.** resulting in

IDENTIFYING PATTERNS

Practice 1

Read the paragraph. Circle the letter of the correct pattern.

I recently took a class in *ikebana,* the traditional art of Japanese flower arranging. Ikebana is similar to Western-style flower arranging in that both styles use a variety of seasonal flowers and greens arranged in an attractive way. However, they differ in several important ways. First, in ikebana, the act of arranging the flowers should be peaceful and calming. The artist is completely silent while creating the arrangement. It is a time to remember our connection to the natural world and appreciate the beauty around us. For me, practicing ikebana has become a wonderful way to forget about the troubles of daily life. Second, in contrast to crowded Western-style arrangements, which use many types of colorful flowers and can look "busy," ikebana features open, pleasing designs of mainly stems and leaves and just a few flowers (or even none at all). Another important aspect of ikebana is the idea that the individual arranger should express his or her own character or emotions through the arrangement. In this way, the ikebana arrangement is more than flowers in a vase. It is a form of human communication. Although I still love making traditional Western bouquets, ikebana has given me a new way to relax and appreciate the beauty of nature.

1 Which best describes the pattern of the paragraph above?

    a sequence   **b** compare and contrast   **c** cause and effect

A MOOC is a new option for people who enjoy learning online. MOOC is an acronym that stands for "massive open online course." Anyone with access to the Internet can take a MOOC, and there are many interesting things you can learn. To join a MOOC, the first thing you need to do is check that your computer has a working microphone. Then get a pair of headphones, if necessary. Next, find a website that lists MOOCs. Large universities usually offer a variety of them. When you have decided on the topic you want to study, you are ready to submit your registration form. Once that step is complete, check your e-mail for the access link to your MOOC. The final step is to log in to the MOOC on the correct date and time, and let the online learning begin!

2 Which best describes the pattern of the preceding paragraph on page 58?

a sequence   **b** compare and contrast   **c** cause and effect

It took many years of searching before Pluto was first discovered in 1930. Long before that, in the late 1800s, an astronomer named Percival Lowell noticed that two planets, Uranus and Neptune, did not go around the sun in a perfect circle as they should. This discovery meant that something else—another large body—must be pulling the two planets out of orbit. The search for a ninth planet began. On February 18, 1930, a young astronomer named Clyde Tombaugh found an object among the stars. After several colleagues confirmed his observations, Tombaugh's discovery was finally named the ninth planet. It was called Pluto after the Roman god of the underworld.

3 Which best describes the pattern of the paragraph above?

a sequence   **b** compare and contrast   **c** cause and effect

Certain types of insects, such as the Asian long-horned beetle, have become a major problem as global trade has expanded. When goods and products are transported between countries by plane or ship, insects or their eggs often come along for the ride and are transported from their native habitats. The population of these insects can then grow too quickly. This can have a terrible effect on the environment, causing major damage to trees and food crops. The Asian long-horned beetle is an insect that is native to Japan, China, and Korea. The beetle makes holes in trees and eats the wood on the inside, eventually killing the tree. In Asia, the beetles are eaten by various birds and other insects, so most trees are safe. However, when the beetle was transported to North America on ships from China, it caused big problems. Since 1996, when it was first identified in New York City, the beetle has destroyed thousands of trees. Teams of environmentalists and scientists have been working hard to find ways to deal with the problem.

4 Which best describes the pattern of the paragraph above?

a sequence   **b** compare and contrast   **c** cause and effect

Anita Caldwell grew up believing that it was her duty to help others. Even as a young girl in elementary school, she was an active member of her community. Her mother recalls a time when Anita was eight years old and an elderly neighbor was sick. Anita visited the woman every day, bringing her food and helping with the housework and gardening. "She was always doing something to help other people," says Anita's mom proudly. Now that she is in her 40s, Anita hasn't changed much. She is the founder of Health-Wise, a program that collects fresh vegetables and fruits donated from local farms and delivers them to the elderly in nursing homes.

5 Which best describes the pattern of the paragraph above?

a sequence   **b** compare and contrast   **c** cause and effect

Hatching order affects birds' behavior later in life. Researchers studied several families of zebra finches. The study found that the order in which baby birds in the same nest hatched from their eggs affected the birds' behavior later. When the birds could fly, the younger birds—those that hatched later—were more adventurous than their older brothers and sisters. Researchers believe this helps the younger birds survive by making them able to travel farther from the nest to find their own food.

6 Which best describes the pattern of the paragraph above?

a sequence   **b** compare and contrast   **c** cause and effect

Comprehension Skills Practice Test

Part 1   Previewing and Predicting

Read the first sentence from a news article. Then write the correct news article title for each sentence. There is one extra title.

Source of Strange Odor Still Unknown	New Website Helps Women Find Jobs
Fewer People Smoking at Work	
Most Female Managers Want to Quit	Scientists Hopeful for Cancer Cure

1 _____ A group of medical researchers met in Paris last week to discuss the exciting results of a five-year study.

2 _____ Employees aren't taking as many cigarette breaks at the office these days, choosing instead to take a walk outside or stay at their desks and surf the web.

3 _____ Police are still not sure where the unusual smell residents noticed on Franklin Street last night is coming from.

4 _____ A recent survey of 110 women in top-level positions in their companies showed that the majority of them would prefer not to work.

Part 2   Skimming

Read the previewing questions. Then skim the passage and circle the letters of the two previewing questions that are answered in the passage.

1

Source of Strange Odor Still Unknown

Police are still not sure where the unusual smell residents noticed on Franklin Street last night is coming from. Several calls came in to the police station between 7:00 and 9:00 P.M., with people reporting an unexplained strong smell outside their homes. Homeowner Christine Takacs said, "It was a very sweet smell, like some sort of candy. But it didn't smell natural; it smelled like chemicals. I got worried, so I called my children inside and called the police." Police are asking residents to stay indoors until they can determine where the smell is coming from and whether it is dangerous. For updates and further information, check the Green Springs town website at www.gstown.net.

a What did the odor smell like?

b How should people protect themselves?

c When will the smell go away?

d What is causing the smell?

2

Most Female Managers Want to Quit

A recent survey of 110 women in top-level positions in their companies showed that the majority of them would prefer not to work. The survey was conducted by a group of graduate students in the Business Administration program at City University. The students sent out a mail-in survey and conducted face-to-face interviews with females working in management positions in fifty-four different companies. The survey and interviews asked questions about job satisfaction, family life, stress levels, and personal likes and dislikes at work. Sixty-five percent of the women responded that if given the opportunity, they would prefer not to work at all. Most cited work-related stress as the reason.

a How many women were surveyed?

b Who conducted the survey?

c Which companies do the women work at?

d How satisfied are the women with their salaries?

Part 3 Previewing Longer Passages

Preview and skim the text. Then read the questions and circle the letters of the correct answer.

Technology and Employment Rates

Fewer jobs, moving jobs

Recent developments in technology and the rapid expansion of the global economy have had a negative effect on some fields of employment.

New types of technology have made it possible for some companies to use machines instead of humans to do jobs such as factory work. While saving companies money, this development has reduced the number of available jobs, especially for those with lower education levels. Moreover, technological developments have also changed global supply routes, creating more job opportunities in some countries and cutting job options in others. In short, there are fewer jobs available overall, and those jobs that are available are concentrated in certain regions of the world.

How governments can help workers

Globalization and the trend toward using technology to replace human workers are not likely to slow down any time soon. Unless political leaders step in to ensure more equal distribution of jobs

and wealth, the world economy is in danger of losing balance. However, these developments aren't entirely bad. In fact, these changes have created a rise in the number of higher-level management jobs. Governments can meet the need for skilled labor by supporting education and training opportunities for unskilled workers who have lost their jobs. In this way, displaced workers may be able to get the qualifications they need to succeed.

Economic and political solutions

Governments can also help balance global employment opportunities by collaborating and communicating with other nations on tax systems, regulations, and trade policies that will help keep manufacturing and trade healthy in all regions of the world.

Of course, even if governments take the problems seriously, there's no guarantee that taking these steps will make a lasting difference. Nevertheless, even if today's government leaders are just beginning to think about ways to protect people's futures, it's a good start.

1 What type of passage is this?

   a a magazine article

   b an e-mail message

   c a travel blog

   d a company memo

2 What is the main topic of this passage?

   a politics

   b science

   c economics

   d history

3 Which topic is NOT discussed in this passage?

   a solutions to the problem

   b reasons why there are fewer jobs

   c how governments can help workers

   d which countries will succeed in the future

Part 4   Scanning

Read each question and then scan the festival poster for the answer. Write the answer to the question.

Celebrate Hartland City's
35th Annual Tomato Festival

Who: Sponsored by the Hartland City Business Association (www.hartlandbiz.com)

What: Three days of food, fun, art, and 50 live musical performances!

Where: Downtown Hartland, between Ralley Street and 7th Avenue

When: July 26, 27, and 28, 2016

How: Tickets are available at Blue Moon Bakery, Chelsea's Ice Cream, Rick's Tavern, and Brown's Hardware.

Adults – $20.00
Kids 12 and under – $8.00
Kids under 5 – FREE
Call for information: (802) 290-1625

---

1 What is the price of an adult ticket to the festival?
$ _____ .00

2 How many years has the city held the festival?
_____

3 How many places can people buy tickets?
_____

4 Where in Hartland City is the festival held?
Between Ralley Street and _____

5 How many musical performances are scheduled?
_____

6 How many days will the festival last?
_____

7 How much does a ticket cost for a three-year-old child?
_____

Part 5 Skimming

Skim the text to find the main idea. Then circle the letters of three true statements on the next page.

New Hands-Free Computer Controls

Information technology experts are always working on innovative ways to solve problems and improve the design and function of computers. The vast increase in computer use over the past two decades has literally been a pain in the neck for many people. Sitting at a desk, staring straight ahead at a screen for several hours, and clicking a mouse hundreds of times can eventually cause muscle and joint stiffness. Soon, there will be relief for those who suffer from computer-related physical pain and discomfort.

This year, a new device will go on sale that will allow people to use the Internet, search files, and scroll through documents without ever touching their computers. The new hands-free motion controller sits on the desk in front of the computer. Users put their hands above the controller and simply point at the screen to browse the web, play games, or open spreadsheets. The device even recognizes and reacts to more complex movements, such as pulling, grabbing, and pinching. This feature allows users to manipulate three-dimensional images on the screen as though they are working with a piece of clay.

Representatives for the product's manufacturing company say the enhanced freedom of movement will help alleviate muscle soreness and other physical issues suffered by so many computer users.

a   The article is about a new type of technology.

b   The device is already sold in stores.

c   The new technology will be helpful for students.

d   The article explains what the product can do.

e   The goal of the product is to help computers work faster.

Part 6   Skimming

Read the question. Then read the passage and circle the letter of the correct answer.

1

Contrary to many countries around the world, the twenty-seven nations of the European Union (EU) have strict policies against the use of animal testing for developing products such as cosmetics. Strict new animal protection legislation bans the sale of all cosmetics that have been developed through animal testing. The EU has had anti-animal-testing laws in place since 2009, but the new law has been expanded to include all ingredients in cosmetic products regardless of where in the world the animal testing took place. For example, French cosmetics corporations can no longer purchase ingredients produced in China or elsewhere if animals were used in lab testing during the development of those ingredients.

What is the purpose of this text?

a   to express the author's opinion on animal testing

b   to compare animal testing policies in different countries

c   to describe a new ban on animal testing for cosmetics

Part 7   Understanding Paragraphs

Read each group of sentences. Decide if they form a unified paragraph. Circle the letter of the correct answer.

1

Australia's Great Barrier Reef is one of the world's most diverse ecosystems. It is the largest structure on Earth that is made by living organisms and can be seen from space. The reef spans an area of 344,400 square kilometers. It is made up of hundreds of breathtakingly beautiful tropical islands and over 2,900 individual reef systems, which are home to an abundance of marine species.

a   unified paragraph

b   not a unified paragraph

2

Australia is the largest island-country in the world and has a population of about 22 million people. Human activities on the island, such as fishing, diving, and tourism, have had a devastating effect on the wildlife in some parts of the reef. The establishment of protected areas, such as the Great Barrier Reef Marine Park, has helped to limit the negative impacts of human use, but environmental scientists and marine biologists say more must be done to preserve this natural wonder of the world.

a   unified paragraph

b   not a unified paragraph

Part 8   Identifying the Topic of a Paragraph

Read each paragraph. Circle the letter of the correct topic.

1

The symptoms of a peanut allergy can be fatal. The reaction primarily affects the respiratory system, causing a swelling of the air passages that makes it difficult for the victim to breathe. If the person has a severe sensitivity, he or she may die. Even a tiny amount of peanut dust in the air is enough to kill some peanut allergy sufferers. For this reason, peanuts are no longer served as snacks on airplanes, and many school cafeterias have become peanut-free zones.

a   types of snacks served on airplanes

b   dangers of peanut allergies

c   peanut allergies in children

2

Identity theft is the crime of stealing someone's identity—data such as a person's name, address, phone number, social security number, or other personal information. Typically, thieves steal people's identities for financial gain. For example, they can access credit cards or bank accounts. Some victims of identity theft have been held accountable for thousands of dollars of debt when thieves obtained their credit card numbers and went on lavish spending sprees, purchasing cars, airline tickets, or other luxury items.

a   a definition of identity theft

b   the victims of identity theft

c   new types of crime

3

Each year, the average family gets numerous sore throats, runny noses, coughs, fevers, and other types of viruses. In these cases, many parents bring their children to their physician's office expecting a prescription for antibiotics to help the child get well faster. These days, however, most doctors are cautious about doling out these drugs when they aren't really necessary. Instead, doctors may be more likely to recommend rest and letting the patient's immune system do its job.

a   family problems

b   doctors' use of medication

c   how the immune system works

Part 9   Identifying the Main Idea

Read each paragraph. Circle the letter of the main idea.

1

Carlo Petrini developed the Slow Food movement to counteract society's tendency to embrace a faster and more convenient—but less healthy and enjoyable—way of living. In his home country of Italy, he saw that because of the globalization of the food industry, many small local farms could no longer compete with the lower-cost producers abroad and were beginning to close down. Petrini promoted Slow Food as an alternative to the global expansion of fast-food culture, in which food products are shipped around the world for mass-production and consumption

a Carlo Petrini is an Italian who is interested in international food trends.

b Carlo Petrini has introduced many important ideas, including Slow Food, to Italy.

c Carlo Petrini developed Slow Food to help people be healthier and to help local farms.

2.

Strict animal protection legislature was recently passed in the European Union (EU). The law bans the sale of all cosmetics that have been developed through animal testing. The EU has had anti-animal-testing laws in place since 2009, but the new law has been expanded to include all ingredients in cosmetic products regardless of where in the world the animal testing took place. For example, French cosmetics corporations can no longer purchase ingredients produced in China or elsewhere if animals were used in lab testing during the development of those ingredients.

a The EU has had anti-animal-testing laws since 2009.

b The EU has introduced new and stricter laws to regulate animal testing.

c China produces some products that are tested on animals.

Part 10   Identifying Supporting Details

Read the sentences. Write *M* next to the main idea. Write *S* next to the supporting details.

_____ Over 100 different types of antibiotics are used to treat all sorts of health problems.

_____ The first antibiotic was penicillin, which was accidentally discovered in a mold culture.

_____ Antibiotics are some of the most frequently prescribed types of medications.

_____ These medicines treat diseases by killing the bacteria that cause them.

Part 11   Making Inferences

Read the conversation. Then circle the letter of the correct answer to complete each sentence.

MAN: I heard Sandra ended up getting the promotion you wanted. Sorry about that.

WOMAN: Yeah. Well, I could live without getting the promotion. It was Sandra's behavior afterward that really bothered me. Did you see her?

MAN: Oh, come on. Don't be a poor sport. You'll have your chance.

WOMAN: Well, she didn't have to go around the office handing out her new business cards right in front of me.

1 The people are _____ .
   a coworkers
   b neighbors

2 The man and woman _____ .
   a just met recently
   b know each other well

3 The woman is feeling _____ .
   a envious
   b relieved

4 Sandra is probably _____ person.
   a a thoughtful
   b an inconsiderate

Part 12   Making Inferences

Read the passage from *Peter Pan* by J. M. Barrie. Then circle the letter of the correct answer to each question.

> Mr. Darling used to boast to Wendy that her mother not only loved him but respected him. He was one of those deep ones who know about stocks and shares. Of course no one really knows, but he quite seemed to know, and he often said stocks were up and shares were down in a way that would have made any woman respect him.
>
> Mrs. Darling was married in white.
>
> Wendy came first, then John, then Michael.
>
> For a week or two after Wendy came, it was doubtful whether they would be able to keep her, as she was another mouth to feed.
>
> Mr. Darling was frightfully proud of her, but he was very honourable, and he sat on the edge of Mrs. Darling's bed, holding her hand and calculating expenses, while she looked at him imploringly. She wanted to risk it, come what might, but that was not his way; his way was with a pencil and a piece of paper, and if she confused him with suggestions he had to begin at the beginning again.

1 Which phrase best describes Mr. Darling's personality?

   a cautious and responsible

   b quiet and shy

   c lazy and unreliable

   d modern and progressive

2 Who are Wendy, John, and Michael?

   a the Darling's neighbors

   b the Darling's friends

   c the Darling's parents

   d the Darling's children

3 How does Mr. Darling feel about the future?

   a excited

   b worried

   c happy

   d strange

4 What can be inferred about the situation?

   a Mr. Darling will leave his job.

   b Mrs. Darling will leave Mr. Darling.

   c Mr. Darling will make a decision.

   d Mrs. Darling will get a job.

Part 13 Making Inferences

Read the passage. Then circle the letters of the sentences that are inferences you can make.

Terrence Park is a student at the University of California, Berkeley, majoring in Applied Mathematics. Park is passionate about math. Last year, he became president of the university's math club. He studies diligently and gets excellent grades. For his lab internship, he is studying mathematical applications in cancer research.

From an outsider's perspective, Park has a bright future ahead of him. He has all the potential to make great contributions to the world, maybe in the field of medical research or chemistry. However, when Park graduates next year, he isn't expecting to find a job at all.

Park is among the hundreds of undocumented students enrolled in California universities. These students, most of whom are the children of immigrants, do not have legal U.S. citizenship. Although Park has lived in the United States for almost his entire life, he is not a legal citizen because he was born in his parents' home country and was brought to this country illegally.

Although undocumented students are allowed to attend school, the law prohibits companies from hiring illegal workers —workers who are not official citizens of the United States. Aside from low-wage labor jobs, even with a college degree, Park has no chance of getting the kind of job for which he is qualified.

Terrence Park plans to become a U.S. citizen after he graduates from Berkeley, but the process takes time— something he doesn't have much of as a busy university student. Therefore, after graduation, instead of putting on a suit and going to job interviews, Park will be taking citizenship classes with other undocumented immigrants from different countries. The classes teach immigrants about American history, government, and culture. It will take Park about a year to complete the requirements to finally become an American.

a Terrence Park enjoys studying.

b Park feels confident and optimistic about his future.

c Park wants to return to his parents' home country.

d Park may need to take a low-wage job after college.

e Park will graduate from college in the United States.

Part 14   Following Ideas in Paragraphs

Read the paragraph. Then write the correct phrase to complete the paragraph.

1

| peanuts are not actually nuts | the problem isn't very serious | no one knows the cause for sure | many other snacks are dangerous |

The reason for the recent rise in peanut allergies is still unknown. Some researchers hypothesize that our increased focus on eliminating germs and the use of medications that kill bacteria, such as antibiotics, have weakened our immune systems. Others blame the fact that peanuts are usually roasted, a process that can bring out harmful allergens in food. However, _____ .

2

| try not to use a computer | switch to a different bank | keep a positive attitude | stay aware of the latest identity scams |

To protect yourself from identity theft, experts recommend carefully monitoring your credit cards and bank accounts and keeping receipts and records of your own purchases. Look through bank statements regularly and check for suspicious transactions. In addition, change your online passwords and log-in information from time to time, especially those on financial accounts. Finally, invest in good Internet security software and _____ .

3

| our own immune systems | other types of illnesses | our friends and relatives | the use of chemicals |

The overuse of antibiotics is risky business. Because bacteria are living organisms, they can mutate or change over time. As a result of decades of antibiotic use, some bacteria have changed and become resistant to certain types of drugs. These so-called "super germs" are stronger, so they no longer respond to the medications. They also have the power to affect larger portions of the population with more serious illnesses, making it more difficult to fight them off naturally with _____ .

Part 15   Recognizing Patterns

Read each paragraph. Underline the correct signal word or phrase to complete each sentence. Then circle the letter of the correct pattern.

1   The overuse of antibiotics is risky business. (Because/First) bacteria are living organisms, they can mutate or change over time. (As a result of/Unlike) decades of antibiotic use, some bacteria have changed and become resistant to certain types of drugs. These so-called "super germs" are stronger, (next/so) they no longer respond to the medications. They also have the power to (affect/cause) larger portions of the population with more serious illnesses, making it more difficult to fight them off naturally with our own immune systems.

Pattern:

a   cause and effect
b   compare and contrast
c   sequence

2   Steve Jobs was born (in the beginning/on February 24, 1955) to Joanne Schieble and Abdulfattah Jandali. (At the time/On the other hand), the two were busy graduate students at the University of Wisconsin, and they decided it was best for them to give up the child for adoption. (A short time later/However), the boy was adopted by Clara and Paul Jobs of Mountain View, California, and named Steven Paul Jobs. The family home was within California's Silicon Valley, an area known for its many computer and electronics companies. (Although/When) Steve was a young boy, he and his father would spend hours in the family's garage taking apart and rebuilding electronics - helpful practice for Steve's future career.

Pattern:

a   cause and effect
b   compare and contrast
c   sequence

3   There are many points to consider in the choice between buying organic food and conventional nonorganic food. (Because/Unlike) conventional food, organic food does not use harmful pesticides or chemicals in growing or processing. This means it's better for the environment than conventional foods. (As a result/On the other hand), some conventional food tends to last longer than organic food because it contains preservatives to keep it fresh. This could help reduce food waste. (Although/Finally) organic fruits and vegetables taste much better than conventional ones, nutritionists say they aren't significantly healthier. (Both/During) options have similar levels of vitamin content.

Pattern:

a   cause and effect
b   compare and contrast
c   sequence

VOCABULARY BUILDING

Dictionary Work

PARTS OF SPEECH

Parts of Speech

In a dictionary entry, one of the first pieces of information given about a word is its part of speech—noun, verb, adjective, adverb, and so forth.

Knowing the parts of speech and how they work in a sentence is helpful for your reading. If you know a word's part of speech, you can better guess its meaning. Knowing the part of speech will also help you use the word correctly.

This chart reviews the basic parts of speech and provides examples of how they are used.

Parts of Speech	Examples
Noun (n.): a word that names a person, place, thing, or idea	**Charles** is studying **geography** in **college**.
Verb (v.): a word or phrase that shows an action or a state of being	We **stood** and **watched** as the jet **was taking off**.
Pronoun (pron.): a word that replaces a noun or noun phrase	I'll show **you** where to hang **your** coat.
Adjective (adj.): a word that describes a noun	No one at the party knew the **tall** stranger with the **long**, **black** coat.
Adverb (adv.): a word that gives more information about a verb, adjective, or other adverb	We were **completely** exhausted after the hike. We **almost** didn't make it to the top.
Preposition (prep.): a word that tells where, when, or how	I had dinner **with** my coworker last night. We ate **at** that new Thai restaurant **on** Main Street.
Conjunction (conj.): a word that connects two or more phrases or sentences	Charlie enjoys team sports like soccer **and** baseball, **but** he doesn't like individual sports such as tennis **or** golf.

Practice 1

Read the sentence and circle the letter of the correct part of speech for each underlined word. Use the dictionary entries to check your answers.

> **measurable** *adj.* **1** able to be measured: *A manager should set measurable goals.* **2** important or large enough to have an effect: *The changes did not achieve any measurable results.*
>
> **measure¹** *v.* **1** to find the size, length, or amount of something: *Measure the wall to see if the bookshelves will fit.* **2** to judge the importance or value of something: *It is too early to measure the effectiveness of the drug.* | *Education cannot be measured by test scores alone.* **3** to be a particular size, length, or amount: *The table measures four feet by six feet.*
>
> **measure²** *n.* **1** an official action that is intended to deal with a problem: *Congress passed a measure to control spending today.* | *We have taken measures to limit smoking in the building.*
>
> **measurement** *n.* **1** the length, height, value of something, or the act of measuring: *We took measurements and realized that the table wouldn't fit through the doorway.*

1 Please call the furniture store and confirm the <u>measurements</u> of the new sofa.

   a noun

   b verb

   c adjective

   d adverb

2 When baking bread, it's important to <u>measure</u> all of the ingredients carefully.

   a adverb

   b conjunction

   c verb

   d adjective

3 Covering a cut with a bandage is one <u>measure</u> you can take to prevent infection.

   a preposition

   b adverb

   c noun

   d verb

4 After high school, Felix went on to achieve <u>measurable</u> success.

   a noun

   b preposition

   c adjective

   d adverb

Practice 2

Read each sentence. Then circle the letter of the part of speech of the underlined word.

> **volunteer** *v.* **1** to offer to do something without expecting any reward: *Ernie volunteered to wash the dishes.* **2** to tell someone something without being asked: *Michael volunteered the information before I had a chance to ask him.* **3** to work without pay, especially work that helps others in need: *I volunteer at a homeless shelter every weekend.*
>
> **volunteer** *n.* someone who does something without pay: *A group of volunteers cleaned up the downtown area after the storm.*
>
> **volunteer** *adj.* unpaid, done without pay: *Jim just signed up to be a volunteer firefighter.*
>
> **volunteerism** *n.* the act of doing unpaid work in order to help others in need: *The new mayor is encouraging citizens to consider volunteerism.*

1 David is writing a paper about <u>volunteerism</u> for one of his university classes.

  a noun

  b verb

  c adjective

2 After a disaster such as a hurricane, hundreds of people <u>volunteer</u> to clean up and help rebuild.

  a noun

  b verb

  c adjective

3 Many organizations recruit <u>volunteers</u> on their websites.

  a noun

  b verb

  c adjective

4 <u>Volunteer</u> tourism has been gaining popularity recently.

  a noun

  b verb

  c adjective

5 At her birthday party, Vivian <u>volunteered</u> that she was turning 50 years old.

  a noun

  b verb

  c adjective

FINDING THE RIGHT MEANING

Finding the Right Meaning

Often, one word has more than one definition (meaning) listed in the dictionary. These different definitions are usually similar or related to one another in some way. For example, look at the three definitions of the word *demonstrate*. Which word is repeated in all of the definitions?

> **demonstrate** v.
>
> **1** to show a fact clearly: *The research demonstrates the need to treat cancer early.*
>
> **2** to show or describe how to use or do something: *Instructors should demonstrate how to use the equipment.*
>
> **3** to show that you have a particular skill, quality, or ability: *The contest gave her a chance to demonstrate her ability.*

The word *show* appears in all three definitions, so the common meaning is *showing something*.

When a word has more than one definition in the dictionary:

• Read the sentence where you found the word and decide on the part of speech.
• Read all of the dictionary definitions for the word with that part of speech.
• Think about the meaning of the word in the sentence, and look for the definition that best matches that meaning. Use the example sentences in the dictionary to help you.

Practice 1

Draw a line to match the underlined word in the sentence on the left with its definition on the right.

1 medium

1 Cook the soup over <u>medium</u> heat.

2 Most businesses today use the Internet as a <u>medium</u> of advertising.

3 Michelangelo's preferred <u>medium</u> for his sculptures was marble.

adj. a middle size or amount

n. the material an artist uses to create something

n. a way of communicating or expressing something

2 iron

1 My job interview is in one hour, and I'm not ready. Could you please <u>iron</u> my shirt?

2 Carol didn't appreciate her birthday gift from her husband. He gave her an <u>iron</u>.

3 The <u>iron</u> bars on the windows were meant to keep thieves out.

n. an object that is heated and pushed across a piece of clothing to make it smooth

v. to make your clothes smooth using a flat, heated electrical appliance

adj. made of iron (a metal)

3 way

1 Do you know the <u>way</u> to Francine's house from here?

2 There are many <u>ways</u> people can help reduce greenhouse gases.

3 I arrived home <u>way</u> before you did. Where did you go?

adv. a large distance or amount of time

n. a manner or method of doing something

n. the road or path that you follow to get to a particular place

4 commit

1 A large portion of the city's budget has been <u>committed</u> to the project.

2 No one knows who <u>committed</u> the robbery.

3 Kim <u>committed</u> to completing the report over the weekend.

v. to decide to use money and time for a particular purpose

v. to say that you will definitely do something

v. to carry our or do something (usually wrong or illegal)

Practice 2

Read the sentence and think about the part of speech and meaning of the underlined word. Then circle the letter of the correct definition.

1 The company plans to <u>launch</u> its new marketing strategy next year.

  a n. an occasion at which a new product is shown or made available

  b v. to start something new, such as a new plan or profession

  c v. to send something high into the air or into space, such as a rocket

2 The politicians worked long and hard to <u>secure</u> an agreement against the war.

  a adj. safe, not in danger of harm

  b v. to get or achieve something important

  c v. to fasten or tie something to something else

3 We are studying different types of mold <u>cultures</u> in our plant biology class.

  a n. the beliefs, customs, and traditions of a particular society

  b n. art, literature, music

  c n. bacteria or cells produced for scientific use or research

4 Unfortunately, this isn't Jim's first <u>scrape</u> with the police.

   a v. to remove something from a surface using the edge of a knife or stick

   b n. a mark or slight injury caused by rubbing against a rough surface

   c n. a situation in which you have difficulties or get into trouble

5 After his speech, the presidential candidate gained a larger <u>following</u> among female voters.

   a prep. immediately after

   b adj. next in time

   c n. a group of people who support or admire something or someone

THE WAY WORDS ARE USED

Presentation

The Way Words Are Used

Dictionary definitions usually give example sentences and phrases to show how words are used and what words are often used together.

For example, read the example sentences and phrases in the following definition:

> **bound** *adj.* **1 be bound to do something** to be certain to do something: *People are bound to spell your name wrong.* **2** having a legal or moral duty to do something: *The company is bound by law to provide safety equipment.* **3 house-bound/wheelchair-bound, etc.** controlled or limited by something, so that you cannot do what you want. **4** intending to go in a particular direction or to a particular place: *a plane bound for Peru* **5 bound and determined** driven to do or achieve something, even if it is difficult: *Lars is bound and determined to win the skiing competition this year.*

Practice 1

Write in the missing word in the sentence. Use the examples in the dictionary entry to help you.

> **distance** *n.* **1** the amount of space between two places or things: *What's **the distance from** Los Angeles **to** San Francisco?* | *the distance between the moon and the sun* | *We had driven **a short distance** when the car broke down.* | *The bus stop is within **walking distance of** my house.* **2** a point or place that is far away but close enough to be seen or heard: *The ruins looked very impressive, **even from a distance**.* | *We could see the Sears Tower **in the distance**.* **3 keep your distance a)** to stay far away from someone or something: *The dog looked fierce, so **I kept my distance**.* **b) keep someone at a distance** to avoid becoming too friendly with someone: *He tends to **keep his distance from** his employees.*

1 I think I have the flu. You'd better _____ your distance.

2 The bus nearly went over a cliff. It stopped a _____ distance from the edge.

3 It was a foggy night, but after we crossed the bridge, we could see the lights of the city _____ the distance.

4 John likes Cara, but she seems to be keeping him _____ a distance.

5 Is your office within _____ distance from your apartment?

6 _____ a distance, the woman looked a lot like my friend Sarah.

Practice 2

Write the word to complete each sentence on the next page. Use the examples in the dictionary entry to help you.

> **moment** *n.* **1** a very short period of time: *Robert paused **for a moment**.* | *I'll be back **in a moment**.* | *He was here **a moment ago**. Denise arrived **moments** later.* **2** a particular point in time: *Just **at that moment**, the bell rang.* | *I knew it was you **the moment that** I heard your voice.* | *He knew he loved her **from the moment** he saw her.* | ***At that very moment**, the phone rang.* **3 at the moment** now: *Japanese food is very popular at the moment.* **4 any moment** soon *The attack could come **at any moment**.* **5 for the moment** used in order to say something is true now but will probably change in the future: *For the moment, I'm borrowing my mother's car.*

For	ago	and	for
that	of	very	any

1 Please wait here _____ a moment. I'll let Mr. Smith know you've arrived.

2 How did you get here so fast? I was just on the phone with you a moment _____ .

3 Although Kay hadn't seen Greg in years, she recognized him the moment _____ he stepped off the plane.

4 He took out the diamond ring, and at that _____ moment, she fainted and fell to the ground.

5 Christine is usually here on time. She should be here _____ moment.

6 _____ the moment, Alex is living with me, but it's just until he finds his own apartment.

Word Parts

ROOTS, PREFIXES, AND SUFFIXES

Presentation

Roots, Prefixes, and Suffixes

Many words in English are made up of more than one part. Adding or taking away different parts can change the grammar or the meaning of the word. Understanding different word parts will help you understand and remember words better.

The **root** is the base of a word. Some roots can stand alone as words, for example, *taste, action, definite*.

A **prefix** is a part added to the beginning of the root. It changes the meaning of the word:

Prefix		**Root**	
dis-	+	taste	= distaste
re-	+	action	= reaction
in-	+	definite	= indefinite

A **suffix** is a part added to the end of the root. It changes the part of speech of the word.

Prefix		**Root**		**Suffix**		
dis-	+	taste	+	-ful	=	distasteful (adj.)
re-	+	action	+	-ary	=	reactionary (adj.)
in-	+	definite	+	-ly	=	indefinitely (adv.)

Note that sometimes the spelling of the root changes slightly when a suffix is added.

Example:

rely + -able = reliable

believe + -able = believable

Practice 1

Write a prefix or suffix to each root to form a new word.

in	non	ible	dis
a	al	un	ness
less	ance	im	
tion	re	able	

1 appear _____

2 _____ approve

3 _____ aware

4 function _____

5 fear _____

6 forgive _____

7 _____ new

8 _____ appropriate

9 _____ proper

10 forsee _____

Presentation

Greek and Latin Roots

Many English words originally come from other languages, especially Latin and Greek.

Studying the meanings of Greek and Latin roots is useful because they can help you guess the meanings of unfamiliar words in English.

Greek and Latin roots often cannot stand alone as words. To form complete words, add a prefix, suffix, or both. For example:

Greek

Root: -frig-

Meaning: cold

Latin

Root: -path-

Meaning: suffering

Prefix Root Suffix Word

re- + -frig- + -erator = refrigerator

em- + -path- + -etic = empathetic

Practice 2

Circle the root in each word. Then circle the meaning of the root.

auto	Greek – self	jec, ject	Latin – throw
dent	Latin – tooth	juven	Latin – young
dic, dict	Latin – say	lat	Latin – side
duc, duct	Latin – lead	loc	Latin – place
form	Latin – shape	meter	Greek – measure
graph	Greek – written	phob	Greek – fear
habit	Latin – live	port	Latin – carry

1 relocate

Root: re / loc / ate

Meaning: side / place

2 inhabit

Root: in / habit

Meaning: write / live

3 biography

Root: bio / graph / y

Meaning: written / say

4 rejuvenate

Root: re / juven / ate

Meaning: young / tooth

5 introduction

Root: intro / duc / tion

Meaning: say / lead

6 thermometer

Root: therm / o / meter

Meaning: measure / tooth

7 rejection

Root: re / jec / tion

Meaning: throw / self

8 important

Root: im / port / ant

Meaning: measure / carry

9 bilateral

Root: bi / lat / eral

Meaning: side / live

10 prediction

Root: pre / dic / tion

Meaning: place / say

11 information

Root: in / form / ation

Meaning: shape / write

12 dentistry

Root: dent / istry

Meaning: tooth / say

Presentation

Prefixes and Meanings

A prefix is a group of letters added to the beginning of a root to make another word. Adding a prefix to a root changes the word's meaning. For example, adding the prefix *il-* to the root word *legal* creates the word *illegal*. It changes the meaning to "not legal."

English has many prefixes that mean "not." Study the following chart.

Negative Prefix	Meaning	Example
a-	not	*atypical*
dis-	not	*disapprove*
il-, im-, in-, ir-	not	*illegal, impossible, inconceivable, irresponsible*
mis-	badly, wrongly	*misunderstand*
non-	not	*nonsense*
un-	not	*unable*

Practice 3

Write the number of each root below the correct negative prefix.

1. avoidable	7. traditional	13. timely	19. lead
2. proper	8. decisive	14. mature	20. complete
3. believe	9. legal	15. assemble	21. common
4. regular	10. alcoholic	16. legible	22. relevant
5. logical	11. rational	17. measurable	23. take
6. regard	12. interpret	18. fat	24. sensitive

dis-	im-	in-

il-	ir-	non-

mis-	un-

Practice 4

Add the correct prefix to the word in parentheses. Write in the word to complete the sentence.

anti-	pre-	super-

1 Yoga and meditation are two types of natural _____ (anxiety) treatments.

2 This small store doesn't have everything we need. We'll have to go to the _____ (market).

3 The seats at the wedding party were _____ (assigned). We couldn't sit where we wanted.

trans-	un-	post-

4 Tom plans to do a year of _____ (graduate) studies after he finishes high school.

5 The doctor tried to wake the girl, but she remained _____ (conscious).

6 The bank teller thought the man looked suspicious, so she did not allow the _____ (action).

en-	over-	sub-

7 These living conditions are really _____ (standard). You should move out and find a better apartment.

8 This tool will _____ (able) you to do the job faster.

9 The Internet makes it easy to work anywhere, anytime. Therefore, it makes it easy to _____ (work).

bi-	extra-	re-

10 My company pays employees twice a month, or _____ (weekly).

11 I'm sorry; I forgot your name. Can you _____ (mind) me?

12 Private schools generally offer more types of _____ (curricular) activities than public schools.

auto-	mono-	de-

13 My grandmother is writing her _____ (biography).

14 At the amusement park, one of my favorite rides is the _____ (rail).

15 To solve its financial problems, the country plans to _____ (value) its currency.

Suffixes and Parts of Speech

When a suffix is added to the end of a root, it usually changes the word's part of speech or verb tense. For example:

Root	**Suffix**		
slow (adjective)	+ -ly	=	slowly (adverb)
walk (present tense)	+ -ed	=	walked (past tense)

Some suffixes change the form and meaning of a word. For example:

Root	**Suffix**		
tall (adjective)	+ -est	=	tallest (superlative adjective)

Study the following chart of common English suffixes.

Suffix	Part of Speech	Examples
-able, -ible	adjective	fashionable, incredible
-ance, -ence	noun	independence, confidence
-ation -ion, -tion	noun	creation, emotion
-ful	adjective	cheerful
-ian, -er, -or	noun	politician, baker, advisor
-ish	adjective	stylish
-ism	noun	racism
-ist	noun/adjective	racist
-ity	noun	gravity
-ly	adverb	sadly
-ment	noun	enjoyment
-ness	noun	greatness
-ship	noun	relationship
-ology	noun	biology
-ous	adjective	outrageous

Practice 5

Look at each word and the underlined suffix. Then complete the missing information in the chart.

Word	Part of Speech	Root	Part of Speech of Root
hope<u>ful</u>			
bad<u>ly</u>			
recycl<u>able</u>			
impress<u>ive</u>			
interest<u>ing</u>			
shy<u>ness</u>			

Practice 6

Add the correct suffix to the root in parentheses. Write in the word to complete the sentence. Remember that you may need to change the spelling of the root.

-able	-ance	-tion

1 Rupa was very upset by the teacher's comment. I didn't expect that kind of _____ (react).

2 Look at these photos of my mother when she was a baby. I can see the _____ (resemble) to my daughter.

3 Tara suffers from a rare skin condition. Her doctors have tried every _____ (imagine) treatment, but nothing has worked so far.

-ful	-ian	-ish

4 Something in her eyes told me she wasn't being _____ (truth).

5 Amelia can sometimes be very _____ (child) when she doesn't get what she wants.

6 Rei plays the piano, guitar, and drums. She hopes to be a professional _____ (music) someday.

-ism	-ist	-ity

7 The actor's _____ (popular) grew quickly after his first live interview.

8 One of the main principles of _____ (capital) is competition among businesses.

9 John is working as an environmental _____ (active). He's helping to stop water pollution.

-ly	-ment	-ness

10 How much do you pay in taxes _____ (annual)?

11 Thank you very much. How can I ever repay your _____ (kind)?

12 This restaurant has been here for over 100 years. It's the oldest _____ (establish) in the downtown area.

13 What is the _____ (relation) between age and happiness?

14 _____ (reflex) is a type of Chinese medical treatment that involves pressing on certain parts on the feet.

15 Melanie was _____ (fury) when her new computer broke for the third time.

WORD FORMS AND FAMILIES

Word Forms and Families

A word family is a group of words formed from the same root. Words in the same family usually have similar meanings, but the parts of speech differ. For example:

Noun	Verb	Adjective	Adverb
freedom	free	free	freely

(Note that sometimes the same word may have different parts of speech. In the example above, *free* is both a verb and an adjective.)

Several words may also have the same part of speech. For example, the word *care* has several adjective forms, including two negative ones:

Noun	Verb	Adjective
care	care	careful caring carefree
Negative Adjective	**Adverb**	
careless uncaring	carefully	

Practice 1

Write in the missing forms in the word families.

Noun	Verb	Adjective	Negative adjective	Adverb
correction	correct	_____	incorrect	_____
strategy	_____	_____	_____	strategically
information	_____	_____	uniformed	_____
logic		_____	_____	logically
_____		friendly	_____	
_____	_____	strong		_____
_____	produce	_____	unproductive	productively
_____		_____	irresponsible	responsibly
energy	_____			energetically
attraction	attract	_____	_____	attractively

Practice 2

Circle the letter of the correct form of the word to complete the sentence.

1 Please drive carefully. This is a _____ highway.

    a danger   **b** dangerous

2 Raul is a very _____ student. He always helps other students in the class.

    a considerate   **b** consideration

3 I have to stay up late and finish my report. I don't have a _____ .

    a choose   **b** choice

4 The menu choices may _____ , depending on the season.

    a vary   **b** various

5 The students were extremely _____ , but the professor didn't notice. He just kept talking and talking.

    a bored   **b** boredom

6 Thank you for your excellent _____ . I tried it, and it worked!

    a suggest   **b** suggestion

7 Rosa's opinion was always highly _____ among her colleagues.

    a value   **b** valued

8 Unfortunately, we were completely _____ for the rain on our camping trip.

    a preparation   **b** unprepared

9 If you want to lose _____ , most doctors recommend lowering calories and increasing exercise.

    a weight   **b** weigh

10 Karen could not hide her _____ when she found out she didn't get the job.

    a disappointment   **b** disappointing

Practice 3

Write the different forms of the word to complete each sentence correctly.

settled	settlements	settlers	unsettled

1 The Portuguese were some of the first European _____ of the northeastern United States. They were excellent shipbuilders and sailors, and they _____ in ports all along the eastern coast. One of the first Portuguese _____ was Cape Cod in Massachusetts.

dissimilar	similar	similarities	similarly

2 Tennis and badminton are two different sports, but there are some _____ between them. One way in which these two sports are _____ is in the use of a racquet. Tennis players use the racquet to hit a ball over a net; _____ , badminton players hit a small object called a birdie over a net.

developed	developer	develop	development

3 Steve Jobs, the former CEO of Apple Computers, was a brilliant software _____ . Jobs was the head of Apple's SuperMicro division, which was responsible for the _____ of Macintosh personal computers. Under Jobs's leadership, the company _____ some of the technology industry's most innovative products.

confident	confidence	confide	confidently

4 Making new friends isn't easy for everyone. Many people simply don't have the _____ to start a conversation with a stranger, or they don't know how to take the relationship to the next step with a coworker or acquaintance. The best way to become more _____ is to remember that everyone feels the same way. If you are interested in making friends with someone, that person probably feels the same way about you. Try approaching people _____ and inviting them for coffee or lunch.

disorganized	organization	organizing	organizer

5 Often, _____ a large event such as a wedding or graduation party is a difficult task. There are so many little details to remember. If too many details are overlooked, the party can seem _____ , and it won't be as enjoyable for the guests. One option, if you don't mind spending a little extra money, is to hire a professional party _____ to help with your plans.

Guessing Meaning from Context
WHAT IS CONTEXT?

> **Presentation**
>
> **What Is Context?**
>
> It is rarely necessary to understand the meaning of every word you read. You can usually follow a story or text and understand the general idea of what you are reading even if there are some unknown words. Before you stop to look up a word in the dictionary, continue reading and try to understand the general idea from the context—the other words and phrases in the sentence or passage. The context of a passage can sometimes help you infer important ideas and the meaning of unknown words. This will help you read more quickly and efficiently.

Practice 1

Read the passage with missing words. This is like reading a passage with unknown words. After you read the passage, circle the letter of the correct answer to each question on p. 90.

There was once a ■■■■■■■■ who lived with his wife in a miserable ■■■■■ near the sea, and every day he went fishing. One day, he was sitting with his rod and looking at the clear water when his ■■■ suddenly went down, far below. When he drew it up again, he brought out a large ■■■■■■■■. Then the ■■■■■■■■ said to him, "Hark, you ■■■■■■■, I pray you, let me live, for I am no ■■■■■■■ really but an ■■■■■■■■ prince. What good will it do you to kill me? I should not be good to eat. Put me in the water again, and let me go."

"Come," said the ■■■■■■■, "there is no need for so many words about it—a fish that can talk I should certainly ■■■■■, anyhow." With that, he put him back again into the clear water. The ■■■■■■■ went to the bottom, leaving a long streak of blood behind him. Then the ■■■■■■■ got up and went home to his wife in the ■■■■■.

"Husband," said the woman, "have you ■■■■■ nothing today?"

"No," said the man, "I did catch a ■■■■■■■ who said he was an ■■■■■■■■ prince, so I let him go again."

"Did you not ■■■■ for anything first?" asked the woman.

"No," said the man, "what should I ■■■■ for?"

"Ah," said the woman, "it is surely hard to have to live always in this dirty ■■■■■; you might have wished for a small ■■■■■■■ for us. Go back and call him. Tell him we want to have a small ■■■■■■■. He will certainly give us that."

"Ah," said the man, "why should I go there again?" "Well," said the woman, "you did ■■■■■ him, and you let him go again; he is sure to do it. Go at once."

The man still did not want to go, but he did not like to ■■■■■■ his wife, so he went to the ■■■■.

1 Who are the main characters of the story?
  a a wealthy businessman, his wife, and a prince
  b a poor fisherman, his wife, and a fish
  c a king, a queen, and a prince

2 Where does the couple live?
  a in a large farmhouse
  b in a tall apartment building
  c in a dirty little house

3 Why is the woman upset with her husband?
  a She thinks he should have asked the fish for a new house.
  b She wanted to cook the fish for their evening meal.
  c She wanted to have a chance to meet a prince.

4 What does the man decide to do?
  a He tells his wife to go.
  b He follows his wife's wishes.
  c He takes his wife to see the fish.

Practice 2

Read the passage with missing words. Then write the missing words in the correct places in the passage.

song	discouraged	fragrance	green
tin	bucket	water	brush
sighing	repeated	morning	

Saturday _____ was come, and all the summer world was bright and fresh, and brimming with life. There was a _____ in every heart; and if the heart was young the music issued at the lips. There was cheer in every face and a spring in every step. The locust trees were in bloom and the _____ of the blossoms filled the air. Cardiff Hill, beyond the village and above it, was _____ with vegetation and it lay just far enough away to seem a Delectable Land, dreamy, reposeful, and inviting. Tom appeared on the sidewalk with a _____ of whitewash and a long-handled _____ . He surveyed the fence, and all gladness left him and a deep melancholy settled down upon his spirit. Thirty yards of board fence nine feet high. Life to him seemed hollow, and existence but a burden. _____ , he dipped his brush and passed it along the topmost plank; _____ the operation; did it again; compared the insignificant whitewashed streak with the far-reaching continent of unwhitewashed fence, and sat down on a tree-box, _____ . Jim came skipping out at the gate with a _____ pail, and singing "Buffalo Gals." Bringing _____ from the town pump had always been hateful work in Tom's eyes, before, but now it did not strike him so.

GUESSING THE MEANING OF WORDS AND PHRASES

Copyright © 2017 by Pearson Education, Inc. Duplication is not permitted.

Presentation

Guessing the Meaning of Words and Phrases

When you encounter a new word in a reading passage, the context—the other words and phrases around it—can help you guess or infer the meaning of the new word. For example, read the following passage:

Job experience is the main **criterion** *for selecting new employees. Other factors include education and employer references.*

From the context, you can tell that *criterion*

- is a noun.
- is something used when selecting new employees.
- is a synonym for *factor*.

In addition, you know that job experience, education, and employer references are characteristics that employers use when selecting new employees to hire. This is your background knowledge about the topic.

From the context and your background knowledge, you can figure out that *criterion* means "a factor considered when making a selection."

Combining the context with your own background knowledge is a strategy you should use to figure out new words as you read.

Practice 1

Read each sentence and figure out the part of speech of the underlined word. Use the context and your background knowledge to choose the letter of the correct definition.

1 To <u>reward</u> the girl for her behavior, her father bought her an ice cream cone.
   a n. something you get because you have done something good
   b adj. making you feel happy or satisfied
   c v. to give something to someone because he or she has done something good or helpful

2 As the team of scientists studied the ancient animal bones, they noticed several <u>grooves</u>, which were probably made by early humans using a stone cutting tool.
   a n. long lines made in the surface of something
   b v. to cause something to move back and forth
   c adv. done quickly and with a lot of force

3 Jane was nervous as she described her actions the night before. The police didn't believe her story. It sounded too <u>contrived</u>.
   a adv. dangerously or carelessly
   b adj. easy to understand
   c adj. seeming false and unnatural

4 The argument began between the two men but ended in a big <u>brawl</u> when several people who tried to stop them joined in.

    a n. a large, noisy fight involving many people

    b n. physical strength or power

    c v. to discuss something with a group of people

5 After an <u>invigorating</u> early morning swim in the lake, Wanda felt energized and clear-minded.

    a v. the act of trying something new

    b adj. making you want to join something

    c adj. making you feel more active and healthy

Practice 2

Circle the letter of the best definition for the underlined word in the sentence.

1 Although her son was far away, the woman knew in her heart that he was in danger. It was a mother's <u>intuition</u>.

    a argument involving many countries or governments

    b knowledge based on feelings rather than facts

    c feelings of anger and frustration

2 The <u>migration</u> of geese and other birds from north to south is one of the earliest signs that winter is on its way.

    a a form of communication between different types of animals

    b the movement of a group of animals or people from one place to another

    c different types of transportation used by humans

3 It is unknown whether Professor Boyle will return to teach this year or next. She is leaving the university <u>indefinitely</u>.

    a for a period of time without any decided end

    b without being certain of the right decision

    c for a very short period of time

4 I've been trying to study for over an hour, but I can't concentrate. I have a <u>nagging</u> headache.

    a causing you to feel nervous and excited

    b continuously making you worry or feel pain

    c making you feel relaxed and stress-free

5 I've just heard that there's an <u>opening</u> for a cook at Paul's Pizza Kitchen. I don't have much experience, but I think I'll apply anyway.

    a a tear or a rip in something

    b a job or a position that is available

    c a business that is just starting

GUESSING MEANING FROM A PASSAGE

Presentation

Guessing Meaning from a Passage

In longer passages, you have many opportunities to use context to help you understand unknown words and phrases. Clues in other sentences and paragraphs can also help you figure out the meaning.

When you find a new word in a longer passage,

- read the sentence and decide on the word's part of speech.
- look at the context—the other words, phrases, and sentences close to the unknown word.
- think about the meaning of the sentence and the topic of the passage.
- use your background knowledge to make a guess about the meaning.
- read the sentence with your guess instead of the unknown word. Does it make sense in the overall context?

Practice 1

Read the passage. Use the context to figure out the part of speech and general meaning of the underlined words. Then draw a line to match each word with its definition.

This weekend <u>brought</u> brutally cold temperatures to much of the Northeast, causing school closings and <u>grounding</u> flights up and down the coast. The blast of <u>frigid</u> air is expected to <u>linger</u> well into the week, when a warm <u>front</u> will finally move in from the south. Forecasters warn that the sub-freezing temperatures combined with precipitation could make roads slippery and have dangerous and deadly <u>consequences</u> throughout the region. Residents are <u>cautioned</u> to dress warmly and not to engage in any unnecessary car travel.

1	precipitation	v. making planes unable to fly
2	consequences	adj. very cold, freezing
3	cautioned	adv. terrible, severely
4	linger	v. warned of danger
5	grounding	n. large mass of air
6	brutally	n. rain or snow
7	frigid	v. stay
8	front	n. results of a particular action

Practice 2

Read the passage. Use the context to figure out the part of speech and general meaning of the underlined words. Circle the correct answer.

> With stress and anxiety on the rise in our culture, many people are beginning to seek new ways to relax and reduce tension. "Mindfulness" is one form of meditation that has been gaining recognition recently. Proponents of mindfulness claim that with regular practice, it can help anyone combat stress and become happier and healthier.
>
> Mindfulness involves being intensely aware of what you're sensing and feeling at every moment. For example, when you are eating food mindfully, you chew slowly, paying attention to the food's flavor and texture in your mouth. According to those who practice mindfulness, this type of constant self-awareness can help us be less distracted and allows us to enjoy each moment of our lives more fully.

1 seek

Part of speech: adjective, adverb, noun, verb

General meaning: becoming more popular; feeling of being stressed or tense; fight against; look for; supporters; the way something feels when you touch it; thinking about too may things at once; very much, strongly

2 tension

Part of speech: adjective, adverb, noun, verb

General meaning: becoming more popular; feeling of being stressed or tense; fight against; look for; supporters; the way something feels when you touch it; thinking about too may things at once; very much, strongly

3 gaining recognition

Part of speech: adjective, adverb, noun, verb

General meaning: becoming more popular; feeling of being stressed or tense; fight against; look for; supporters; the way something feels when you touch it; thinking about too may things at once; very much, strongly

4 proponents

Part of speech: adjective, adverb, noun, verb

General meaning: becoming more popular; feeling of being stressed or tense; fight against; look for; supporters; the way something feels when you touch it; thinking about too may things at once; very much, strongly

5 combat

Part of speech: adjective, adverb, noun, verb

General meaning: becoming more popular; feeling of being stressed or tense; fight against; look for; supporters; the way something feels when you touch it; thinking about too may things at once; very much, strongly

6 intensely

Part of speech: adjective, adverb, noun, verb

General meaning: becoming more popular; feeling of being stressed or tense; fight against; look for; supporters; the way something feels when you touch it; thinking about too may things at once; very much, strongly

7 texture

Part of speech: adjective, adverb, noun, verb
General meaning: becoming more popular; feeling of being stressed or tense; fight against; look for; supporters; the way something feels when you touch it; thinking about too may things at once; very much, strongly

8 distracted

Part of speech: adjective, adverb, noun, verb
General meaning: becoming more popular; feeling of being stressed or tense; fight against; look for; supporters; the way something feels when you touch it; thinking about too may things at once; very much, strongly

Practice 3

Read the passage. Use the context to figure out the meaning of the underlined words. Draw a line to match each definition to the correct word.

The tall youth, turning to the right, went down a gentle slope until he came to a little stream where he knelt and drank. Despite his weariness, his thirst, and his danger, he noticed the silvery color of the water, and its soft sighing sound as it flowed over its pebbly bed made a pleasant murmur in his ear. Robert Lennox always had an eye for the beautiful, and the flashing brook, in its setting of deep, intense forest green, soothed his senses, speaking to him of comfort and hope.

He drank again and then sat back among the bushes, still breathing heavily, but with much more freedom. The sharp pain left his chest, new strength began to flow into his muscles, and, as the body was renewed, so the spirit soared up and became sanguine once more. He put his ear to the earth and listened long, but heard nothing, save sounds natural to the wilderness—the rustling of leaves before the light wind, the whisper of the tiny current, and the occasional sweet note of a bird in brilliant dress, pluming itself on a bough in its pride. He drew fresh courage from the peace of the woods and resolved to remain longer there by the stream. Settling himself into the bushes and tall grass, until he was hidden from all but a trained gaze, he waited, body and soul alike growing steadily in vigor.

1 slope		hill
2 pebbly		decided
3 soothed		confident, positive
4 sanguine		strength, energy
5 rustling		crackling sound
6 bough		tree branch
7 resolved		covered with small rocks
8 vigor		calmed, relaxed

Practice 4

Read the passage. Use the context to figure out the meaning of the underlined words. Draw a line to match each word with its meaning.

Many animals migrate. In general, they travel for feeding or breeding purposes. For instance, in late autumn, flocks of Canadian geese fly from the chilly north to more temperate southern climates.

Whales are another type of animal that migrates long distances, heading toward the colder poles in the summer and toward the tropical waters of the equator in the winter. This allows whales to take advantage of abundant food in colder waters in the summer. Then, when food productivity lowers, they migrate to warmer waters and give birth to their calves there.

Adult female sea turtles, when they are ready to lay their eggs, return to the same beach where they were born, often journeying hundreds of miles to get there.

How do the animals find their way? In their recent book, *Nature's Compass: The Mystery of Animal Navigation*, scientists James and Carol Gould write that in these acts of long-distance navigation, animals "are performing feats far beyond anything humans can manage without specialized instruments, equipment, and training." Their research findings showed that some animals navigate via instinct and others through learning and experience. Other recent research indicates that some animals utilize the position of the sun and stars as well as Earth's magnetic fields to determine their routes.

1. migrate   traveling

2. temperate   natural sense or feeling

3. abundant   use

4. calves   amazing accomplishments

5. journeying   move from one place to another

6. feats   baby whales

7. instinct   plenty

8. utilize   warm and mild

Phrases and Collocations
COMMON TYPES OF COLLOCATIONS

Presentation

Common Types of Collocations

Collocations are groups of words that are used together so frequently that they become fixed phrases. For example:

- The bump on her head *grew and grew* until it was the size of a golf ball.
- *Let me know* if you're planning to come to the party.
- Please check your answers carefully; it's easy to *make a mistake*.

Common types of collocations in English include the following:

Verb + Noun:

Steven wants to *take a class* at the university.

Do you want to *make dinner*, or should I?

Noun (+ preposition) + Noun:

Do you like this **radio program**?

Please buy a **gallon of milk**.

Verb + Adverb:

I think I'll go home early. I don't **feel well**.

Please **talk quietly** in the halls.

Adjective + Noun:

I need to make a **quick trip** to the supermarket.

Exercising is the **best way to lose weight**.

Prepositional Phrase:

Over time, he started to enjoy his work.

The thief came sometime **during the night**.

Phrasal Verb (Verb + Preposition):

I ran into an old friend from high school the other day.

Hans didn't **show up** for class today.

Practice 1

Complete each sentence with a word from the box to form a common English collocation.

verb + noun

have	do	get
take	make	

1 I'll cook, and you can _____ the dishes.
2 The students were getting tired, so the teacher said they could _____ a break.
3 I'm thirsty. Let's stop here and _____ a drink.
4 Did you _____ a haircut? Your hair looks really nice.
5 Kenji is working part time now. He needs to _____ money to pay his rent.

noun + (preposition) + noun

company	heart	cup
office	bowl	

6 Fast food is one reason for the increase in _____ attacks in this country.
7 We each ordered a sandwich and a _____ of soup for lunch.
8 The _____ president announced that the firm would be closing.
9 They're planning to build a new _____ building downtown.
10 Would you like a _____ of coffee or tea?

verb + adverb

fluently	well	carefully
quickly	early	

11 Paul ran so _____ that no one could catch him.
12 After five years in France, Wanda could speak the language _____ .
13 Akeem studied hard. He wanted to do _____ on the test.
14 Listen _____ while I give the instructions.
15 If we want to be on time for the flight, we'll have to leave _____ .

Practice 2

Complete each sentence with a word from the box to form a common English collocation.

adjective + noun

old	low	good
bad	difficult	

1 Many people shop at Farrelly's Supermarket because of the _____ prices.

2 Social networking sites such as Facebook are a great way to reconnect with _____ friends.

3 Jennifer doesn't look very happy. I think she's had a _____ day.

4 It's a _____ idea to stretch before and after you exercise.

5 Eugene made the _____ decision to leave his job after 20 years.

prepositional phrase

in	under	during
at	on	

6 The cat is hiding _____ the sofa.

7 I'm too tired to do the dishes now. I'll do them _____ the morning.

8 My cousins are planning to come and visit us _____ the summer.

9 Do you prefer to watch movies in a theater or _____ home?

10 Be sure to arrive _____ time for the show.

phrasal verb (verb + preposition)

keep	make	figure
get	take	

11 Looking out the window, Rob watched the plane _____ off.

12 You're doing a great job. Please _____ up the good work.

13 Let's take a trip someplace warm this winter. I really want to _____ away.

14 My sister and I never stay mad at each other for long. If we have a fight, we always _____ up quickly.

15 The math problem was difficult to _____ out. Most students got the answer wrong.

PHRASAL VERBS

Presentation

Phrasal Verbs

Phrasal verbs are very common in English. A phrasal verb consists of a verb and a small word called a particle. Together, the verb and particle form a special meaning.

Read the following example:

Never bring up the topic of vacation time at a job interview

In this sentence, the words *bring* and *up* form a phrasal verb meaning "to talk about" or "to introduce a topic of conversation."

Phrasal verbs are different from verb + preposition combinations, as in this sentence:

My mother asked me to bring the basket of laundry up the stairs.

In this sentence, *bring up* is not a phrasal verb because you could replace *up the stairs* with a different prepositional phrase such as *to her*. Moreover, prepositions in prepositional phrases always have an object.

Here are some common examples of phrasal verbs:

- My car *broke down* on the way home.
- *Call* me *back* when you get this message.
- After the school fire alarm *went off*, it took a long time for the children to *calm down*.
- If you need anything, you can *count on* me.
- The cookie *fell apart* when she tried to eat it.
- Let's *find out* what's playing at the movie theater tonight.
- *Hang on*; I'll be right back.
- That teacher never says anything nice. She just *points out* everyone's mistakes.

Practice 1

Underline the phrasal verbs in the passage. Do not underline the verb + preposition combinations.

I always wake up early on Saturdays, even though I don't have to go to work. My alarm goes off at 5:30 A.M. I get out of bed, and I'm ready to take on the day. My morning routine is simple. First, I wash up and get dressed, and then, if the weather's good, I head out for a quick walk. I usually stop by Mr. Baker's newsstand, chat with him for a few minutes, and pick up a newspaper and a cup of coffee to enjoy on a bench in the park. I take my time, sipping my coffee and reading the newspaper from cover to cover. When I'm finished, I still have the whole day ahead of me. I wouldn't give up my Saturday mornings for anything!

Practice 2

Write in the correct verb from the box to complete the phrasal verb in each sentence. Use a dictionary if you need help. Change the form of the verb if necessary.

do	make	look
get	take	

1 I think it's time to _____ away with that rule. It just doesn't make sense anymore.

2 The story wasn't true. The boy just _____ up a lie to avoid punishment.

3 _____ out! There's a tree in the road up there!

4 Amelia is still heartbroken. I wonder if she'll ever _____ over John.

5 Please _____ over the report carefully before you send it to the head office.

6 Ian wanted to try a new hobby, so he decided to _____ up snowboarding.

7 This book is confusing and not very interesting. It's difficult to _____ into the plot.

8 During the war, people had to _____ without unnecessary items, such as sweets or cosmetics.

9 The speaker's voice was very quiet. We could barely _____ out what she was saying.

IDIOMS

Presentation

Idioms

An idiom is a type of collocation. It is a group of words (a phrase) that has a special meaning when used together. You usually cannot tell the meaning of an idiom just by understanding the separate words in the phrase. That is why it is important to make idioms part your vocabulary study.

Idioms are not only useful but also fun to learn.

Here are some examples of common idioms in English:

* Yolanda said she was *sick and tired* of waiting for Roberto to call. ("frustrated and impatient")

* You don't have to make a decision now. Why don't you *sleep on it* and give me your answer tomorrow? ("wait until the next day")

* The test was a *piece of cake*. Every student got an A. ("very easy")

Practice 1

Read the sentences and think about the meaning of each underlined idiom. Then draw a line to match each idiom to its meaning on the next page.

This bag is very heavy. Can you <u>give me a hand</u>?

The ambulance arrived at the accident <u>in the nick of time</u>. The injured woman is now recovering in the hospital.

Paola <u>bends over backwards</u> to make Anthony happy, but no matter what she does, he's never satisfied.

You look very tired. Why don't you stay home and <u>take it easy</u> tonight?

I just paid for an expensive car repair, and now <u>I'm broke</u>.

If you have time, <u>drop me a line</u> and let me know how you're doing.

We were very tired after skiing all day, so we decided to <u>hit the hay early</u>.

I've seen this movie at least five times. I <u>know it like the back of my hand</u>.

1 give me a hand		rest and relax
2 in the nick of time		go to bed
3 bend over backwards		try very hard
4 take it easy		be very familiar with something
5 be broke		call or email someone
6 drop me a line		help someone
7 hit the hay		have no money
8 know something like the back of my hand		quickly

Practice 2

Read the sentences and think about the meaning of each underlined idiom. Then draw a line to match the idiom to its meaning.

With the weak economy, it's very difficult for some families to <u>make ends meet</u>.

Usually, students must hand in homework every Monday, but the professor said she would <u>make an exception</u> this week because Monday is a holiday.

There are too many different types of tablet computers. I can't <u>make up my mind</u>. They all look great.

If you're late to the office, don't try to explain or <u>make excuses</u>. Just apologize and get to work.

Volunteer work is one way you can <u>make a difference</u> in the world.

Whenever I visit my hometown, I always <u>make time</u> to visit my neighbor, Mrs. Hobbs.

1 make ends meet	have enough money to pay the bills
2 make an exception	include something in your schedule or plans
3 make up my mind	give reasons for bad behavior
4 make excuses	do something good for others
5 make a difference	decide
6 make time	give special permission

Practice 3

Read the definition. Then write the word from the box to complete the idiom correctly.

sweet	nose	eyes	shoulder
heart	green	leg	stomach
head			

1 When you feel sad and need to talk to someone about your problems, you cry on someone's _____ .

2 If you are a very kind person, then people say you have a _____ of gold.

3 If you are very intelligent, then you have a good _____ on your shoulders.

4 If you don't mind things that others find scary, then you have a strong _____ .

5 When you are careful to stay out of trouble, you keep your _____ clean.

6 When you want to wish someone luck before they perform on stage, you can say "break a _____ ."

7 If you like to garden and take care of plants, then you have a _____ thumb.

8 If you love to eat candy, cake, and ice cream, you have a _____ tooth.

9 If you always see and hear everything that's going on, then people say you have _____ in the back of your head.

PHRASES IN CONTEXT

Presentation

Phrases in Context

As you read, you will find many collocations in the form of phrases, phrasal verbs, and idioms. Being able to recognize phrases quickly is part of becoming a faster, more fluent reader.

Many collocations include the word or concept of *money*. For example:

- Bill Gates *makes* a lot of *money*. ("to earn")
- My sister *raises money* for the American Cancer Society. ("persuade people to donate money")
- We *spend* too much *money* on food. ("use")
- Gloria does not *take* any *money* from her parents.
- Mrs. Dhu likes to *give money* to her grandchildren.

Practice 1

Circle the letter of the verb that correctly completes each collocation about money.

1 I don't need a big salary to be happy. As long as I _____ enough money to pay my bills, I'm satisfied.

    a make

    b pay

2 If you want to _____ money for your vacation, you should stop buying expensive electronics.

    a raise

    b save

3 Food prices are so high. We _____ a lot of money on groceries every week.

    a pay

    b spend

4 The children are selling cookies and candy in order to _____ money for their trip to the beach.

    a give

    b raise

5 Mrs. Langley is very generous. Every year, she _____ a lot of money to charity.

    a gives

    b makes

Presentation

Phrases in Context

As you read, you will find many collocations in the form of phrases, phrasal verbs, and idioms. Being able to recognize phrases quickly is part of becoming a faster, more fluent reader.

Many collocations include the word or concept of *time*. For example:

- I paid my phone bill just *in time*. ("before it was too late")
- The bus never comes *on time*. ("at the proper or expected time")
- Rana is having a *hard time* in school. ("trouble")
- I didn't finish the project yesterday. I *ran out of time*. ("did not have enough time")
- In her *spare time*, Lisa likes to read mysteries. ("extra time")
- *Take your time*. It's early. ("Go slowly without rushing.")
- He often *wastes time* playing video games. ("uses time in a foolish or useless way")
- My aunt frequently spends *time* at the gym. ("uses time")

Practice 2

Write the word or phrase to complete each collocation correctly.

spend	hard	take your	on
waste	run out of	just in	spare

1 I'm glad you're finally here. You've arrived _____ time for dessert!

2 Kelly was having a _____ time eating because of her toothache.

3 You'd better get to work on your science project. It's due on Friday, and you don't want to _____ time.

4 In her _____ time, Roberta plays tennis and golf and paints beautiful landscapes.

5 The train was late, but there wasn't much traffic, so we still made it to the theater _____ time.

6 You learn a lot of interesting things about people when you _____ a lot of time with them.

7 Children shouldn't _____ time indoors watching TV. They need to get out and explore the world.

8 There's no need to rush. Just relax and _____ time.

Presentation

Phrases in Context

As you read, you will find many collocations in the form of phrases, phrasal verbs, and idioms. Being able to recognize phrases quickly is part of becoming a faster, more fluent reader.

Many collocations are related to sports. For example:

- I like to *play basketball*. (*play* + name of sport)
- Let's *go swimming*. (go + verb + *-ing*)

Practice 3

Circle the letter of the verb that correctly completes each collocation.

1 There's nothing happening on campus tonight. Do you want to _____ bowling or something?
   a go
   b play
   c do

2 There's a joke that says that some Canadian children learn to _____ hockey before they can walk.
   a do
   b play
   c go

3 I'm going on a business trip to Switzerland. If I have any spare time, I think I'll _____ hiking in the Alps.

   a do

   b play

   c go

4 Jason decided not to join any sports teams at school. He's been _____ karate since he was three years old, and he wants to continue.

   a doing

   b playing

   c going

5 Every time I _____ swimming, I get water in my ear.

   a play

   b go

   c do

Presentation

Phrases in Context

As you read, you will find many collocations in the form of phrases, phrasal verbs, and idioms. Being able to recognize phrases quickly is part of becoming a faster, more fluent reader.

Many collocations use the verbs *do* or *make*. For example:

- do business
- do research
- do your best
- make a reservation
- make a suggestion
- make the most of something ("take advantage of it")

Practice 4

Write in *make* or *do* to complete each collocation.

In today's global economy, most companies _____ business in foreign countries, and business travel is more common and convenient than ever. You can save time and money if you _____ your travel reservations online. If you're planning to visit a country you've never traveled to before, it's important to _____ some research about the country's customs. There are plenty of websites that _____ suggestions and offer useful information for business travelers. If you know some basic information about the culture, you won't _____ a mistake that could embarrass you or your hosts. While in the country, you should _____ your best to follow the cultural rules and _____ the most of your trip by taking some time to _____ some sightseeing.

Presentation

Phrases in Context

As you read, you will find many collocations in the form of phrases, phrasal verbs, and idioms. Being able to recognize phrases quickly is part of becoming a faster, more fluent reader.

Many collocations use the verbs *have* or *take*. For example:

- have an effect on ("influence, affect")
- have access
- have trouble
- have fun
- take time; take a moment
- take notice
- take a chance
- take a break

Practice 5

Write in *have* (*has*) or *take* to complete each collocation.

New developments in technology _____ a huge effect on the way we live our daily lives. Today, from almost anywhere on Earth, you _____ access to the rest of the world via the Internet. Just _____ a moment to look around whenever you're in a crowded public place. _____ notice of how many people are looking at some kind of handheld device. Smart phones, tablet computers, and laptops all offer new ways to _____ fun. Of course, the technology explosion _____ some negative effects on our lives, too, especially when it comes to children. Many young children, when they _____ free time, are allowed to play video games or watch TV for hours. As a result, doctors report treating many overweight children who _____ trouble doing even small amounts of physical exercise. Health officials warn parents not to _____ chances with their children's health. If children are allowed to use computers, make sure they _____ breaks often and get physical exercise.

Practice 6

Write in a preposition from the box to complete each collocation correctly.

along	by	in	to
between	from	of	with

Certain types _____ insects, such as the Asian long-horned beetle, have become a major problem as global trade has expanded. When goods and products are transported _____ countries _____ plane or ship, insects or their eggs often come _____ for the ride and are transported _____ their native habitats. The insects can have a terrible effect _____ the environment, causing major damage _____ trees and food crops. The Asian long-horned beetle is an insect that is native _____ Japan, China, and Korea. The beetle makes holes _____ trees and eats the wood on the inside, eventually killing the tree. In Asia, the beetles are eaten _____ various birds and other insects, so most trees are safe. However, when the beetle was transported _____ North America _____ ships from China, it caused big problems. Since 1996, when it was first identified _____ New York City, the beetle has destroyed thousands _____ trees. Teams _____ environmentalists and scientists have been working hard to find ways to deal _____ the problem.

Following Ideas in Text

KEY PARTS OF SENTENCES

Part 1

Presentation

Key Parts of Sentences

To understand sentences in English, you need to understand the words and the structure of the sentence—the relationships between and among the words.

The key parts of an English sentence are the subject and the verb.

The **subject** tells who or what is doing the action in the sentence or clause.

The **verb** describes the action of the sentence or clause.

The subject may be

- a pronoun: *I, you, he, she, it, we, they, who, this, that,* etc.
- a name: *Donald, New York, Atlantic Ocean,* etc.
- a phrase: *my favorite book, the old race car,* etc.

The verb may be

- in different forms/tenses: *has, had, is having, has had,* etc.
- a modal: *can, might, would, should,* etc.
- negative: *does not have, didn't have,* etc.

A sentence can have more than one subject and/or more than one verb. For example:

<u>Grace and her sister</u> [subjects] <u>stood up and left</u> [verbs] the room.

Practice 1

Underline all of the subjects in the passage.

A lucky New Jersey man was saved from spending a cold night in the woods when he was found by a furry, four-footed friend. Tom Fahner was hiking on Mount Gilmore last Saturday. He reached the top of the mountain and noticed that the sun was setting. "I knew I had to hurry to get down before dark." On the way down, Tom took a wrong turn and found himself lost in the deep forest. "I looked down and couldn't see the trail anymore," the hiker said. Tom called for help, but no one came, so he made a shelter with tree branches and decided to camp for the night. "It was too cold to sleep; I just tried to stay warm." Sometime during the night, Tom heard something running through the woods. It stopped in front of the shelter and started to bark loudly. It was Bruce Edwards's hunting dog, Rosco. The two were hunting. Rosco called his owner, who came to Tom's rescue and guided him back to the trail and down the mountain to safety.

Part 2

Underline all of the verbs in the passage.

A lucky New Jersey man was saved from spending a cold night in the woods when he was found by a furry, four-footed friend. Tom Fahner was hiking on Mount Gilmore last Saturday. He reached the top of the mountain and noticed that the sun was setting. "I knew I had to hurry to get down before dark," he said. On the way down, Tom took a wrong turn and found himself lost in the deep forest. "It was getting dark fast. I looked down and couldn't see the trail anymore," the hiker said. Tom called for help, but no one came, so he made a shelter with tree branches and decided to camp for the night. "It was too cold, so I just tried to stay warm." Sometime during the night, Tom heard something running through the woods. It stopped in front of the shelter and started to bark loudly. It was Bruce Edwards's hunting dog, Rosco. The two were hunting. Rosco called his owner, who came to Tom's rescue and guided him back to the trail and down the mountain to safety.

Practice 2

Part 1

Underline all of the subjects in the passage.

Washington High School track star Crispin Matthews will have to sit out the spring season as he recovers from ankle surgery. Matthews, a senior this year, says he is disappointed to miss this last season at Washington, but he understands that it is for the best. Matthews's ankle was injured during the high-jump event last year. The injury did not heal properly and required surgery to repair the bone. Matthews had hoped to join the track team at Holden University, where he will be a student next year, but he says he isn't sure that will be possible. "I will do whatever the doctors tell me to do," he says. "I want to start running again as soon as possible." Well-wishers may send cards and flowers to Howard Medical Center.

Part 2

Underline all of the verbs in the passage.

Washington High School track star Crispin Matthews will have to sit out the spring season as he recovers from ankle surgery. Matthews, a senior this year, says he is disappointed to miss this last season at Washington, but he understands that it is for the best. Matthews's ankle was injured during the high-jump event last year. The injury did not heal properly and required surgery to repair the bone. Matthews had hoped to join the track team at Holden University, where he will be a student next year, but he says he isn't sure that will be possible. "I will do whatever the doctors tell me to do," he says. "I want to start running again as soon as possible." Well-wishers may send cards and flowers to Howard Medical Center.

SIGNAL WORDS AND PHRASES

Presentation

Signal Words and Phrases

Certain words and phrases are used to signal new ideas, examples, or the relationship among ideas in a passage. Studying signal words and phrases can help you better understand the flow of ideas as you read.

The following chart includes common categories of signal words and phrases used in English.

Purpose in the Passage	Signal Words and Phrases
to give an example	*for example, for instance, in particular, to give an example*
to explain causes and results or effects	*as a result, because of, due to, therefore, so, consequently*
to add a new idea to a series of ideas	*in addition, furthermore, moreover, as well as, another*
to explain steps in a sequence or events in time	*at first, first, then, finally, next year, in 1945, last month, recently*
to introduce a contrasting idea	*however, but, although*
to emphasize a fact or detail or to clarify a point	*in fact, as a matter of fact*

Practice 1

Circle the letter of the signal word or phrase that correctly completes each sentence.

1 Mrs. Brown's son is polite and intelligent, _____ handsome.

    a as a result

    b as well as

2 _____ to its beautiful architectural and historical sights, Rome offers tourists great parks, restaurants, and nightlife.

    a In addition

    b Since

3 The new president promised to lower taxes and create new jobs, _____ he knew these goals would be difficult to achieve.

    a although

    b moreover

4 The traffic problem downtown is getting worse. _____ , just last week there were three accidents on Main Street.

    a As a matter of fact

    b Finally

5 There are a hundred things that kids can do besides sitting in front of the TV or a computer. _____ , they can play a musical instrument, do an art project, or go outside and enjoy nature.

    a Consequently

    b For instance

6 Last night's storm caused numerous fallen trees and power outages all over the city; _____ , residents should be careful and only travel if absolutely necessary.

    a as well as

    b therefore

Practice 2

Circle the best signal or phrase in brackets that would indicate a logical division of ideas in the essay.

Air travel has changed drastically [as a result of / at first / however / in recent years / in the past], especially when it comes to safety measures. [As a result of / At first / However / In recent years / Such as] increased crime and terrorist events [as a result of / at first / furthermore / in the past / such as] the September 11 attacks, airports and airlines have had to apply strict new security measures. [As a result of / At first / However / In the past / Such as], there were no long lines to get through airport security; people were allowed to bring what they wanted on the airplane. This included many items that are now taken away by security officials if travelers forget to leave them behind, [as a result of / at first / furthermore / in recent years / such as] bottled water, nail files, and regular-sized tubes of toothpaste. [As a result of / At first / However / In recent years / In the past], some people complained about the new security measures because they weren't used to having to wait in line or have their bags searched. [As a result of / At first / Furthermore / In fact / In the past /], they felt that some of the new security procedures were a violation of their privacy. [As a result of / At first / Furthermore / However / In recent years], over time, people have come to accept the new systems and realize they are safer because of them.

PERSONAL PRONOUNS AND POSSESSIVE ADJECTIVES

Presentation

Personal Pronouns and Possessive Adjectives

Writers use pronouns and possessive adjectives to avoid repeating the same words in a sentence or passage. Personal pronouns and possessive adjectives are used to refer to people.

Here are the most common types:

Subject pronouns:

I, you, he, she, it, we, they

Object pronouns:

me, you, him, her, it, us, them

Possessive adjectives:

my, your, his, her, its, our, their

Personal pronouns take the place of a noun or noun phrase. They can function as the subject or object of a sentence or as the object of a preposition:

- Subject: Gemma kept saying that she didn't want to go. (she = Gemma)
- Object: We loved our cats, but we gave them away when we moved overseas. (them = cats)
- Object of a preposition: Francois said he needed time to think about which decision would be the best for him. (him = Francois)

Possessive adjectives show that something belongs to a person or group of people:

Young people have their whole future ahead of them. They can do anything they want with their lives. (their = young people's)

Practice 1

Part 1

Read the excerpt from *The Fisherman and His Wife*. Underline the personal pronouns in the passage.

A There was once a fisherman who lived with his wife in a miserable hovel near the sea, and every day he went fishing. One day, as he was sitting with his rod and looking at the clear water, his line suddenly went down, far below. When he drew it up again, he brought out a large flounder. Then the flounder said to him, "Hark, you fisherman, I pray you, let me live. I am no flounder really but an enchanted prince. Why kill me? I should not be good to eat. Please take this sharp hook out of my mouth. Put me in the water again, and let me go."

B "Come," said the fisherman, "there is no need for so many words about it—a fish that can talk I should certainly let go, anyhow." With that, he put him back again into the clear water. The flounder went to the bottom, leaving a long streak of blood from its mouth. Then the fisherman got up and went home to his wife in their hovel.

C "Have you caught nothing today?" the woman asked her husband.

"No," said the man. "I did catch a flounder who said he was an enchanted prince, so I let him go again."

"Did you not wish for anything first?" asked the woman.

"No," said the man. "What should I wish for?"

"Ah," said the woman, "it is surely hard to have to live always in this dirty hovel; you might have wished for a small cottage for us. Go back and call him. Tell him we want to have a small cottage; he will certainly give us that."

"Ah," said the man, "why should I go there again?"

"Well," said the woman, "you did catch him, and you let him go again; he is sure to do it. Go at once."

D The man still did not want to go, but he did not like to oppose his wife, so he went to the sea.

Part 2

Read the excerpt from *The Fisherman and His Wife*. Underline the possessive adjectives in the passage.

There was once a fisherman who lived with his wife in a miserable hovel near the sea, and every day he went fishing. One day, as he was sitting with his rod and looking at the clear water, his line suddenly went down, far below. When he drew it up again, he brought out a large flounder. Then the flounder said to him, "Hark, you fisherman, I pray you, let me live. I am no flounder really but an enchanted prince. What good will it do you to kill me? I should not be good to eat. Please take this sharp hook out of my mouth. Put me in the water again, and let me go."

"Come," said the fisherman, "there is no need for so many words about it—a fish that can talk I should certainly let go, anyhow." With that, he put him back again into the clear water. The flounder went to the bottom, leaving a long streak of blood from its mouth. Then the fisherman got up and went home to his wife in their hovel.

"Have you caught nothing today?" the woman asked her husband.

"No," said the man. "I did catch a flounder who said he was an enchanted prince, so I let him go again."

"Did you not wish for anything first?" asked the woman.

"No," said the man. "What should I wish for?"

"Ah," said the woman, "it is surely hard to have to live always in this dirty hovel; you might have wished for a small cottage for us. Go back and call him. Tell him we want to have a small cottage; he will certainly give us that."

"Ah," said the man, "why should I go there again?"

"Well," said the woman," you did catch him, and you let him go again; he is sure to do it. Go at once."

The man still did not want to go, but he did not like to oppose his wife, so he went to the sea.

Practice 2

Read the excerpt from *The Fisherman and His Wife*. Circle the letter of the correct function in the sentence for each pronoun or adjective.

When the fisherman got there, the sea was all green and yellow and no longer so smooth; so (1) he stood still and said, "Flounder, flounder in the sea, Come, I pray thee, here to (2) me; for (3) my wife, good Ilsabil bade me speak to you again." Then the flounder came swimming to (4) him and said, "Well, what does (5) she want, then?" "Ah," said the man, "as I did catch you, my wife says I really ought to have wished for something. (6) She does not like to live in a wretched hovel any longer. She would like to have a cottage." "Go, then," said the flounder, "she has (7) it already." When the man went home, his wife was no longer in the hovel, but instead of (8) it there stood a small cottage, and she was sitting on a bench before the door. Then (9) she took him by the hand and said to him, "Just come inside, look, now isn't this a great deal better?" So (10) they went in, and there was a small porch, and a pretty little parlor and bedroom, and a kitchen and pantry, with the best of furniture, and fitted up with the most beautiful things made of tin and brass, whatsoever was wanted. Behind the cottage was a small yard with hens and ducks and a little garden with flowers and fruit. "Look," said the wife, "is not that nice!" "Yes," said the husband, "and so we must always think it—now (11) we will live quite contented." "We will think about that," said the wife. With that, (12) they ate something and went to bed.

1 In this item, *he* is
  a the subject
  b an object
  c a possessive adjective

2 In this item, *me* is
  a the subject
  b an object
  c a possessive adjective

3 In this item, *my* is
  a the subject
  b an object
  c a possessive adjective

4 In this item, *him* is
  a the subject
  b an object
  c a possessive adjective

5 In this item, *she* is
  a the subject
  b an object
  c a possessive adjective

6 In this item, *she* is
  a the subject
  b an object
  c a possessive adjective

7 In this item, *it* is
  a the subject
  b an object
  c a possessive adjective

8 In this item, *it* is
  a the subject
  b an object
  c a possessive adjective

9 In this item, *she* is
  a the subject
  b an object
  c a possessive adjective

10 In this item, *they* is
  a the subject
  b an object
  c a possessive adjective

11 In this item, *we* is
  a the subject
  b an object
  c a possessive adjective

12 In this item, *they* is
  a the subject
  b an object
  c a possessive adjective

Practice 3

Read the excerpt from *The Fisherman and His Wife*. Circle the letter of the subject or object pronoun that correctly completes each sentence in the passage.

Everything went well for a week or a fortnight, and then the woman said, "Hark you, husband, this cottage is far too small for (1), and the garden and yard are little; the flounder might just as well have given (2) a larger house. (3) should like to live in a great stone castle; go to the flounder, and tell (4) to give (5) a castle." "Ah, wife," said the man, "the cottage is quite good enough; why should (6) live in a castle?" "What!" said the woman, "just go there, the flounder can always do that." "No, wife," said the man, "the flounder has just given (7) the cottage. (8) do not like to go back so soon. (9) might make (10) angry." "Go," said the woman, "he can do it quite easily and be glad to do (11); just you go to (12)."

1 **a** they
    b us
    c we

2 **a** he
    b I
    c us

3 **a** I
    b It
    c Me

4 **a** him
    b us
    c you

5 **a** it
    b them
    c us

6 **a** them
    b us
    c we

7 **a** her
    b us
    c we

8 **a** I
    b She
    c Us

9 **a** Him
    b It
    c They

10 **a** her
    b him
    c them

11 **a** it
    b me
    c them

12 **a** her
    b him
    c you

DEMONSTRATIVE PRONOUNS AND ADJECTIVES

Presentation

Demonstrative Pronouns and Adjectives

Writers use demonstrative pronouns and adjectives to refer back to something they mentioned earlier in a passage.

Demonstrative pronouns:

this, that, these, those

Demonstrative adjectives:

this experiment, that theory,

these creatures, those people

Like personal pronouns, **demonstrative pronouns** take the place of a phrase or an idea called the referent—the word or idea the pronoun refers back to. Demonstrative pronouns function as subjects or objects in a sentence. For example:

- We're going to have a *test* [referent] on Friday. I'll tell you more about *that* [demonstrative pronoun] later.
- *Cars cause pollution.* [referent] *That* [demonstrative pronoun] is why many cities encourage residents to use public transportation.

Demonstrative adjectives are used before a noun. They usually replace a longer phrase or idea. For example:

A *group of about 300 teachers* [referent] has decided to go on strike. *These* [demonstrative adjective] employees believe they have been receiving unfair pay.

Practice 1

Circle the letter of the correct referent for the underlined pronoun or adjective.

1 Graphic novels, especially Japanese *manga*, have become extremely popular in recent years. These books are similar to traditional comic books, but they're longer.

   a comic books

   b graphic novels

   c recent years

2 I baked some chocolate chip cookies. Please don't eat the ones on the counter. Those are for the neighbors.

   a the neighbors

   b some chocolate chip cookies

   c the ones on the counter

3 Animals and humans can form strong bonds. For instance, cats are highly intelligent. That is why they make such good pets.

   a cats are highly intelligent

   b make good pets

   c can form strong bonds

4 Plants make their own food through photosynthesis. <u>This process</u> allows plants to convert light energy into chemical energy.

   a Photosynthesis

   b their own food

   c chemical energy

5 In 2008, Barack Obama was elected president of the United States. <u>This</u> was significant because he was the country's first African American leader.

   a president of the United States

   b first African American leader

   c Barack Obama was elected president

Practice 2

Read the passage. Find the referent for each of the underlined phrases. Then draw lines to match the phrases on the left to their referents on the right.

The *aurora borealis*—also known as the northern lights—is a natural phenomenon that occurs at the northernmost points of Earth. <u>These amazing light displays</u> are most commonly seen in the sky in areas near the North Pole, such as northern Canada, the U.S. state of Alaska, Greenland, and Scandinavia. Auroras are caused when the sun creates high-energy gas called solar wind. When <u>this wind</u> reaches our planet, it hits Earth's magnetic field, and <u>this</u> creates electrical currents. The electrical currents begin to travel along the surface of Earth's atmosphere, and they gather more and more energy until they reach the poles. The light of the aurora is created when <u>these high-energy electrical particles</u> mix with other gases, such as oxygen and nitrogen. Auroras may be very different in size and appearance. <u>These colors and shapes</u> depend on the amounts and types of gases that are present in the atmosphere at the time the auroras happen. There are also auroras that occur at the southernmost tip of Earth. <u>Those</u> are known as *aurora australis*.

1 these amazing light displays	auroras that occur at the southernmost tip of Earth
2 this wind	aurora borealis
3 this	solar wind
4 these high-energy electrical particles	it hits Earth's magnetic field
5 these colors and shapes	electrical currents
6 those	size and appearance

RELATIVE PRONOUNS

Presentation

Relative Pronouns

Relative pronouns appear in sentences with two clauses: a main clause and an adjective clause that modifies a noun in the main clause. In other words, a relative pronoun takes the place of a noun or an idea already mentioned in the sentence. Relative pronouns include *who*, *which*, and *that*.

- *who* is used to refer to people

Pierre de Coubertin was the French educator and historian *who* started the modern-day Olympics.

(The referent for *who* = Pierre de Coubertin)

- *that* is used to refer to people or objects

She was the same customer service representative that I had spoken to the day before.

(The referent for *that* = the same customer service representative)

We're planning to stay at the hotel *that* we stayed at last year. (The referent for *that* = the hotel)

- *which* can be used to refer to objects or ideas

I read many books online, *which* weren't even available a few years ago.

(The referent for *which* = many books)

Howard has decided to start saving money, *which* is an entirely new concept for him.

(The referent for *which* = saving money)

Practice 1

Circle the letter of the relative pronoun that completes each sentence correctly.

1 This isn't the sweater _____ I loaned you. That one was red.

  a who

  b that

2 Nathan is a great example of someone _____ worked his way up to the top. He started out as a janitor and now is the president of the company.

  a who

  b which

3 The man announced to his children that they would be going camping for the weekend, _____ didn't seem to thrill them.

  a who

  b which

4 Did you see the expensive sports car _____ was parked outside the hotel? I think it belongs to a celebrity.

  a who

  b that

5 Of all the teachers I've had in my life, Mrs. Johanna Merritt was by far the one _____ had the greatest positive influence on me.

   a who

   b which

Practice 2

Read the passage and write the correct referent to complete each sentence.

The male head of the house, Lord Grantham	massive estate	actors	their servants
	television show	reasons	show
a task	the couple	dresses	

Downton Abbey is a popular British _____ that

was created by Julian Fellowes. The _____ , which

is set in Yorkshire, England, in the early 1900s, is filmed at Highclere Castle in Hampshire.

The castle and its grounds form a _____ that is

the real-life country home of the Earl of Carnarvon and his family. By tradition, wealthy

British nobles named their homes, so *Downton Abbey* refers to the house and its gardens

and grounds. The show's plot gives viewers a glimpse into the complex lives of the

aristocratic Crawley family as well as of _____ ,

who are in charge of keeping the home and its inhabitants in perfect shape.

_____ , who is played by actor Hugh Bonneville,

made his fortune in part by marrying his wife, Cora, an American woman born to a wealthy

New York family. In the show's first season, _____ ,

who have three daughters but no sons, must decide what to do when the *Titanic* sinks,

killing Lord Grantham's cousin, the sole heir to Downton Abbey and Lord Grantham's

fortune.

There are a variety of _____ that

the show is so popular. For one thing, portraying the historical details accurately is

_____ that requires an enormous amount

of research. In addition, the scenery and costumes are beautiful, especially the

_____ that are worn by the Crawley

women. Of course, another thing that makes the show work so well are all of the

_____ who make the fictional characters come to life.

Vocabulary Building Practice Test

Part 1   Parts of Speech

Read the sentence and circle the letter of the correct part of speech for each underlined word.

1 You can't force Sarah to do her homework. It's her responsibility, not yours.
   a noun
   b verb
   c adjective
   d adverb

2 Jimmy wants to join the police force after he graduates.
   a adverb
   b conjunction
   c noun
   d adjective

3 The washing machine is very old, and the buttons don't work well. Just press gently; don't force it.
   a preposition
   b adverb
   c noun
   d verb

4 There are many different forces that can affect a child's life, both positively and negatively.
   a noun
   b preposition
   c adjective
   d adverb

Part 2   Finding the Right Meaning

Read the sentence and think about the part of speech and meaning of the underlined word. Then circle the letter of the correct definition.

1 Many women juggle several part-time jobs along with parenting their children.
   a v. to keep three or more objects in the air at one time
   b v. to try to fit several things into your schedule at the same time
   c v. to carry several things at the same time without dropping them

2 You shouldn't judge people based on what they look like or what they wear. In many cases, you'd be wrong.
   a n. the official in control of a court and who makes the final decision in a legal case
   b v. to form or give an opinion about someone
   c v. to make a guess about an amount, distance, or size

3 John is <u>facing</u> one of the most difficult times in his life.

   a n. the front surface of something, such as a building

   b n. an expression someone makes with his or her eyes, nose, and mouth to express emotion

   c v. to deal with a challenging situation

Part 3 The Way Words Are Used

Read the dictionary entry. Then complete each sentence by circling the letter of the correct word.

> **silence** *n.* **1** the complete absence of sound; quiet: **shatter the silence** *The silence was suddenly shattered by a loud scream* | **dead silence** *the dead silence of the forest at night* | **awkward silence** *There was an awkward silence when the boy asked the girl to dance.* | **moment of silence** *The president asked for a moment of silence to remember the soldiers who had died.*

1 Did you notice the _____ silence when the professor asked David if he had studied for the test?

   a dead

   b awkward

   c moment

   d shatter

2 On the country road in the middle of the night, there was not a sound, just _____ silence.

   a dead

   b awkward

   c moment

   d shatter

3 The funeral began and ended with a/an _____ of silence.

   a dead

   b awkward

   c moment

   d shatter

4 I was enjoying a peaceful morning until a noisy flock of crows arrived to _____ the silence.

   a dead

   b awkward

   c moment

   d shatter

Part 4   Roots, Prefixes, and Suffixes

Write a prefix or suffix to each root to form a new word.

less	ance	re	tion
ness	dis	in	ible
im	non	ity	
un	al	able	

1 perform _____

2 _____ able

3 _____ believable

4 ration _____

5 hope _____

6 sick _____

7 _____ apply

8 _____ edible

9 _____ polite

10 break _____

Part 5   Greek and Latin Roots

Underline the root in each word. Then underline the meaning of the root.

1 local

Root: loc / al

Meaning: self / place

2 habitual

Root: habit / ual

Meaning: say / live

3 monolingual

Root: mono / lingual

Meaning: one / down, from

4 biography

Root: bio / graph / y

Meaning: written / under

5 juvenile

Root: juven / ile

Meaning: young / carry

6 reduction

Root: re / duc / tion

Meaning: measure / lead

7 speedometer

Root: speedo / meter

Meaning: measure / carry

8 injection

Root: in / jec / tion

Meaning: throw / live

9 porter

Root: port / er

Meaning: measure / carry

10 automobile

Root: auto / mobile

Meaning: self / under

11 unilateral

Root: uni / lat / eral

Meaning: side / under

12 dictation

Root: dic / ta / tion

Meaning: place / say

13 reformation

Root: re / form / ation

Meaning: shape / write

14 dental

Root: dent / al

Meaning: tooth / say

Part 6 Negative Prefixes

Write the number of each root below the correct negative prefix.

1. migrate	5. planned	9. logical	13. popular
2. qualify	6. governmental	10. able	14. use
3. treat	7. literate	11. destructible	15. sincere
4. replaceable	8. perfect	12. fiction	16. recoverable

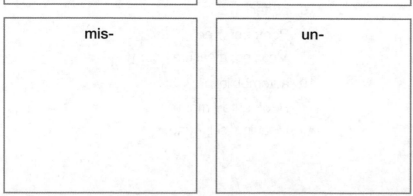

dis-

im-

in-

il-

ir-

non-

mis-

un-

Part 7 Prefixes and Meanings

Write the correct prefix to complete the word in each sentence.

anti-	pre-	super-

1 The students went out in the streets for _____ government protests.

2 Tom has such a great voice. He's going to be the next pop _____ star.

3 Is your son old enough to start _____ school?

trans-	semi-	post-

4 The coach will have a _____ game party if the team wins tonight.

5 If they win the _____ final game, the team will go to the championship.

6 This airline is giving discounts on all of its _____ atlantic flights.

Part 8 Suffixes and Parts of Speech

Look at each word and the underlined suffix. Then complete the missing information in the table.

Word	Part of Speech	Root	Part of Speech of Root
joy**ful**	_____	_____	_____
warm**ly**	_____	_____	_____
remov**able**	_____	_____	_____
locat**ion**	_____	_____	_____
disgust**ing**	_____	_____	_____
fond**ness**	_____	_____	_____

Part 9 Suffixes and Parts of Speech

Add the correct suffix to the root in parentheses. Write in the word to complete the sentence. Remember that you may need to change the spelling of the root.

-able	-ence	-tion

1 Hannah has been baking and decorating a cake all day. She is proud of her delicious _____ (create).

2 These days, most people use email for written _____ (correspond).

3 Since Carla stopped working full time and studying, her schedule is more _____ (manage).

-ful	-ian	-ish

4 Our trip to Spain was absolutely _____ (wonder).

5 Don't drink that water. It looks a little _____ (brown).

6 Kevin is quite a _____ (history). He knows all about the Renaissance.

Part 10   Word Forms and Families

Circle the letter of the correct form of the word to complete the sentence.

1 I just read a very _____ book about how to start exercising.

   a motivation

   b motivating

2 When you go to the beach, it's very important to _____ yourself from the sun.

   a protect

   b protection

3 Tom is very serious about sports. He hates to _____ .

   a lose

   b loss

4 British English and American English _____ in several key ways.

   a differ

   b different

5 The children were very _____ about the field trip to the zoo.

   a excited

   b exciting

Part 11   What Is Context?

Read the passage from *Anne of Green Gables* with missing words. This is like reading a passage with unknown words. After you read the passage, circle the letter of the correct answer to each question on the next page.

> It was broad daylight when Anne awoke and sat up in ▆▆, staring confusedly at the window through which a flood of cheery ▆▆▆▆▆▆ was pouring and outside of which something white and feathery waved across glimpses of blue ▆▆.
>
> For a moment, she could not remember where she was. First came a delightful thrill, as something very pleasant; then a ▆▆▆▆▆▆ remembrance. This was Green Gables, and they didn't want her because she wasn't a ▆▆!
>
> But it was ▆▆▆▆▆ and, yes, it was a cherry-tree in full bloom outside of her ▆▆. With a bound she was out of bed and across the floor. She pushed up the sash—it went up stiffly and creakily, as if it hadn't been ▆▆▆▆▆ for a long time, which was the case; and it stuck so tight that nothing was needed to hold it up.
>
> Anne dropped on her knees and gazed out into the June ▆▆▆▆▆, her eyes glistening with delight. Oh, wasn't it beautiful? Wasn't it a ▆▆▆▆▆ place? Suppose she wasn't really going to stay here!
>
> She would ▆▆▆▆▆ she was. There was scope for imagination here.
>
> A huge cherry-tree grew outside, so close that its boughs tapped against the house, and it was so thick-set with ▆▆▆▆▆▆ that hardly a leaf was to be seen. On both sides of the house was a big orchard, one of apple-trees and one of cherry-trees, also showered over with ▆▆▆▆▆; and their grass was all sprinkled with dandelions. In the garden below were lilac-trees purple with flowers, and their dizzily sweet ▆▆▆▆▆ drifted up to the window on the morning wind.

1 Where does the story happen?
   a in the countryside
   b in the city
   c in a foreign country

2 What time of day is it?
   a evening
   b afternoon
   c morning

3 Who is the character in this scene?
   a a young girl
   b a teenage boy
   c an elderly woman

4 What season is it?
   a winter
   b spring
   c fall

5 How is the girl feeling?
   a tired
   b optimistic
   c afraid

Part 12 Guessing the Meaning of Words and Phrases

Read each sentence and figure out the part of speech of the underlined word. Use the context and your background knowledge to circle the letter of the correct definition.

1 The overzealous fans finally chased the movie star back into the waiting car.
   a v. to know someone well
   b n. a feeling of concern or worry
   c adj. too eager or excited about something

2 My legs were still trembling hours after I finished giving my presentation.
   a adj. very long
   b v. shaking very slightly
   c adv. fast moving

3 We retraced our steps all the way back to the theater, but we never found Jackie's missing scarf.
   a n. a colorful drawing
   b adj. mysterious and frightening
   c v. to go back exactly the same way

4 I understand that you're upset, but I really don't think this situation warrants a big fight.
   a v. to cause problems
   b n. an official document
   c v. to be worth the trouble

Part 13 Guessing Meaning from a Passage

Read the passage. Use the context to figure out the part of speech and general meaning of the underlined words. Then draw a line to match each word with its definition.

Technology and Employment Rates

Fewer jobs, moving jobs

The rapid expansion of both the global economy and new developments in the field of technology have had a negative effect on some fields of employment.

New types of technology have made it possible for some companies to use machines instead of humans to do various jobs such as factory work. While saving companies money, this development has reduced the number of available jobs, especially for those with lower education levels. Moreover, technological developments have also changed global supply routes, creating more job opportunities in some countries and cutting job options in others. In short, there are fewer jobs available overall, and those jobs that are available are concentrated in certain regions of the world.

How governments can help workers succeed

Globalization and the trend toward using technology to replace human workers are not likely to slow down any time soon. Unless political leaders step in to ensure more equal distribution of jobs and wealth, the world economy is in danger of losing balance. However, these developments aren't entirely bad. In fact, these changes have created a rise in higher-level management jobs. Governments can meet the need for skilled labor by supporting education and training opportunities for unskilled workers who have lost their jobs. In this way, displaced workers may be able to get the qualifications they need to succeed.

Economic and political solutions

Governments can also help balance global employment opportunities by collaborating and communicating with other nations on tax systems, regulations, and trade policies that will help keep manufacturing and trade healthy in all regions of the world.

Of course, even if governments take the problem seriously, there's no guarantee that taking these steps will make a lasting difference. Nevertheless, even if today's government leaders are beginning to think about ways to protect people's futures, it's a good start.

1. expansion   n. placement

2. concentrated   v. working together

3. distribution   n. rules and laws

4. collaborating   adj. close together in one area

5. policies   n. growth or development

Part 14 Common Types of Collocations

Complete each sentence with a word from the box to form a common English collocation.

verb + noun

do	have	take

1 I can't play basketball after school today. I have to stay home and _____ my homework.

Please don't hurry to finish the test. Just _____ your time.

Do you and your sister _____ a lot in common?

noun + noun

taxi	staff	cake

2 James's first part-time job was as a _____ driver in New York City.

Several members of the sales _____ left the company this month.

Can you recommend a good bakery? I need to buy a birthday _____ for a friend.

adverb + verb

finally	partly	completely

3 Congratulations! I hear you _____ finished your research study.

While hiking in the rain forest, try to remain _____ silent. That way you won't scare away the animals.

Tomorrow's weather looks nice. It's going to be _____ sunny and 70 degrees.

Part 15 Idioms

Read each sentence and circle the letter of the correct word to complete the idiom.

1 Rhonda is always too busy to get together. She doesn't have any _____ time.

   a work

   b spare

   c hang

2 Karen is so mean. Everyone _____ over backward to try to make her happy, but she still complains.

   a smiles

   b walks

   c bends

3 I'm sorry, but you're too young to see this movie. If I make an _____ for you, I'll have to do it for everyone.

   a answer

   b exception

   c obsession

4 We arrived at the school just _____ time to see the beginning of the holiday concert.

   a on

   b in

   c at

Part 16   Signal Words and Phrases

Circle the letter of the signal word or phrase that correctly completes each sentence.

1 The university's international fair will continue this weekend, _____ the weather report says it may rain.

   a as well as

   b although

2 _____ , the speaker concluded the presentation by inviting audience questions.

   a Finally

   b In addition

3 Smoking is no longer allowed on company grounds. _____ , employees must quit smoking in order to be eligible for manager positions.

   a As a result

   b Moreover

4 Only three students have enrolled in the filmmaking course this semester. _____ , we will need to cancel the course.

   a Therefore

   b In addition

Part 17   Personal Pronouns and Possessive Adjectives

Read the passage and circle the pronouns and possessive adjectives that correctly complete the sentences.

Each year, the average family gets numerous sore throats, runny noses, coughs, fevers, and other types of viruses. In these cases, many parents bring (their / her) children to their physician's office, expecting a prescription for medication to help the child get well faster. These days, some in the healthcare industry are being more cautious about doling out these drugs when (it / they) aren't really necessary. Instead, doctors may be more likely to recommend rest and letting the patient's own immune system do (its / their) job.

The overuse of antibiotics is risky business. Because bacteria are living organisms, (they / he) can mutate—that is, (we / they) can change over time. As a result of years or decades of antibiotic use, some bacteria have changed and become resistant to certain types of the drugs. These new "super germs" are stronger, so (they / their) no longer respond to the medications. (They / He) also have the power to affect larger portions of the population with more serious illnesses, making (its / it) more difficult to fight them off naturally with (our / his) own immune system.

Part 18 Demonstrative Pronouns and Adjectives

Circle the letter of the correct referent for the underlined pronoun or adjective.

1 Each year, the average family gets numerous sore throats, runny noses, coughs, fevers, and other types of viruses. In these cases, many parents bring their children to their physician's office, expecting a prescription for medication to help the child get well faster.

   a the average family

   b sore throats, runny noses, coughs, and fevers

   c other types of viruses

2 In these cases, many parents bring their children to their physician's office, expecting a prescription for medication to help the child get well faster. These days, some in the healthcare industry are being more cautious about doling out these drugs when they aren't really necessary.

   a some in the healthcare industry

   b their physician's office

   c prescriptions for medication

3 As a result of decades of antibiotic use, some bacteria have changed and become resistant to certain types of the drugs. These new "super germs" are stronger, so they no longer respond to the medications.

   a some bacteria

   b decades of antibiotic use

   c certain types of the drugs

Part 19 Relative Pronouns

Circle the letter of the relative pronoun that completes each sentence correctly.

1 The first type of antibiotic was penicillin, _____ was accidentally discovered from a mold culture.

   a who

   b which

2 Education companies began mass producing classical-music CD sets combined with video DVDs, _____ children could watch as they listened and magically became geniuses.

   a who

   b which

3 In addition to the increased costs, which will undoubtedly be passed on to cosmetics consumers, cosmetics firms are concerned that the ban on certain ingredients will reduce their ability to innovate new products _____ are genuinely safe for humans.

   a who

   b that

READING FASTER

Introduction Strategies for Reading Faster

INTRODUCTION: STRATEGIES FOR READING FASTER

> **Presentation**
>
> #### Strategies for Reading Faster
>
> Sometimes it is important to read slowly and carefully, such as when you are reading instructions or technical or scientific passages. Other kinds of reading materials, such as newspaper articles, can be read more quickly. It is important to be able to adjust your reading speed up and down as needed.
>
> The purpose of this section is to encourage you to read faster. Learning to read faster will help you
>
> - read more efficiently and get the information you need from the text more quickly.
> - read more. The more you read, the more your general English skills will improve—not only in reading but also in listening, speaking, and writing.
> - focus on the idea and meaning of the whole passage rather than on individual words.
>
> To read faster, follow this advice:
>
> - Don't translate. Try to think in English as you are reading.
> - Skip unknown words or try to guess meaning from context.
> - Time yourself when you are reading.

Read the instructions for timed reading below. Read the passage, following the instructions. Then go to *Reading Faster Practice* activity to answer the comprehension questions.

Instructions for Timed Reading

1. Print a copy of the Reading Rate Table and the Reading Rate Log from the Appendices on pp. 194–195.

2. Before you start reading, write your exact start time (minutes and seconds) on the Reading Rate Log.

3. Start the timer.

4. Preview the passage by skimming it quickly.

5. Read the passage, skipping over unknown words or guessing their meaning.

6. Stop the timer and write your exact finish time on the Reading Rate Log.

7. Calculate your reading time (your finish time minus your start time), and check your reading rate on the Reading Rate Table.

8. Make a check mark next to your reading rate on the Reading Rate Log.

9. Check your reading rate progress after a few passages. Your number should get higher. If it does not, challenge yourself to read faster.

10. Answer the comprehension questions. Do <u>not</u> look back at the passage. Then write the number of correct answers on the Reading Rate Log.

Palm Oil and Endangered Orangutans

Do you usually read the list of ingredients when you buy something? If you do, then you probably know that palm oil—the oil that comes from the African oil palm tree—is found in hundreds of products, from cosmetics to baked goods to cleaning supplies. Because palm oil is useful for so many products and is cheap to produce, it is in high demand around the world. Around 50 million tons of palm oil are produced each year, mostly in Indonesia, Malaysia, and a handful of African countries.

Borneo and Sumatra, two islands in Indonesia, both have many large palm oil plantations. These tropical Southeast Asian islands are home to thousands of animal species, including the endangered orangutan.

Because of the huge international demand for palm oil, thousands of acres of rainforest land in Borneo and Sumatra have been cleared to make way for palm oil plantations. This rainforest land used to be the native habitat of the orangutan. By some estimates, over the past two decades, more than 90 percent of the orangutan's habitat has been destroyed.

Similar to the chimpanzee, the orangutan is one of humans' closest relatives. In fact, the word orangutan comes from the Malay and Indonesian words meaning "person of the jungle." Orangutans are gentle animals that do not pose any danger to humans.

Unfortunately, however, humans pose a great threat to the orangutans. Many orangutans are killed by humans, especially because of the production of palm oil. In the process of clearing large areas of rainforest to plant palm trees, the palm oil companies leave the orangutans with nowhere to live and nothing to eat. In addition, the companies often burn large areas of land for clearing, which results in the deaths of many of the animals from inhaling smoke or burning to death.

Some sources have reported that six to twelve endangered orangutans are killed every day due to the actions of the palm oil industry. An estimated 50,000 orangutans have already died as a result of deforestation in the past twenty years. In Sumatra alone, the orangutan population is just 6,000—down from 100,000 fifty years ago.

Animal rights activists say that if this pattern is allowed to continue, orangutans in the wild could be extinct within ten to twelve years. In twenty years, their rainforest habitat, home to thousands of other species of plants and animals, will also be gone.

Many people want to know what they can do to help. There are many international animal rights organizations that are working to protect the orangutan. These groups have websites that offer useful information about how concerned citizens can support their efforts and how to tell which products contain palm oil, which may be listed under different names on product labels.

Introduction Practice Questions

Introduction: Practice Questions

Answer the questions based on the reading "Palm Oil and Endangered Orangutans" in the Introduction on p. 133. Do not go back to the reading. Write the number of correct answers on the Reading Rate Log.

1 What types of products contain palm oil?

a mainly cosmetics

b mainly food products

c many kinds of products

2 Where is most palm oil produced?

a all around the world

b in Southeast Asia

c all over Africa

3 In order to build palm oil plantations, companies _____ .

a search for land where no animals live

b destroy large areas of the rainforest

c move orangutans to safe locations

4 The word *orangutan* means _____ .

a "gentle to people"

b "person of the jungle"

c "human's relative"

5 The decline in the orangutan population _____ .

a began years ago

b came on suddenly

c has not been proven

6 Which of the following is NOT mentioned in this passage?

a why palm oil is in high demand

b what orangutans usually eat

c how orangutans are killed

7 Animal rights activists say that, in the near future, orangutans may _____ .

a be dangerous to humans

b not exist in the wild

c adapt to other habitats

8 From this passage, we can infer that the author recommends _____ .

a donating money to help orangutans

b not buying products made with palm oil

c taking a trip to see wild orangutans

Timed Reading Practice

PRACTICE 1 STEVE JOBS: A PORTRAIT OF SUCCESS

Timed Reading 1

Guidelines for Timed Reading

To read faster, follow this advice:

- Don't translate. Try to think in English as you are reading.
- Skip unknown words or try to guess meaning from context.
- Time yourself when you are reading.

Instructions for Timed Reading

1 Print a copy of the Reading Rate Table and the Reading Rate Log from the Appendix.
2 Before you start reading, write your exact start time (minutes and seconds) on the Reading Rate Log.
3 Start the timer.
4 Preview the passage by skimming it quickly.
5 Read the passage, skipping over unknown words or guessing their meaning.
6 Stop the timer and write your exact finish time on the Reading Rate Log.
7 Calculate your reading time (your finish time minus your start time), and check your reading rate on the Reading Rate Table.
8 Make a check mark next to your reading rate on the Reading Rate Log.
9 Check your reading rate progress after a few passages. Your number should get higher. If it does not, challenge yourself to read faster.
10 Answer the comprehension questions. Do not look back at the passage. Then write the number of correct answers on the Reading Rate Log.

Practice the strategies for faster reading. Read the passage. Then go to *Timed Reading 1 Comprehension Questions* activity on p. 137 to answer the questions.

Steve Jobs—A Portrait of Success

The Early Years

Many people would agree that Steve Jobs, former CEO of Apple Computers, was one of the most influential people in the world, certainly in the field of technology. Under Jobs's direction, Apple Inc. developed some of the world's most innovative and exciting technological inventions.

Jobs was born on February 24, 1955, to Joanne Schieble and Abdulfattah Jandali. At the time, the two were busy young graduate students at the University of Wisconsin, and they decided it was best for them to give up the child for adoption.

A short time later, the boy was adopted by Clara and Paul Jobs of Mountain View, California, and named Steven Paul Jobs. The family home was within California's Silicon Valley, an area known for its many computer and electronics companies.

Steve's father, Paul, was a machinist, and when Steve was a young boy, the two would spend hours in the family's garage taking apart and rebuilding electronics—helpful practice for Steve's future career.

In elementary school, Steve didn't stand out—at least not in a good way. He preferred playing jokes on his classmates and teachers to completing his school work. In the fourth grade, a teacher named Imogene Hill saw that young Steve had potential. Hill was finally able to convince Steve to take his studies more seriously. How did she do it? She rewarded him with candy and five-dollar bills from her own money. Later, Steve spoke about Mrs. Hill fondly, calling her "one of the saints of my life."

In 1969, at age thirteen, Steve met an eighteen-year-old university freshman named Steve "Woz" Wozniak, his future Apple cofounder. Although they were different ages, the two had a lot in common. They shared a love of electronics and computer design, and they were both leaders rather than followers. In his book *Woz*, Steve Wozniak said of their meeting, "Typically, it was really hard for me to explain to people the kind of design stuff I worked on, but Steve got it right away. And I liked him. He was kind of skinny and wiry and full of energy. Steve and I got close right away, even though he was still in high school. We talked electronics, we talked about music we liked, and we traded stories."

Steve and Woz's first "business" together began in 1972. Woz had read an article in an electronics magazine about a device that could be attached to a telephone and could hack into the telephone company's main computer and allow people to make free long-distance phone calls. They decided to try to make one, and they succeeded. The pair began selling their devices to students living in college dormitories. Of course, the devices were illegal, so the business didn't last long. Steve and Woz stopped selling them after they were nearly caught by the police.

When Steve finished high school, he enrolled in classes at Reed College, a private liberal arts college in Oregon. The tuition for Reed was very expensive, and Steve's parents could barely afford it. Nevertheless, they wanted their son to succeed, so they were prepared to spend almost their entire life's savings on his education.

However, as it turned out, Steve didn't stay at Reed for a long time. He dropped out after just six months, later saying, "I couldn't see the value in it. I had no idea what I wanted to do with my life and no idea how college was going to help me figure it out. And here I was spending all of the money my parents had saved their entire life. So I decided to drop out and trust that it would all work out OK."

Timed Reading 1

Answer the questions based on Reading 1, "Steve Jobs: The Early Years." Write the number of correct answers on the Reading Rate Log.

1 Which of the following is true about Steve Jobs's early childhood?

   a He was born in California.

   b He was given up for adoption.

   c His parents owned a computer company.

2 Steve's interest in electronics came from _____ .

   a reading electronics and computer magazines

   b visiting computer companies in his hometown

   c building electronics in the garage with his father

3 It can be inferred from this passage that _____ .

   a Steve was never a very good student

   b Steve's teachers did not think he could be successful

   c Steve had trouble making friends in school

4 Imogene Hill was _____ .

   a Steve's high school girlfriend

   b a teacher who influenced Steve

   c Steve's elementary school classmate

5 Jobs met his future business partner, Steve Wozniak, when _____ .

   a he was still in high school

   b they were attending college together

   c they worked at a computer company together

6 Which of the following was NOT mentioned in this passage?

   a what Steve Wozniak studied in college

   b what year Steve and Woz first met

   c where Steve first attended college

7 Steve's first business with Woz did not succeed because _____ .

   a no one bought the product

   b it was not legal

   c they were still in college

8 Which of the following is true about Steve Jobs's college experience?

   a He graduated from Reed College.

   b He graduated from college later in life.

   c He never graduated from college.

Timed Reading 2

Practice the strategies for faster reading. Read the passage. Then go to *Timed Reading 2 Comprehension Questions* activity on p. 138 to answer the questions.

Steve Jobs—A Portrait of Success

Apple's Beginnings

Steve Jobs dropped out of Reed College, but he stayed near the campus for the next year and a half taking a few classes in creative subjects that interested him. One class in calligraphy sparked his interest in creating different styles of type.

In the early 1970s, Jobs continued to try different paths for his life. He worked for a short time as a video game designer for Atari in 1974 and then traveled around India and other parts of Asia for several months. Meanwhile, his old friend Steve Wozniak was still in California, working for the computer company Hewlett-Packard. Wozniak spent his spare time learning more about computers and trying to build his own personal computer.

When Jobs returned from his travels, Wozniak showed him the computer board he had finally finished building. Jobs knew right away that his friend's clever invention had big possibilities. He told Wozniak that he thought they should start a company together. Apple Computer, Inc. was born on April 1, 1976, when Jobs was just twenty-one years old.

The two first worked out of Jobs's garage, where, as a boy, he had first discovered his passion for technology while building electronics with his dad. To get the money to fund their start-up, Jobs sold his Volkswagen bus and Wozniak sold his scientific calculator. According to Wozniak, the name Apple Computers was suggested by Jobs while the two were on a car trip. At the time, Jobs was working part-time caring for apple trees on a farm. Wozniak also said that Jobs may have borrowed the name from Apple Records, the record label for The Beatles.

Together, Jobs and Wozniak brought the power of computer technology into the hands of everyday people. Instead of giant, expensive computers that only businesses could afford to use, Apple created smaller machines that were user friendly and affordable for many more people. Their first product, the Apple I, released in 1976 and sold for $666.66.

For the next three years, the two men continued to make improvements to the design of the Apple I, and in 1979, they released the Apple II. This system was much more powerful, and it was able to display color graphics. When the Apple II hit the market, sales increased by 700 percent. Jobs and Wozniak were millionaires after just three years in business.

Despite their early successes, the next several years brought challenges and disappointments. Design problems caused a few products to be recalled. Other manufacturers, such as IBM, created new software and options for consumers and soon started to outperform Apple's sales. Some of Apple's top executives began to feel that Jobs was hurting the company, and they started to question his leadership.

Steve Jobs left his position as CEO of Apple in 1985 and started his own company, called NeXT, Inc. This company had only limited success, and in 1997, Jobs sold the company to Apple for $429 million. By this time, the top leaders at Apple had changed their minds about Jobs's ability to run the company, and they asked him to come back as CEO.

The 1980s and early 1990s were a tough time for Apple. IBM products continued to grow in popularity, and Apple needed innovation to get its products noticed again. Back in the top seat at Apple, Jobs provided the marketing and creative genius that put Apple back on top when, during the late 1990s, the company introduced the stylish new iMac line.

Timed Reading 2

Answer the questions based on Reading 2, "Apple's Beginnings." Write the number of correct answers on the Reading Rate Log.

1 After college, Steve Jobs worked _____ .
   a for a tour company in India
   b as a video game designer
   c at Hewlett-Packard

2 It was Steve Wozniak who _____ .
   a designed Apple's earliest computer
   b first had the idea to start a company
   c got all of the money to start Apple

3 We can infer from this passage that _____ .
   a Jobs and Wozniak disagreed about starting a company
   b Apple was started without much money
   c Steve Jobs tried to get a job at IBM after he left Apple

4 The name Apple may have come from _____ .
   a the name of a song
   b Steve's love of music
   c Steve's favorite fruit

5 The Apple II _____ .
   a was more popular than the Apple I
   b had many design problems
   c was smaller than IBM's computers

6 As a company, Apple _____ .
   a always out-sold its competitors
   b had some challenging times
   c almost went out of business during the 1980s

7 Which of the following is NOT mentioned in this passage?
   a Steve Jobs's salary at Apple
   b the reason Steve Jobs left Apple
   c what happened to NeXT

8 In the late 1990s, Steve Jobs _____ .

    a helped Apple become more successful

    b left Apple and became the CEO of IBM

    c created a new company called NeXT

Timed Reading 3

Practice the strategies for faster reading. Read the passage. Then go to *Timed Reading 3 Comprehension Questions* activity on p. 141 to answer the questions.

Steve Jobs—A Portrait of Success

Finishing on Top

Steve Jobs's return to Apple was challenging. At the time, he was also running Pixar Animation Studios, which he had purchased after selling NeXT. Jobs's biography, written by Walter Isaacson, mentions how hard Jobs worked during his first few months back at Apple, saying that he was so tired, he could hardly speak when he arrived home in the evening.

Steve Jobs was a tough boss, and he had high expectations of the people who worked for Apple. When he first came back to the company, he met with every team and every employee at Apple. Each team had to explain why they felt they were important to the company. Jobs told them that if the team didn't present enough good reasons, he would cancel their product and they would be asked to leave.

No one questioned Jobs's ability to run Apple successfully, especially after the introduction of the iMac in 1998. Its sleek, see-through design and bright colors were revolutionary—a fresh and welcome change from the plain, boxy white PCs that had been common since the mid-1980s. Through the 2000s, other Apple products, such as the iBook and iPod, made Apple the trendiest computer company around. PC users started switching to Macs, and Apple was back on top again.

In 2003, Jobs's life changed drastically when he learned that he had a rare form of pancreatic cancer. Doctors told Jobs that the cancer could be treated with surgery. However, he wanted to wait and research nonsurgical and alternative medical treatments. Jobs put off having surgery for nine months, keeping his illness a secret from the public because executives worried that if investors learned that Apple's top man was seriously ill, they would begin to sell their shares of stock in the company.

In 2004, Jobs had a successful surgery to remove the cancer, and for several years after that, he remained well and continued to push Apple to its creative limits. In many ways, Apple went far beyond previous achievements. In 2007, each share of Apple stock was worth a record-breaking $199.99. That same year, the company reported $1.58 billion in profit.

In early 2009, Jobs's health began to fail again, and once again he did his best to keep the information from reaching the ears of the public. He appeared in public less frequently, and he even took a leave of absence for nearly a full year. On October 5, 2011, Apple announced that Steve Jobs had passed away. He was 56 years old.

Until today, the little computer company that Steve Jobs started in his garage with his friend Steve Wozniak hasn't slowed down. Apple's small *i* continues to appear in front of new words, from iTunes to iPhone to iPad—each time sending consumers rushing to electronics stores and competitors scrambling to create similar products.

Apple is the second most profitable information technology company (after the South Korean company Samsung Electronics), and it is the third largest manufacturer of mobile phones (after Samsung and Nokia). Apple employs about 75,000 people worldwide and operates close to 400 retail stores in fourteen different countries, in addition to its online store and iTunes marketplace. The company is estimated to be worth $414 billion.

Timed Reading 3

Answer the questions based on Reading 3, "Steve Jobs: Finishing on Top." Write the number of correct answers on the Reading Rate Log.

1 When Steve Jobs returned to Apple, he _____ .
  a started working part-time only
  b shared duties with Steve Wozniak
  c had to work very hard

2 Jobs met with each team at Apple to _____ .
  a learn all of his new employees' names
  b explain why he had returned as CEO
  c make sure they were all important to the company

3 The iMac was an important product because it _____ .
  a made Apple a trendy company again
  b was Apple's first new product since 1985
  c was faster and less expensive than a PC

4 From this passage, we can infer that _____ .
  a at first, Jobs did not want to return to Apple because he wanted to retire
  b some people did not have confidence in Jobs's ability to lead Apple
  c Jobs was more talented than other Apple executives

5 Which of the following is NOT mentioned in this passage?
  a Jobs was married and had three children.
  b Jobs believed in alternative forms of medicine.
  c Jobs took a year's leave of absence when he was ill.

6 After recovering from his first surgery, Steve Jobs _____ .
  a took several months off
  b continued to work for Apple
  c focused more on his family

7 Which of the following is NOT included in this passage?
  a when Steve Wozniak stopped working at Apple
  b how old Steve Jobs was when he died
  c how much Apple is worth today

8 Since Steve Jobs's death, Apple has _____ .
   a continued to move forward
   b slowed down its production
   c opened 400 new stores worldwide

PRACTICE 2 WAYS OF LEARNING

Timed Reading 1

Practice the strategies for faster reading. Read the passage. Then go to *Timed Reading 1 Comprehension Questions* activity on p. 143 to answer the questions.

Ways of Learning

Multiple Intelligences

The traditional belief about human intelligence is that people are born with a certain capacity for it. Simply put, some people are just more intelligent than others. According to this belief, a person's level of intelligence can be measured by a simple short-answer test called an Intelligence Quotient (IQ) test.

The theory of Multiple Intelligences was developed in 1983 by Harvard psychologist Dr. Howard Gardner. Gardner defines intelligence as the skills that make it possible for a person to gather new knowledge and solve problems in life. His idea is that all humans have a combination of nine different types of intelligence. Within each person, Gardner says, each of these intelligences is stronger or weaker, and this makes us able to process information and learn in different ways.

Gardner's nine multiple intelligences are:

1. **Linguistic Intelligence:** the ability to use language to express your ideas and to understand others' ideas. Lawyers, writers, and other people who use spoken or written language for their work have high levels of linguistic intelligence.

2. **Logical/Mathematical Intelligence:** the ability to easily understand and create mathematical systems and formulas or scientific concepts. Chemists, engineers, and others in scientific fields are generally strong in this area.

3. **Musical/Rhythmic Intelligence:** the ability to hear, recognize, and create musical patterns. People with this intelligence can remember and learn to play musical pieces quickly and easily, and they may "hear" music in their minds all the time.

4. **Bodily/Kinesthetic Intelligence:** the ability to use your body or the movement of your body to process information, solve a problem, or put on some kind of performance. Dancers, athletes, and actors are some examples of people with this type of intelligence.

5. **Spatial Intelligence:** the ability to understand spatial arrangements and the distance, direction, and connections between and among spaces. People who have a good sense of direction or those involved in visual arts or design high spatial intelligence.

6. **Naturalist Intelligence:** the ability to have an understanding of and sensitivity to the natural world and living things (plants and animals). Those who work with plants and animals, such as farmers, herbalists, and veterinarians are intelligent in this way.

7. **Intrapersonal Intelligence:** the ability to know yourself and have an understanding of your own likes, dislikes, emotions, and reactions. Individuals with this intelligence are typically confident leaders and aren't afraid to express their opinions.

8. **Interpersonal Intelligence:** the ability to understand and communicate well with other people. People who work with groups of people in education or psychology, such as teachers and therapists, have strong interpersonal intelligence.

9. **Existential Intelligence:** the capacity and tendency to ask and wonder about questions of life, death, truth, and reality. Philosophers and spiritual leaders are strong in this area.

We all know someone who is exceptionally good at math or music or who seems to learn new languages very quickly. Most people can probably identify one or more of Gardner's intelligences that they feel describes their strengths or special skills.

The theory of Multiple Intelligences has been popular among those in the education field; if teachers can recognize when a student shows intelligence in one or more areas, then they can teach that student in the way he or she learns best.

Some have criticized Gardner, saying that his theory has not been researched thoroughly enough to be proven. These sources agree that different people may be more skilled than others in certain of the nine intelligence areas, but they say it's important to recognize that people also have varying capacities for general intelligence.

Timed Reading 1

Answer the questions based on Reading 1, "Multiple Intelligences." Write the number of correct answers on the Reading Rate Log.

1 The traditional belief about intelligence is that _____.
   a different people have different types of intelligence
   b people are born with a certain level of intelligence
   c people become more or less intelligent with age

2 Dr. Howard Gardner's theory _____.
   a is a brand new concept in education
   b was developed about thirty years ago
   c is one of the earliest theories about human intelligence

3 According to Gardner, lawyers and writers are more likely to have _____.
   a spatial intelligence
   b linguistic intelligence
   c mathematical intelligence

4 High levels of spatial intelligence may help us _____.
   a find our way when we are lost
   b use our bodies to create performances
   c understand what other people are feeling

5 Which of the following is NOT mentioned in this passage?
   a where and when Gardner developed his theory
   b how Gardner's theory has been applied
   c how multiple intelligences can be measured

6 According to this passage, which of the following people are most likely to know about Gardner's theory?

   a painters

   b teachers

   c musicians

7 Critics of Gardner's theory say that _____ .

   a only general intelligence can be measured

   b it is completely false and should be ignored

   c it has not been sufficiently researched

8 From this passage, we can infer that the author _____ .

   a has probably met Dr. Gardner in person

   b most likely works in the field of education

   c agrees that people have multiple intelligences

Timed Reading 2

Practice the strategies for faster reading. Read the passage. Then go to *Timed Reading 2 Comprehension Questions* activity on p. 145 to answer the questions.

Ways of Learning

Acquired Savant Syndrome

Forty-year-old Derek Amato is a professional musician. He composes original classical pieces and plays beautiful, complicated melodies on the piano. To listen to him, you would think Amato has been playing the piano his entire life. He hasn't. In fact, Amato has only been playing for a few years, and he didn't learn to play in any of the usual ways—neither through years of lessons nor by ear. Amato's talent came to him suddenly, literally overnight.

Amato is one of about thirty people in the world who have been diagnosed with what is known as "acquired savant syndrome," a medical condition caused by a serious head injury that results in the sudden ability to do something the person has never done before—and do it well. Acquired skills include the ability to paint, draw, do complex mathematical calculations without writing down even one number, or—as in Amato's case—play music like a virtuoso.

In October, 2006, while at a party at a friend's backyard pool, Amato jumped into the shallow end and hit his head on the hard bottom. He remembers knowing that something was terribly wrong and that he had hurt himself badly. Amato suffered a serious concussion and was hospitalized briefly. After a few days, Amato stopped by the home of a musician friend for a visit. When he saw the friend's piano across the room, he said he was mysteriously drawn to it. He walked over, sat down, and immediately started playing his own composition. It was as if he had been playing piano his entire life. He described the experience in a televised interview: "It just all came out. It was almost like it was just flowing with no limitations. Really."

Before the accident, Amato had always loved music, and he played a little bit of guitar, but he'd never played any instrument seriously and had never taken a piano lesson in his life. Amato cannot read music. He says the music comes to him in his mind's eye when he sees lines of black and white squares flowing from left to right. "That's my notation," Amato says. "When those black and white squares are going, that's what my hands do."

Researchers believe that acquired savant syndrome occurs when the right brain takes over when there is an injury to the left brain. Dr. Andrew Reeves, a neurologist at the Mayo Clinic, examined Amato and explained the phenomenon. He said that Amato's head injury rewired his brain, leading to his acquired musical skills.

Before the accident, Amato had had various kinds of jobs without knowing what he wanted to do. Once, he had even been homeless for several months and lived in his car while looking for a job. His new skills gave his life a renewed purpose and an unexpected way to support himself. Amato recorded an album of his original work and is currently working on another one.

Amato still has some health problems as a result of the accident. However, despite those negative side effects, he says he wouldn't change what happened to him. "I think the headaches and the loss of hearing—those things are kind of the price tag on this particular gift. And I'm OK with that. I look at it as a blessing."

Timed Reading 2

Answer the questions based on Reading 2, "Acquired Savant Syndrome." Write the number of correct answers on the Reading Rate Log.

1 Derek Amato's musical talent is unusual because _____ .
  a he is better than a professional musician
  b he never took music lessons of any kind
  c he learned how to read music overnight

2 Amato's case of acquired savant syndrome is _____ .
  a the only reported case of this type
  b one of about thirty cases in the world
  c similar to many other reported cases

3 Amato's accident happened when he _____ .
  a jumped into the shallow end of a pool
  b fell and hit his head on a friend's piano
  c was visiting the home of a musician friend

4 Researchers believe that Amato's condition _____ .
  a was caused by a rewiring of the brain
  b will probably go away over time
  c is more common than most people know

5 Which of the following is NOT mentioned in this passage?
  a Amato's childhood and family life
  b Amato's previous experiences with music
  c Amato's health problems after the accident

6 Before the accident, Amato _____ .

    a had always wanted to be a professional musician

    b had a difficult time financially and professionally

    c had a mysterious feeling that something bad would happen

7 From this passage, we can infer that Amato _____ .

    a no longer goes near swimming pools

    b is planning to start his own music school

    c will continue to play music for the rest of his life

8 From this passage, we can infer that Amato feels the accident _____ .

    a was the home owner's fault

    b changed his life for the better

    c could not have been avoided

Timed Reading 3

Practice the strategies for faster reading. Read the passage. Then go to *Timed Reading 3 Comprehension Questions* activity on p. 147 to answer the questions.

Ways of Learning

The Self-Taught Electrical Engineer

William Kamkwamba grew up on his family's farm in rural Malawi, Africa. His young life was not easy. William, his parents, and his six sisters all lived together in a small house made of clay. Even as a young boy, William was expected to help his parents on the farm for several hours every day in addition to keeping up with his studies at school. Every evening, he had to finish his homework and go to bed early. This was because his family could not afford to use much of the kerosene needed to burn the lamps they used for lighting.

The year William was thirteen years old, his life changed forever. He was finishing eighth grade and had been accepted at a nearby high school for the following year. The weather had been very dry in Malawi—much too dry. Month after month, it did not rain, and there was a massive drought. Farmers could not grow food, and many people around the country were starving.

William's parents were farmers, and because they could not grow food, they did not have enough money to pay for William to attend high school. After attending just a few months of his freshman year, he was forced to drop out of school. For the next five years, William was unable to go to school at all.

He stayed at home, helping his parents on the farm. Day to day, he saw how hard life was in his village, how hard his parents and sisters worked, and how tired they all were. He wanted to do something to make life easier and more comfortable for his family and for the other people in his village.

After he left school, William started to borrow books from the local library. One book, a textbook called Using Energy, was especially interesting. The cover of the book showed a wind turbine—the type of windmill used for making electricity. The picture gave William an idea. He wanted to make a windmill to provide electric power for his family's house. The only problem was that the book didn't explain what materials were needed to build a windmill or give instructions for how to do it.

Over the next year, with only an eighth grade education and that picture, William taught himself how to build a working windmill. He collected bits of trash and broken items from all over his village—scraps of wood, broken bicycles, old shoes—and started to build a windmill next to his family's house.

Other people in William's village called him crazy, but nothing could stop him. Finally, when William was fourteen, he completed his first windmill. It was five meters high and made from a broken bicycle, a tractor fan blade, car parts, and tree branches. It provided enough power to run four light bulbs. When the village people saw the windmill turning and saw electric lights coming from William's house, they came running. William had succeeded.

News of his achievement spread quickly around the country and, before long, international visitors came to meet William and see his work.

Kamkwamba's autobiography, *The Boy Who Harnessed the Wind*, tells the story of how the world learned about this boy who dropped out of school and used his time to improve the lives of his country's people. With the help of several international organizations, his village now has clean running water, solar powered lighting, and electric power. In addition, William was finally able to complete his schooling. He went on to complete high school and then studied English in the United Kingdom. He currently studies engineering at Dartmouth College, one of the best universities in the United States, and travels around the world speaking about how his dream became a reality.

Timed Reading 3

Answer the questions based on Reading 3, "The Self-Taught Electrical Engineer." Write the number of correct answers on the Reading Rate Log.

1 As a young boy, William Kamkwamba _____ .

    a built a clay house for his family

    b dropped out of elementary school

    c helped his parents run the family farm

2 William's parents went to bed early every night because _____ .

    a they were so tired from working on the farm

    b they couldn't pay for the fuel to run the lights

    c there was nothing to do in the small village

3 William was forced to stop attending school _____ .

    a on his thirteenth birthday

    b just after he started high school

    c before he finished eighth grade

4 From this passage, we can infer that _____ .

    a most people had more money than William's family

    b there is still a massive drought affecting Malawi

    c people in Malawi must pay for children's education

5 William learned how to build a windmill using _____ .

    a a picture and his own knowledge

    b ideas from international organizations

    c instructions in his school textbook

6 From this passage, we can infer that people in William's village _____ .

    a did not believe he would succeed

    b were not interested in getting electricity

    c still do not have running water

7 Which of the following is NOT mentioned in this passage?

    a William's village now has running water.

    b William went on to finish high school.

    c William's parents now live in the United States.

8 William attended university _____.

    a in the United Kingdom

    b in Malawi

    c in the United States

PRACTICE 3 LANGUAGES AND CULTURES IN DANGER

Timed Reading 1

Practice the strategies for faster reading. Read the passage. Then go to *Timed Reading 1 Comprehension Questions* activity on p. 149 to answer the questions.

Languages and Cultures in Danger

The Ainu

The world has changed a great deal since its prehistoric beginnings. Over the hundreds of thousands of years that people have been living on Earth, many different factors have affected our various cultural and linguistic traditions. Events such as climate changes or wars over land or cultural beliefs have caused some groups of people to move great distances or to change or give up their traditions. In addition, people from different cultures have married one another, creating new blended cultures. The rise of modern technology has also contributed to the loss of some of the old ways of doing things.

Luckily, some of the traditions and languages from many of the original cultures still remain and have been preserved by the people who cherish them and want them to continue.

The Ainu are a group of people from northern Japan. Their culture is one example of a traditional culture that still exists today—but in a much smaller and very different capacity. The Ainu culture was one of the first to live on the Japanese islands during the Jômon period (14,000–300 BCE). An Ainu legend tells that the Ainu people "lived in this place a hundred thousand years before the Children of the Sun" (the people we now know as Japanese).

The original ancestors of today's Ainu inhabited the northernmost part of Japan on the islands of Honshu and Hokkaido and on islands farther north in the Sea of Okhotsk between Japan and Russia. They were experts at living off the land. For many years, their culture thrived, and they lived peacefully, hunting, fishing, and gathering. During the Meiji period (1868–1912), the Japanese government encouraged people living in the southern areas to move north and create settlements in Hokkaido. The government believed that a nation of people who shared just one set of cultural traditions would help make Japan a stronger, more powerful nation.

As the incoming Japanese settlers flooded onto Hokkaido and began to build their own farming and fishing villages, many Ainu had to leave their land and move to areas where farming was less productive. Instead of fishing for themselves, many had to take jobs working for the newly established Japanese fishing industry. Ainu were asked to change their names and take on new Japanese names. Some of their most important cultural traditions, such as tattooing women's faces and their bear sacrificing ceremony, were now outlawed. The government created special schools for Ainu children where they were allowed to speak only Japanese, and Ainu parents were encouraged to speak Japanese at home. Over time, many Ainu married Japanese. As a result of these factors, some aspects of traditional Ainu culture and language disappeared over several generations.

Today, only about 25,000 people claim to be Ainu. Fewer than 100 of those—mainly the elderly—can speak the native Ainu language fluently.

There is hope of preserving the Ainu culture before it completely dies out, however. The Ainu Association of Hokkaido is an active organization dedicated to keeping Ainu culture and language alive and well. The group holds educational and cultural events to promote Ainu heritage and raise money to help support education and professional training for young Ainu—those who hold the future of the Ainu culture in their hands.

Timed Reading 1

Answer the questions based on Reading 1, "The Ainu." Write the number of correct answers on the Reading Rate Log.

1 This passage lists all of the following factors that have caused cultures to change EXCEPT that _____ .

   a people from different cultures intermarried

   b there were wars over land and cultural beliefs

   c young people do not care about old traditions

2 The author says that the rise in modern technology _____ .
  a has caused cultures to stop doing things in the old ways
  b has made it easier for people to communicate
  c created many interesting new cultural traditions

3 The Ainu started to live in northern Japan _____ .
  a when they had to leave their farmland
  b many thousands of years ago
  c around the same time as the Japanese

4 From this passage, we can infer that _____ .
  a some Ainu were not treated well in the past
  b Ainu culture will probably die out completely
  c many people in Japan do not know about the Ainu

5 Ainu culture began to change when _____ .
  a there were no more speakers of the Ainu language
  b many Japanese moved to the far north of Japan
  c Ainu had to move because there were no more fish

6 From this passage, we can infer that most Ainu people _____ .
  a moved farther south to find better farmland
  b followed the Japanese government's orders
  c did not want to live on Hokkaido

7 Which of the following is NOT mentioned in this passage?
  a the current population of Ainu
  b how many people currently speak Ainu
  c whether there are still special schools for Ainu children

Timed Reading 2

Practice the strategies for faster reading. Read the passage. Then go to *Timed Reading 2 Comprehension Questions* **activity on p. 151 to answer the questions.**

Languages and Cultures in Danger

The Ayapaneco Language of Mexico

Manuel Segovia is seventy-five years old. He lives in the village of Ayapa, Tabasco, which is in the tropical southern part of Mexico. His neighbor Isidro Velasquez is sixty-nine and lives in a house about 500 yards from Segovia's.

The two have something very important in common. They are the last two living speakers of the Ayapaneco language. Unfortunately, although Segovia and Velasquez know each other and have this linguistic connection, the two men refuse to speak to each other.

In addition to Spanish, the language spoken by most Mexicans, Mexico has 364 different indigenous languages and dialects. Many of these indigenous languages are also in danger of dying out; however, with only two living speakers, Ayapaneco is in the greatest peril.

Ayapeneco is an ancient language that was spoken for centuries in Mexico. The native name for the language is Nuumte Oote, which means "true voice." Until the mid-1900s, the language was spoken by hundreds of people in the area where Segovia and Velasquez live. Things began to change when the Mexican government passed a law requiring all schools to use Spanish in their classes. For several decades, children were forbidden to speak anything but Spanish at school. As a result, young Ayapaneco speakers began to speak their native language only at home. In addition, with Mexico's urban development, younger people moved away from rural areas to find jobs. This meant that they moved away from their families and stopped speaking the language of their ancestors. With so many obstacles, it's amazing that the Ayapaneco language has lasted so long.

Manuel Segovia grew up speaking Ayapaneco with his parents and older brother. After their parents died, the two brothers continued to speak the language to each other. When his brother died about ten years ago, Manuel became one of the last living fluent Ayapaneco speakers. He says he still speaks the language to his wife and son who understand him but can only speak a few words themselves. "When I was a boy, everybody spoke it," Segovia says. "It's disappeared little by little, and now I suppose it might die with me." Even so, Segovia has no interest in speaking with Velasquez, and Velasquez shares the feeling. It isn't clear why the two men prefer to avoid each other, but people who know them both say they have never been good friends.

Linguist Daniel Suslak is working on a project to create a dictionary of Ayapaneco before the language disappears. Of Segovia and Velasquez, Suslak says, "They don't have a lot in common." He says neither of the men is easy to get along with, adding that Segovia can be a little "prickly" and Velasquez rarely leaves home. Suslak's project is a race against time. He must work to finish the dictionary before it's too late.

In addition to Suslak's dictionary efforts, Mexico's National Indigenous Language Institute asked Manuel Segovia to offer classes in Ayapaneco so he can pass his language on to other local people in the region. However, the classes did not continue due to lack of funding and low enrollment. "I bought pencils and notebooks myself," Segovia complains. "The classes would start off full and then the students would stop coming."

Without linguists such as Daniel Suslak, indigenous languages like Ayapaneco will simply be lost forever. When Suslak's project is done, there will at least be a dictionary for those interested in looking up words in Ayapaneco. The question is whether anyone will be interested enough to do so.

Timed Reading 2

Answer the questions based on Reading 2, "The Ayapaneco Language of Mexico." Write the number of correct answers on the Reading Rate Log.

1 Manuel Segovia and Isidro Velasquez _____ .
   a are old friends
   b don't know each other
   c live in the same area

2 The language of Ayapaneco is _____ .

   a one of many languages in danger

   b the only indigenous language spoken in Mexico

   c closely related to the Spanish language

3 The native name for Ayapaneco means _____ .

   a "true voice"

   b "young voice"

   c "speak the truth"

4 This passage lists all of the following reasons for the decline of Ayapaneco EXCEPT _____ .

   a wars between neighboring rural towns

   b young people moving to the cities

   c Spanish being taught in schools

5 From this passage, we can infer that _____ .

   a Segovia and Velasquez both want to help preserve their language

   b Segovia has done more than Velasquez to help preserve Ayapaneco

   c Velasquez is hoping to write his own Ayapaneco dictionary

6 One thing that has NOT been done to preserve the Ayapaneco language is to _____ .

   a offer Ayapaneco language classes

   b record Segovia and Velasquez speaking

   c write an Ayapaneco dictionary

7 Which of the following is NOT mentioned in this passage?

   a the real reason why Segovia and Velasquez refuse to speak to each other

   b the number of people who speak Ayapaneco in Mexico

   c the name of the organization that preserves indigenous languages

8 From this passage, we can assume that _____ .

   a many people will buy the Ayapaneco dictionary

   b Ayapaneco will die with Segovia and Velasquez

   c Segovia's son will continue to speak Ayapaneco

Timed Reading 3

Practice the strategies for faster reading. Read the passage. Then go to *Timed Reading 3 Comprehension Questions* activity on p. 154 to answer the questions.

Languages and Cultures in Danger
The Cajuns

The Cajuns are a group of people who live in the southern U.S. state of Louisiana. Theirs is one of the most fascinating cultures of any group living in the United States today. Restaurants serving traditional Cajun dishes such as gumbo, a spicy seafood stew, and red beans and rice are popular around the world. Cajun folk music, with its fiddle and accordion harmonies, has a large international following.

However, the Cajun people haven't had it easy. In fact, for many Cajuns, the journey to Louisiana was long and full of heartbreak. Their history is not taught in most schools, but it is a rich and remarkable story.

The word *Cajun* comes from the original French word *Acadian*, which refers to the French settlers of the Acadia region of northern Canada.

In the early 1600s, several hundred French citizens left France and sailed across the Atlantic Ocean in search of a better life that would be free from the high taxes the French government forced citizens to pay. The northeastern coast of Canada, in the area now known as Nova Scotia and New Brunswick, provided plenty of rich farmland, forests for hunting, and ocean for fishing. The settlers of New France made friends with the native Wabenaki Indians. They built farms and villages, traded furs, fished, and collected oysters. For the most part, they lived a peaceful, independent life for nearly a hundred years.

In the late 1600s and early 1700s, conflicts arose between the French and the British governments. The land that the French Acadians had settled in Canada was a border area between French and British territories, and the two powers began to fight over the right to govern Acadia. Over a period of about seventy-five years, there were several battles between British and French forces. The Acadian settlers and the Wabenaki joined in and kept the British from taking over the region.

In 1710, the British navy, led by General Charles Lawrence, succeeded in beating the French and took over Acadia. For the next forty-five years, the Acadians lived under British rule with few problems. However, everything changed for the Acadians in 1755—the start of the French and Indian War. Between 1755 and 1763, thousands of Acadians were driven out of Canada by the British. The Acadians' homes and villages were set on fire and burned to the ground. Families were separated as men were put on ships and taken away to build new British colonies. Meanwhile, their wives and children were loaded onto other ships and sent back to France or other areas of Europe. Approximately one-third of the Acadians drowned or died from disease.

Many Acadians who survived made their way south to Louisiana, which was still ruled by France at the time. Some made the entire journey on foot, taking many months and relying on kind strangers for food and shelter. In Louisiana, they were safe. Once again, there was land where they could farm and hunt and rivers and swamps where they could trap animals and fish. Once again, they made friends and shared the land with the local Native Americans. Men and woman from the two cultures even married each other. Over time, the Acadian culture and language blended with those of the Native Americans and the local Africans, who had been brought to Louisiana as slaves. Soon, an original Louisiana Cajun culture emerged.

Modern Cajuns speak a unique dialect of French called Cajun French, and many Cajuns keep up the traditions of their Acadian ancestors. However, as time passes and the older members of the culture die, some younger Cajuns have begun to forget their cultural roots and have stopped speaking their language.

Fortunately, with the huge popularity of Cajun food and music, at least some aspects of the culture are likely to survive and continue to be appreciated by people around the world.

Timed Reading 3

Answer the questions based on Reading 3, "The Cajuns." Write the number of correct answers on the Reading Rate Log.

1 Most Cajuns now live _____ .
   a in northeastern Canada
   b all around the world
   c in the southern United States

2 Two popular aspects of Cajun culture are _____ .
   a music and clothing
   b clothing and food
   c food and music

3 Cajun history is _____ .
   a taught in most schools
   b not well known around the world
   c not written down in formal records

4 The Cajuns left France because they wanted _____ .
   a a better place to hunt and fish
   b to live under British rule
   c more economic independence

5 In Canada, the new French settlers _____ .
   a fought with Native Americans
   b lived peacefully for a long time
   c nearly died from disease

6 The French and British governments disagreed over _____ .
   a who should govern Acadia
   b what language should be taught in schools
   c how much the Cajuns should be taxed

7 For the Cajuns, the period between 1755 and 1763 can best be described
   as _____ .
   a a dark time in their history
   b a time of peaceful British rule
   c a period of great economic growth

8 From this passage, it can be inferred that the Cajuns _____ .
   a were happy in Louisiana
   b wanted to return to Canada
   c decided to give up their culture

Choosing Words to Learn

Choosing Words to Learn

Reading is one of the best ways to improve your English vocabulary. However, it would be very difficult to try to learn *all* of the new words and phrases you find as you read. Good language learners select words that are useful for them. How do you know which words you should choose to learn? Here are some guidelines for choosing the most useful vocabulary words to write down, study, and learn.

- Learn the words that are used most frequently in general and in academic English. Lists of these words can be found on the Internet. You can search for the 3000 most frequently used words in English. You will probably already know many of the words. If you learn all of the words, then you will know about 90 percent of the words used in most English texts.
- Choose the words and phrases that are most useful to you. These include (1) words and phrases you see or hear frequently, and (2) words and phrases you can use for school, your current or future job, or your personal interests.

Practice 1

1 Read the passage on the next page to the end. Do not stop to look up new words or phrases.

2 Read the passage again and make a list of new words and phrases on a separate piece of paper.

3 Check the word list in the Appendix, Transition Words and Phrases on p. 193, for the words you chose. On your paper, circle the words you find.

4 For the words that are not included in the Appendix, decide which are useful to learn and circle them on your paper. A word is probably useful if
- you have seen it before or it occurs more than once, or
- the topic of the reading is useful to your studies, job, or personal interests.

5 In a dictionary, look up the words you circled and make an entry for each one. In the space below, type in the following information for each word:
- word
- part of speech
- meaning
- sample sentence

6 Submit your work to your teacher.

Antibiotics are some of the most frequently prescribed types of medications. These medicines treat diseases by killing the bacteria that cause them. The first type of antibiotic was penicillin, which was accidentally discovered from a mold culture. Today, more than 100 different types of antibiotics are used to treat all sorts of health problems, from minor infections to life-threatening illnesses.

Each year, the average family gets numerous sore throats, runny noses, coughs, fevers, and other types of viruses. In these cases, many parents bring their children to the doctor's office, expecting a prescription for medication that will help the child get well faster. These days, some in the healthcare industry are being more cautious about doling out these drugs when they aren't really necessary. Instead, doctors may be more likely to recommend rest and letting the patient's own immune system do its job.

The overuse of antibiotics is risky business. Because bacteria are living organisms, they can mutate—that is, they can change over time. As a result of years or decades of antibiotic use, some bacteria have changed and become resistant to certain types of the drugs. These new "super germs" are stronger, so they no longer respond to medications. They also have the power to affect larger portions of the population with more serious illnesses, making it more difficult to fight them off naturally with our own immune system.

Therefore, don't be surprised if your doctor doesn't immediately reach for the prescription pad the next time you're ill. He or she may be doing you—and all of us—a big favor.

Practice 2

Information technology experts are always working on innovative ways to solve problems and improve the design and function of computers. The vast increase in computer use during the past two decades has literally been a pain in the neck for many people. Sitting at a desk, staring straight ahead at a screen for several hours, and clicking a mouse hundreds of times a day can eventually cause muscle and joint stiffness. Soon, however, there will be relief for those who suffer from computer-related physical pain and discomfort.

This year, a new device will go on sale that will allow people to use the Internet, search files, and scroll through documents without ever touching their computers. The new hands-free motion controller sits on your desk in front of the computer. A user can put his or her hand above the controller and simply point at the screen to move the cursor around, browse the web, play games, or open spreadsheets. The device even recognizes and reacts to more complex movements, such as pulling, grabbing, and pinching. This feature allows users to manipulate three-dimensional images on the screen as though they were working with a piece of clay.

Representatives from the product's manufacturing company say that the enhanced freedom of movement the device offers will help alleviate muscle soreness and other physical issues suffered by so many computer users.

_____

_____

_____

_____

_____

_____

_____

_____

_____

_____

_____

_____

_____

_____

_____

Practice 3

Have you ever heard of the Mozart effect? It's the notion that if babies or young children listen to classical music, especially music by the Austrian composer Wolfgang Amadeus Mozart, they will become more intelligent.

The idea became popular in the early 1990s after an article appeared in the scientific journal *Nature*. The article discussed the idea that listening to classical music improves brain function in children and specifically mentioned Mozart's music as an example. The idea that playing Mozart's music to babies could potentially create a whole generation of extra-intelligent adults captured the public's imagination.

Soon, hopeful parents around the world began playing classical symphonies for their babies and toddlers. Education companies began mass-producing classical CD and DVD sets, so children could "magically" become geniuses. Some hopeful mothers even tried loading their home and car stereos with Mozart CDs in the months preceding their baby's birth, turning up the volume so their unborn children could hear.

Mozart mania extended beyond babies. Teachers began playing classical music in their elementary school classrooms to help their students learn more effectively, and some farmers even tried playing Mozart to their cows in the hopes that it would help them produce better milk.

Does this quick and convenient method really generate more intelligent humans? The answer isn't actually found in the research. The original study cited in the *Nature* article didn't focus on children but on a group of 36 young adult students. These students were divided into three groups and asked to perform a task. Before the task, each group listened to ten minutes of silence, a ten-minute recording of relaxation instructions, or ten minutes of a Mozart sonata.

The students who had listened to Mozart did do better at tasks where they had to create shapes in their minds, but the effect was only temporary. After listening to the music, students were better at spatial tasks where they had to look at folded pieces of paper of different shapes and predict how they would appear when unfolded. However, according to the study, the effect only lasted for about fifteen minutes. Nevertheless, people continued to believe that listening to music had a permanent positive effect on the human intellect.

In reality, all that can be determined from the research is that music leads to a short-term improvement in some spatial tasks, but the benefits are only short-lived. Unfortunately, music doesn't make us more intelligent overall.

Practice 4

Unlike many other parts of the world, the countries of the European Union (EU) have strict policies against the use of animal testing for developing products such as cosmetics.

New and stricter animal protection legislature was passed recently in the EU. The law bans the sale of all cosmetics that have been developed through animal testing.

The EU has had anti-animal testing laws in place since 2009, but the new law has been expanded to include all ingredients in cosmetic products, regardless of where in the world the animal testing took place. For example, French cosmetics corporations can no longer purchase ingredients produced in China or elsewhere if animals were used in lab testing during the development of those ingredients.

The expanded legislation was a huge triumph for European animal rights activists, who have been lobbying for the change for more than two decades. Prior to the 2009 ban, cosmetics companies had still been allowed to use lab animals to test products for serious effects on human health, such as cancer. However, the new law bans that level of testing as well.

In addition to the increased costs that will undoubtedly be passed on to cosmetics consumers, cosmetics firms are concerned that the ban will reduce their ability to innovate new products that are genuinely safe for humans.

The EU commission that approved the ban says it is working with the cosmetics industry to develop alternatives to animal testing so they won't experience a competitive disadvantage.

_____
_____
_____
_____
_____
_____
_____
_____
_____
_____
_____
_____
_____
_____

Storing and Studying New Words

Vocabulary Notebooks

Are you an active vocabulary learner? What do you do when you find a new word or phrase in your reading? Many students use vocabulary notebooks to store and study new words. This is a good way to remember vocabulary and improve your English skills.

There are many ways to organize a vocabulary notebook. You can organize new words by date, by parts of speech, by topic, or alphabetically—like the dictionary. You can write the words in a notebook, on index cards, or in a computer file. The important thing is to choose a way that is convenient and makes it easy for you to find and study new words.

Below is a basic example of a vocabulary notebook entry. Read the instructions and look at the sample.

- Draw a line down the middle of the page.
- Write the new word on the left side of the page.
- Beside the new word, write its part of speech (noun, verb, adjective, adverb).
- Write the definition of the word on the right side of the page.
- Below the word, write the sentence where you found the word. If needed, add another sample sentence from the dictionary.

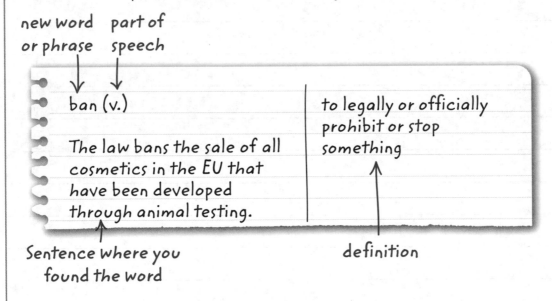

new word or phrase

part of speech

ban (v.)

The law bans the sale of all cosmetics in the EU that have been developed through animal testing.

to legally or officially prohibit or stop something

Sentence where you found the word

definition

Practice 1

Read the text and choose five new words. Write the following information for each word:

Word	Part of Speech	Sample Sentence	Definition

You've heard of fast food, but what about slow food? The Slow Food movement is actually a lifestyle philosophy founded in 1986 by Italian culinary expert Carlo Petrini. Petrini first gained worldwide recognition when he led protests against the opening of a new McDonald's franchise near the Spanish Steps in Rome.

Petrini developed the Slow Food idea to counteract society's tendency to embrace a faster and more convenient, but less healthy or enjoyable, way of living. In his home country, he saw that because of the globalization of the food industry, many small, local farms could no longer compete with the lower-cost producers abroad and were beginning to close down. Petrini promoted Slow Food as an alternative to the global expansion of fast-food culture in which food products are shipped around the world for mass production and consumption.

The main premise of the Slow Food movement is "keep it local." According to the organization's website, it "strives to preserve traditional and regional cuisine and encourages farming of plants, seeds, and livestock characteristic of the local ecosystem." Petrini hopes to keep local farms alive so people will be able to enjoy high-quality, healthy food from their local farmers for centuries to come.

_____

_____

_____

_____

_____

_____

_____

_____

_____

_____

_____

_____

Practice 2

Read the text and choose five new words. Write the following information for each word:

Word	Part of Speech	Sample Sentence	Definition

Australia's Great Barrier Reef is one of the world's most diverse ecosystems. It is the largest structure on Earth made by living organisms that can be seen from space.

The reef spans an area of 344,400 square kilometers. It includes hundreds of breathtakingly beautiful tropical islands and more than 2,900 individual reef systems, which are home to an abundance of marine species. The reef is also home to the world's largest collection of coral reefs—with 400 types of coral, 1,500 species of fish, and 4,000 types of mollusks—and it serves as a habitat for several endangered species, including the dugong, a relative of the manatee, and the large green turtle.

Human activities, such as fishing, diving, and tourism, have had a devastating effect on the wildlife in some parts of the reef. According to a study published in 2012, the reef has lost more than half of its coral since 1985.

The establishment of protected areas, such as the Great Barrier Reef Marine Park, has helped limit the negative impacts of human use, but environmental scientists and marine biologists say more must be done to preserve this natural wonder of the world.

Presentation

Word Maps

Word maps are a good way to collect and store important information about new vocabulary. The more you work with new words and are able to make meaningful connections to them, the faster you will learn and be able to remember them. Creating word maps for new words helps you learn and remember new vocabulary so you can understand and use those words in the future.

Style 1

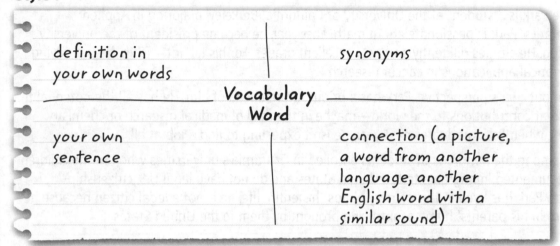

Style 2

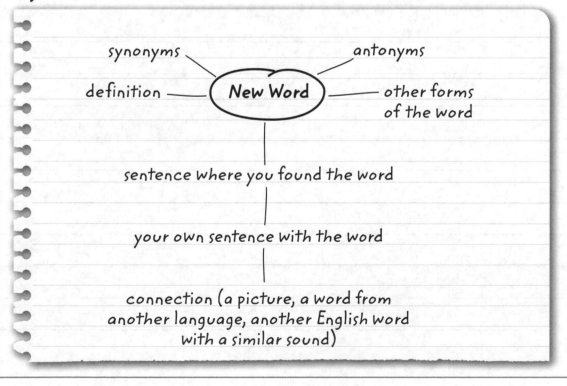

Practice 3

Read the text. Choose two new words. Complete the following information about each word. Then use the information to make a word map below. Follow Style 1 in the Presentation on p. 163.

New word Definition in your own words	Synonyms Your own sentence	Connection (to another word)

Terrence Park is a student at the University of California, Berkeley, majoring in Applied Mathematics. Park is passionate about math. Last year, he became president of the university's math club. He studies diligently and gets excellent grades. For his lab internship, he is studying mathematical applications in cancer research.

From an outsider's perspective, Park has a bright future ahead of him. He has all the potential to make great contributions to the world—maybe in the field of medical research or chemistry. However, when Park graduates next year, he isn't expecting to find a job at all.

Park is among the hundreds of students enrolled in California's universities who are the children of undocumented immigrants to the United States and do not have legal U.S. citizenship. Although Park has lived in this country almost his entire life, he is not a legal citizen because he was born in his parents' home country and brought by them to the United States.

_____

_____

_____

_____

_____

_____

_____

_____

_____

_____

Practice 4

Read the text. Choose two new words. Complete the following information about each word. Then use the information to make a word map below. Follow Style 2 in the Presentation.

New word Synonyms Antonyms	Definition Other forms of the word	Sentence where you found the word Your own sentence	Connection (to another word)

Although all students, regardless of their citizenship status, are allowed to attend school, the law prohibits companies from hiring undocumented workers—workers who are not citizens or legal residents of the United States. Aside from low-wage labor jobs, Park has no chance of getting the kind of job for which he is qualified, even with a college degree.

Terrence Park plans to become a U.S. citizen after he graduates from Berkeley, but the process takes time—something he doesn't have much of as a busy university student. Therefore, after graduation, instead of putting on a suit and going to job interviews, Park will take citizenship classes with other undocumented immigrants from different countries. The classes teach immigrants about American history, government, and culture. It will take Park about a year to complete the requirements to finally become a U.S. citizen.

Study Cards

Study cards are small cards you can use to study new vocabulary at home, in a café, on the train or bus, or anywhere else.

Use the words in your vocabulary notebook and follow these instructions to make study cards.

- Write the word in big letters in the middle of the card.
- Write the word's part of speech in the top right-hand corner of the card.
- Write a sample sentence below the word.
- Write the definition on the back of the card. Draw a picture that represents the word or make a connection with another word, if possible.

Use your study cards to practice the words. Follow these tips for practicing the words on your own.

- Look at the cards. Say the words aloud and try to remember their meanings. If you don't remember a word, look at the definition on the other side of the card. Put the words you don't know in a separate pile. Review those words again.
- Look at the definition side of each card. Say and spell the words aloud. Put the words you don't know in a separate pile. Review those words again.
- Practice your words with another student. Test each other by saying a word and asking for the definition or by giving a definition and asking for the word.
- Make new cards that have the word on one card and the definition on a different card (single-sided study cards). Play matching games, memory games, or categorizing games with these cards.

Practice 5

Read the text and choose five new words. Write the information below for each word. Then make your own study card with this information and use it for study and review.

Study Card (front)

Part of Speech

Word

Sample sentence

Study Card (back)

Definition

Have you taken the time to read a food label recently? If so, chances are you've seen a warning that indicates the food contains peanuts or was prepared or processed in a facility that uses peanuts in other products.

These warnings are relatively new. They have been added in response to the drastic rise in peanut allergies among children. According to some statistics, 1 in 100 children born today will experience a peanut allergy at some point. The prevalence of peanut allergies has skyrocketed over the past 20 years, and the figure tripled between 1997 and 2008.

The symptoms of a peanut allergy can be fatal. The reaction primarily affects the respiratory system, causing a swelling of the air passages and making it difficult for the victim to breathe. If the person has a severe sensitivity, he or she may die. Even a tiny amount of peanut dust in the air is enough to kill some peanut allergy sufferers. For this reason, peanuts are no longer served as snacks on airplanes, and many school cafeterias have become peanut-free zones.

The reason for the recent rise in peanut allergies is still unknown. Some researchers hypothesize that our increased focus on eliminating germs and the use of medications such as antibiotics that kill bacteria have weakened our immune systems. Others blame the fact that peanuts are usually roasted, a process that can bring out harmful allergens in food. However, no one knows the cause for sure.

_____

_____

_____

_____

_____

_____

_____

Practice 6

Read the text and choose five new words. Write the information below for each word. Then make your own study card with this information and use it for study and review.

Study Card (front)

Part of Speech

Word

Sample sentence

Study Card (back)

Definition

Identity theft is the crime of stealing someone's identity—personal data such as a person's name, address, phone number, social security number, or other personal information. Typically, thieves steal people's identities for financial gain. For example, they can access credit cards or bank accounts. Some victims of identity theft have been held accountable for thousands of dollars of debt when thieves obtained their credit card numbers and went on lavish spending sprees, purchasing cars, airline tickets, or other luxury items.

Since the rise of the Internet, criminals have gained access to all kinds of private information that they can use to their own advantage. Despite increased security measures online, computer hackers are able to find ways around many of the systems designed to prevent identity theft. For example, they may pose as credit card companies and send e-mails asking people to respond with private account information, such as passwords.

In addition to the computer experts who use their skills to become identity thieves, some criminals also use low-tech methods to achieve their goals. They may steal wallets, research public files or documents, or even rummage through garbage, collecting personal information from telephone bills.

To protect yourself from identity theft, experts recommend carefully monitoring your credit cards and bank accounts and keeping receipts and records of your purchases. Look through bank statements regularly and check for suspicious transactions. In addition, change your online passwords and login information from time to time, especially those on financial accounts. Finally, invest in a good Internet security software program and stay aware of the latest identity scams.

_____

_____

_____

_____

_____

_____

_____

Reading for Study

Text Marking and Study Outlines

Longer passages, such as research articles or textbook chapters, often include a lot of important information. How do you make sure you understand the key points you need to know for your tests, papers, or other assignments? Here are some strategies you can use to understand and remember information in longer academic passages.

Marking and Underlining

As you read each paragraph, use a pencil or highlighter to underline or mark the main idea and supporting details. Keep the following in mind when you mark a text:

- Underline only the most important points and ideas. If you underline too much, you will not be able to tell what's important.
- Put a star (*) in the margin next to the sentence that gives the main idea of the paragraph.
- Write comments, questions, or short summaries in the margins.

Look at this example of a student's marked paragraph:

47

Geographic Location

The *aurora borealis*—also known as the northern lights—is
✶ a natural phenomenon that <u>occurs at Earth's northernmost
points</u>. These amazing light displays are most commonly
seen in the sky in areas <u>near the North Pole, such as northern
Canada, the U.S. state of Alaska, Greenland, and the
countries of Scandinavia</u>. It was the astronomer <u>Galileo who
first named the phenomenon</u> in 1616. In Latin, *aurora* means
"dawn," and *borealis* means "north." The <u>name translates to
"northern dawn."</u>

Study Outlines

After you read a passage, use the information you underlined to create a brief outline of the main and supporting ideas. This will help you remember the information and use it to write essays or research papers. Look at this sample outline for the passage above:

<u>Main idea:</u>
The aurora borealis occurs at Earth's northernmost points.

<u>Supporting ideas:</u>
- near the North Pole, northern Canada, Alaska, Greenland, Scandinavia
- Astronomer Galileo named the phenomenon
- Name translates to "northern dawn"

Practice 1

Use the marked information in the following passage to write a study outline for each paragraph. Then submit your work to your teacher.

49

Appearance of Auroras

Auroras may occur at any time of the year. However, because the North Pole has daylight for 24 hours a day for several months of the year, they <u>can only be seen from about</u>
＊ <u>October through April.</u> Depending on the exact location and atmospheric conditions, <u>they may look very different.</u> They may <u>range in color</u> from blue or violet to green, red, or orange. They can look like a faint glow on the horizon—like a sunrise or sunset—or they can appear as <u>moving beams or rays of brightly colored light.</u> They are also sometimes described as looking like <u>curtains or ribbons</u> waving in the sky.

Causes and Formation

＊ Auroras are <u>caused when the sun creates high-energy gas called solar wind.</u> When this solar wind approaches our planet, it hits Earth's magnetic field, which <u>creates an electrical current.</u> The electricity begins to travel along the surface of Earth's atmosphere and gathers more energy until it reaches the poles. The light of the aurora is then created when these high-energy electrical <u>particles mix with other gases,</u> such as oxygen and <u>nitrogen.</u> The different <u>colors depend on the amounts and types of gases</u> that are present in the atmosphere at the time the aurora occurs.

Practice 2

Part 1

> ### Presentation
>
> #### Graphic Organizers and Charts
>
> Graphic organizers and charts are two ways of representing information visually. You can use these tools to make important information from a reading easier to find and understand.
>
> Charts are especially useful for articles that are organized in a pattern and discuss more than one topic or theme. Charts may have two or more columns, depending on the amount and type of information in the text.

Read the following article. Then study the sample graphic organizer.

Palm Oil and Endangered Orangutans

Do you usually read the list of ingredients when you buy something? If you do, then you probably know that palm oil—the oil that comes from the African oil palm tree—is found in hundreds of products, from cosmetics to baked goods to cleaning supplies. Because palm oil is useful for so many products and is cheap to produce, it is in high demand around the world. Around 50 million tons of palm oil are produced each year, mostly in Indonesia, Malaysia, and a handful of African countries.

Borneo and Sumatra, two islands in Indonesia, both have many large palm oil plantations. These tropical Southeast Asian islands are home to thousands of animal species, including the endangered orangutan.

Because of the huge international demand for palm oil, thousands of acres of rainforest land in Borneo and Sumatra have been cleared to make way for palm oil plantations. This rainforest land used to be the native habitat of the orangutan. By some estimates, over the past two decades, more than 90 percent of the orangutan's habitat has been destroyed.

Similar to the chimpanzee, the orangutan is one of humans' closest relatives. In fact, the word orangutan comes from the Malay and Indonesian words meaning "person of the jungle." Orangutans are gentle animals that do not pose any danger to humans.

Unfortunately, however, humans pose a great threat to the orangutans. Many orangutans are killed by humans, especially because of the production of palm oil. In the process of clearing large areas of rainforest to plant palm trees, the palm oil companies leave the orangutans with nowhere to live and nothing to eat. In addition, the companies often burn large areas of land for clearing, which results in the deaths of many of the animals from inhaling smoke or burning to death.

Some sources have reported that six to twelve endangered orangutans are killed every day due to the actions of the palm oil industry. An estimated 50,000 orangutans have already died as a result of deforestation in the past twenty years. In Sumatra alone, the orangutan population is just 6,000—down from 100,000 fifty years ago.

Animal rights activists say that if this pattern is allowed to continue, orangutans in the wild could be extinct within ten to twelve years. In twenty years, their rainforest habitat, home to thousands of other species of plants and animals, will also be gone.

Many people want to know what they can do to help. There are many international animal rights organizations that are working to protect the orangutan. These groups have websites that offer useful information about how concerned citizens can support their efforts and how to tell which products contain palm oil, which may be listed under different names on product labels.

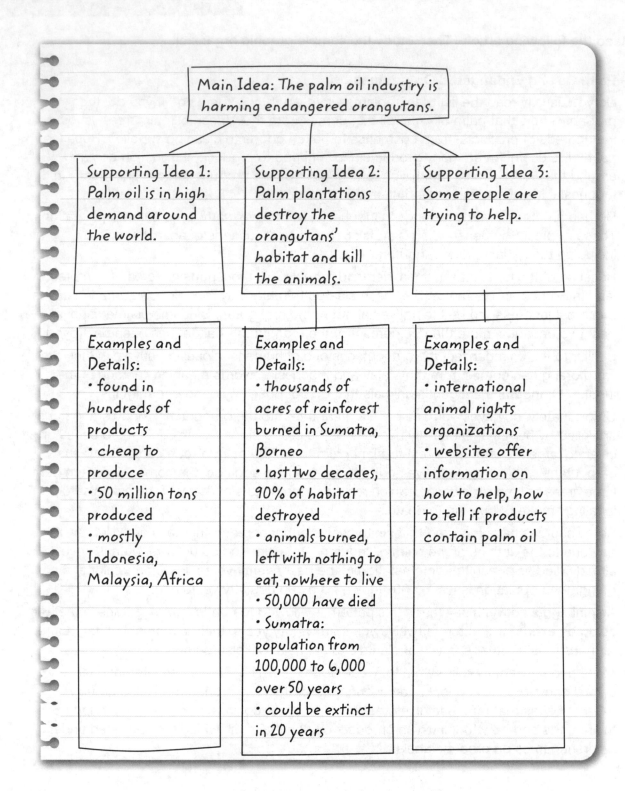

Main Idea: The palm oil industry is harming endangered orangutans.

Supporting Idea 1: Palm oil is in high demand around the world.

Supporting Idea 2: Palm plantations destroy the orangutans' habitat and kill the animals.

Supporting Idea 3: Some people are trying to help.

Examples and Details:
- found in hundreds of products
- cheap to produce
- 50 million tons produced
- mostly Indonesia, Malaysia, Africa

Examples and Details:
- thousands of acres of rainforest burned in Sumatra, Borneo
- last two decades, 90% of habitat destroyed
- animals burned, left with nothing to eat, nowhere to live
- 50,000 have died
- Sumatra: population from 100,000 to 6,000 over 50 years
- could be extinct in 20 years

Examples and Details:
- international animal rights organizations
- websites offer information on how to help, how to tell if products contain palm oil

Part 2

Read the following article. Then study the sample chart for the article.

High-Context and Low-Context Cultures

The anthropologist Edward T. Hall first introduced the idea of "high-context" and "low-context" cultures to explain cultural differences in communication. According to Hall, high-context cultures are more common in Eastern countries such as Japan and China, whereas most Western countries are low-context cultures. Of course, communication is important in high-context as well as low-context cultures; it is just the communication style that differs.

According to Hall, both types of culture use nonverbal cues to communicate. However, unlike low-context conversation, high-context conversation involves greater use of nonverbal features such as voice, tone, and gestures. By contrast, people in low-context cultures, such as the United States and Germany, rely more on words to convey meaning. They tend to speak directly, but people from high-context cultures, such as Japan or China, often communicate indirectly.

Conversation is used to begin personal relationships in both high- and low-context cultures. People from high-context cultures share a lot of detailed personal information with friends and coworkers. By contrast, people in low-context cultures generally share only necessary information with smaller, select groups of people.

High-Context Cultures	Low-Context Cultures	Both High- and Low-Context Cultures
Common in Eastern (Asian) countries.	Common in Western countries.	Communication is important.
People communicate indirectly.	People rely on words to convey meaning; they tend to speak directly.	Conversations are used to begin personal relationships.
People share detailed personal information with friends and coworkers.	People share only necessary information with a smaller group of close friends.	People use nonverbal cues to communicate.
People use a large amount of nonverbal features, such as voice, tone, and gestures.		

Practice 3

Read the text and take notes. Use your notes to create a graphic organizer and a chart on a separate piece of paper.

Languages and Cultures in Danger: The Ainu

The Ainu culture was one of the first to live on the Japanese islands during the prehistoric Jômon period (14,000–300 BCE). An Ainu legend tells that the Ainu people "lived in this place a hundred thousand years before the Children of the Sun" (the people we now know as Japanese).

The original ancestors of today's Ainu inhabited the northernmost part of Japan on the islands of Honshu and Hokkaido, as well as islands farther north in the Sea of Okhotsk between Japan and Russia. They were experts at living off the land. For many years, the Ainu culture thrived, and the people lived peacefully, hunting, fishing, and gathering. Much later, during the Meiji period (1868–1912), Japanese government officials came to believe that a nation of people who shared just one set of cultural traditions was better for Japan. They thought it would make Japan a stronger, more powerful nation.

For this reason, the government began to encourage people living in the southern areas of Japan to move north and create settlements on Hokkaido. As the incoming Japanese settlers flooded onto Hokkaido and began to build their own farming villages, many Ainu had to leave their land and move to areas where farming was less productive. Because many of the new settlers were fishermen with bigger fishing boats, many Ainu stopped fishing for themselves and had to take jobs working for others in the new fishing industry.

The government wanted a new Japan with one pure culture. As a result, Ainu were asked to change their names and take on new Japanese names. Some of their most important cultural traditions, such as tattooing women's faces and their bear sacrificing ceremony, were now outlawed. The government created special schools for Ainu children where they were allowed to speak only Japanese, and Ainu parents were encouraged to speak Japanese at home. Over time, many Ainu married Japanese. As a result of these factors, some aspects of traditional Ainu culture and language disappeared over several generations.

LANGUAGE IN CONTEXT

Practice 1

Part 1

Complete the passage using the appropriate words and phrases from the box. Adjust the tense as needed.

civilizations	crime	army	simply
throughout	affect	agriculture	
factor	take pride in	society	

The End of an Era

Ancient Rome was one of the most powerful _____ in history. The Roman Empire lasted about 500 years, from 27 BCE to 476 CE. The emperors of ancient Rome, famous rulers such as Augustus and Nero, were both respected and feared. The large Roman _____ traveled far, spreading the emperors' power _____ Europe, the Near East, and North Africa. Most Roman people were wealthy and lived well. So why didn't the empire continue? What caused such a strong government and society to become weak and fail?

Romans' Changing Attitudes

Experts agree that the main reason for the fall of the Roman Empire was a change in the attitude of the Roman people and the culture of Rome. During the first part of the empire, people worked hard and _____ their _____ , government, and culture. However, later records show that the people began to disapprove of the emperors, the economy became weak, and people became lazy and dissatisfied. The next section explains possible reasons for these changes.

The change in Roman culture and society was probably not caused by just one _____ ; rather, it was a combination of reasons. Historians point to three main ones:

1 A decreasing belief in religion caused the Roman people to think less about honesty and good behavior, which resulted in increased _____ and social problems.

2 The use of the poisonous metal lead in water pipes and cosmetics created health problems and mental illness in much of the population.

3 Climate change _____ the environment and resulted in cooler summers. This had a negative effect on _____ . There was _____ not enough food for the people of Rome.

Part 2

Read the text. Circle the letter of the correct answer.

The End of an Era

Ancient Rome was one of the most powerful civilizations in history. The Roman Empire lasted about 500 years, from 27 BCE to 476 CE. The emperors of ancient Rome, famous rulers such as Augustus and Nero, were both respected and feared. The large Roman army traveled far, spreading the emperors' power throughout Europe, the Near East, and North Africa. Most Roman people were wealthy and lived well. So why didn't the empire continue? What caused such a strong government and society to become weak and fail?

Romans' Changing Attitudes

Experts agree that the main reason for the fall of the Roman Empire was a change in the attitude of the Roman people and the culture of Rome. During the first part of the empire, people worked hard and took pride in their society, government, and culture. However, later records show that the people began to disapprove of the emperors, the economy became weak, and people became lazy and dissatisfied. The next section explains possible reasons for these changes.

Reasons for a Weakened Society

The change in Roman culture and society was probably not caused by just one factor; rather, it was a combination of reasons. Historians point to three main ones:

1. A decreasing belief in religion caused the Roman people to think less about honesty and good behavior, which resulted in increased crime and social problems.
2. The use of the poisonous metal lead in water pipes and cosmetics created health problems and mental illness in much of the population.
3. Climate change affected the environment and resulted in cooler summers. This had a negative effect on agriculture. There was simply not enough food for the people of Rome.

1 The passage is mainly about two Roman rulers: Augustus and Nero.

  a true

  b false

2 It took a long time for the Roman Empire to fall.

  a true

  b false

3 The passage says that the Roman Empire fell because the army was weak.

  a true

  b false

4 The Roman people lost respect for their government.

  a true

  b false

5 A lack of water is one factor given for the fall of the Roman Empire.

  a true

  b false

Part 3

Read each sentence. Circle the letter of the best meaning for the underlined word.

1 Ancient Rome was one of the most powerful underline{civilizations} in history.
   a small towns
   b shopping centers
   c human cultures
   d tourist attractions

2 The large Roman <u>army</u> traveled far, spreading the emperors' power throughout Europe.
   a leader
   b people
   c farmers
   d military

3 The large Roman army traveled far, spreading the emperors' power <u>throughout</u> Europe.
   a all over
   b nearby
   c next to
   d instead of

4 During the first part of the empire, people worked hard and <u>took pride in</u> their society, government, and culture.
   a did not respect
   b were happy with
   c did not understand
   d were surprised by

5 During the first part of the empire, people worked hard and took pride in their <u>society</u>, government, and culture.
   a community
   b education
   c housing
   d clothes

6 The change in Roman culture and society was probably not caused by just one <u>factor</u>; however, it was a combination of reasons.
   a person
   b statement
   c reason
   d question

7 A decreasing belief in religion caused the Roman people to think less about honesty and good behavior, which resulted in increased <u>crime</u> and social problems.
   a building construction
   b illegal activity
   c road traffic
   d sports events

8 Climate change <u>affected</u> the environment and resulted in cooler summers.
   a warmed
   b moved
   c created
   d changed

9 Climate change affected the environment and resulted in cooler summers. This had a negative effect on <u>agriculture</u>.
   a health
   b education
   c farming
   d government

10 There was <u>simply</u> not enough food for the people of Rome.
   a just
   b definitely
   c strangely
   d quite

Part 4

Write the words into the correct sentences.

factor	simply	army	take pride in
affected	society	civilizations	
agriculture	crime	throughout	

1 Overcrowding, pollution, and _____ are some of the problems facing modern cities.

2 The storm caused delays and _____ air travel schedules all over the country.

3 The Mayans and the Aztecs are two early examples of advanced _____ .

4 When there isn't enough rain, _____ suffers.

5 There are some people who want to do things their own way; they don't want to follow the rules of _____ .

6 Instead of going to university after high school, Terrence joined the _____ .

7 It's important to do your best and _____ your work.

8 McDonald's and Starbucks are two companies that can be found _____ the world.

9 All reports of the celebrity's death were _____ not true.

10 Pollution from cars is just one _____ that causes global warming.

Practice 2

Part 1

Read the words in the box. Then complete the passage with the correct words.

noticed	confirmed	doubt	realized
planet	debate	status	various

It took many years of searching before Pluto was first discovered in 1930. Long before that, in the late 1800s, an astronomer named Percival Lowell _____ that two planets, Uranus and Neptune, did not go around the sun in a perfect circle as expected. This discovery meant that something else—another large body—must be pulling on the two planets. The search for a ninth planet began. On February 18, 1930, a young astronomer named Clyde Tombaugh found an object among the stars. After several colleagues _____ his observations, Tombaugh's discovery was finally named the ninth planet. It was called Pluto after the Roman god of the underworld.

In 2006, another discovery caused astronomers to _____ whether Pluto was a planet. Pluto had been considered a planet for 76 years without any _____ . Then astronomers found a group of huge floating rocks—asteroids—near the same area as Pluto. One of these asteroids was actually bigger than Pluto. Some astronomers began to say that Pluto was actually just part of this group of asteroids and not really a planet. Others disagreed and said Pluto should be considered a planet. The debate over the _____ of Pluto continues to this day.

As a result of the Pluto debate, astronomers _____ that there was no clear definition of the word *planet*. There were many ideas about what a planet was and was not. Consequently, a group of astronomers from the International Astronomical Union got together and created a definition on which they could all agree. The definition states that a planet is a body that 1) moves around the sun, 2) is large enough for its own gravity to make it round, and 3) has "cleared its neighborhood" of smaller objects. Under this new definition, the scientists decided that Pluto was too small to be a _____ , and they changed its status to "dwarf planet." Today, there are still varying opinions about Pluto's status. Some astronomers agree that Pluto's size makes it unworthy of the "planet" title. However, many others disagree with the new definition and think it should be changed. They think Pluto should again be counted as the ninth planet. There are many different opinions and _____ arguments on both sides. The only thing that seems clear is that the debate will continue.

Part 2

Read the text. Circle the letter of the correct answer.

It took many years of searching before Pluto was first discovered in 1930. Long before that, in the late 1800s, an astronomer named Percival Lowell noticed that two planets, Uranus and Neptune, did not go around the sun in a perfect circle as they should. This discovery meant that something else—another large body—must be pulling on the two planets. The search for a ninth planet began. On February 18, 1930, a young astronomer named Clyde Tombaugh found an object among the stars. After several colleagues confirmed his observations, Tombaugh's discovery was finally named the ninth planet. It was called Pluto after the Roman god of the underworld.

In 2006, another discovery caused astronomers to debate whether Pluto was a planet. Pluto had been considered a planet for 76 years without any doubt. Then astronomers found a group of huge floating rocks—asteroids—near the same area as Pluto. One of these asteroids was actually bigger than Pluto. Some astronomers began to say that Pluto was actually just part of this group of asteroids and not really a planet. Others disagreed and said Pluto should be considered a planet. The debate over the status of Pluto continues to this day.

As a result of the Pluto debate, astronomers realized that there was no clear definition of the word *planet*. There were many ideas about what a planet was and was not. Consequently, a group of astronomers from the International Astronomical Union got together and created a definition on which they could all agree. The definition states that a planet is a body that 1) moves around the sun, 2) is large enough for its own gravity to make it round, and 3) has "cleared its neighborhood" of smaller objects. Under this new definition, the scientists decided that Pluto was too small to be a planet, and they changed its status to "dwarf planet."

Today, there are still varying opinions about Pluto's status. Some astronomers agree that Pluto's size makes it unworthy of the "planet" title. However, many others disagree with the new definition and think it should be changed. They think Pluto should again be counted as the ninth planet. There are many different opinions and various arguments on both sides. The only thing that seems clear is that the debate will continue.

1 The passage is an introduction to how planets are formed.

    a true

    b false

2 Percival Lowell was the astronomer who discovered Pluto.

    a true

    b false

3 Astronomers began to argue about Pluto when they found a larger object near it.

    a true

    b false

4 According to the new definition, Pluto is no longer considered a planet.

    a true

    b false

5 Today, most experts agree on the status of Pluto.

    a true

    b false

Part 3

Read each sentence. Circle the letter of the best meaning for the underlined word.

1 In the late 1800s, an astronomer named Percival Lowell <u>noticed</u> that two planets, Uranus and Neptune, did not go around the sun in a perfect circle as expected.

    a dreamed

    b observed

    c told

    d warned

2 In the late 1800s, an astronomer named Percival Lowell noticed that two <u>planets</u>, Uranus and Neptune, did not go around the sun in a perfect circle as expected.

    a scientific subjects

    b astronomical bodies

    c European countries

    d world wonders

3 After several colleagues <u>confirmed</u> his observations, Tombaugh's discovery was finally named the ninth planet.

    a checked

    b refused

    c played

    d became

4 In 2006, another discovery caused astronomers to <u>debate</u> whether Pluto was a planet.

    a reply

    b understand

    c discuss

    d feel

5 Pluto was considered a planet for 76 years without any <u>doubt</u>.

    a question

    b anger

    c threat

    d loss

6 As a result of the Pluto debate, astronomers <u>realized</u> that there was no clear definition of the word *planet*.

    a discussed

    b read

    c understood

    d denied

7 The scientists changed its <u>status</u> to "dwarf planet."

    a location

    b rank

    c color

    d size

8 There are many different opinions and <u>various</u> arguments on both sides.

    a nervous

    b dangerous

    c humorous

    d numerous

Part 4

Write the words into the correct sentence.

debate	various	doubt	realized
status	planet	confirm	notice

1 The city officials are having a _____ about what to name the new park.

2 Jupiter is the largest _____ in our solar system.

3 I can honestly say, without any _____ , that this is the best day of my life.

4 As the hurricane got smaller and weaker, its _____ was changed to a tropical storm.

5 When the thieves _____ they were on camera, they quickly covered their faces and ran out of the store.

6 Please call the airline 72 hours in advance to _____ your reservation.

7 Karla has a lot of experience in business. She has worked for _____ types of companies.

8 I borrowed my sister's shirt without asking yesterday. Thankfully, she didn't _____ it was missing.

Practice 3

Part 1

Complete the passage using the appropriate words from the box.

despite	remain	youth	setting
courage	renewed	occasional	resolved

The tall _____ , turning to the right, went down a gentle slope until he came to a little stream, where he knelt and drank. _____ his weariness, his thirst and his danger, he noticed the silvery color of the water, and its soft sighing sound, as it flowed over its pebbly bed, made a pleasant murmur in his ear. Robert Lennox always had an eye for the beautiful, and the flashing brook, in its _____ of deep, intense forest green, soothed his senses, speaking to him of comfort and hope.

He drank again and then sat back among the bushes, still breathing heavily, but with much more freedom. The sharp pain left his chest, new strength began to flow into his muscles, and, as the body was _____ , so the spirit soared up and became sanguine once more. He put his ear to the earth and listened long, but heard nothing, save sounds natural to the wilderness, the rustling of leaves before the light wind, the whisper of the tiny current, and the _____ sweet note of a bird in brilliant dress, pluming itself on a bough in its pride.

He drew fresh _____ from the peace of the woods, and _____ to _____ longer there by the stream. Settling himself into the bushes and tall grass, until he was hidden from all but a trained gaze, he waited, body and soul alike growing steadily in vigor.

Part 2

Read the text. Circle the letter of the correct answer.

The tall youth, turning to the right, went down a gentle slope until he came to a little stream, where he knelt and drank. Despite his weariness, his thirst and his danger, he noticed the silvery color of the water, and its soft sighing sound, as it flowed over its pebbly bed, made a pleasant murmur in his ear. Robert Lennox always had an eye for the beautiful, and the flashing brook, in its setting of deep, intense forest green, soothed his senses, speaking to him of comfort and hope.

He drank again and then sat back among the bushes, still breathing heavily, but with much more freedom. The sharp pain left his chest, new strength began to flow into his muscles, and, as the body was renewed, so the spirit soared up and became sanguine once more. He put his ear to the earth and listened long, but heard nothing, save sounds natural to the wilderness, the rustling of leaves before the light wind, the whisper of the tiny current, and the occasional sweet note of a bird in brilliant dress, pluming itself on a bough in its pride. He drew fresh courage from the peace of the woods, and resolved to remain longer there by the stream. Settling himself into the bushes and tall grass, until he was hidden from all but a trained gaze, he waited, body and soul alike growing steadily in vigor.

1 Robert Lennox, the main character in the passage, is on vacation.
  a true
  b false

2 Lennox feels very lonely and worried.
- **a** true
- **b** false

3 Lennox is running away from someone or something.
- **a** true
- **b** false

4 Lennox hears his enemy coming toward him.
- **a** true
- **b** false

5 At the end of the passage, Lennox decides to stay where he is.
- **a** true
- **b** false

Part 3

Read each sentence. Circle the letter of the best meaning for the underlined word.

1 The tall youth, turning to the right, went down a gentle slope until he came to a little stream, where he knelt and drank.
- **a** fruit tree
- **b** wild animal
- **c** young person
- **d** old building

2 Despite his weariness, his thirst and his danger, he noticed the silvery color of the water, and its soft sighing sound, as it flowed over its pebbly bed, made a pleasant murmur in his ear.
- **a** because of
- **b** even with
- **c** along with
- **d** away from

3 Robert Lennox always had an eye for the beautiful, and the flashing brook, in its setting of deep, intense forest green, soothed his senses, speaking to him of comfort and hope.
- **a** surroundings
- **b** direction
- **c** sounds
- **d** creation

4 The sharp pain left his chest, new strength began to flow into his muscles, and, as the body was renewed, so the spirit soared up and became sanguine once more.
- **a** replied
- **b** remembered
- **c** recognized
- **d** repaired

5 He put his ear to the earth and listened long, but heard nothing, save sounds natural to the wilderness, the rustling of leaves before the light wind, the whisper of the tiny current, and the <u>occasional</u> sweet note of a bird in brilliant dress, pluming itself on a bough in its pride.

    a rare

    b quiet

    c unknown

    d frequent

6 He drew fresh <u>courage</u> from the peace of the woods, and resolved to remain longer there by the stream.

    a question

    b strength

    c fear

    d sadness

7 He drew fresh courage from the peace of the woods, and <u>resolved</u> to remain longer there by the stream.

    a waited

    b decided

    c tried

    d shouted

8 He drew fresh courage from the peace of the woods, and resolved to <u>remain</u> longer there by the stream.

    a fall

    b stay

    c run

    d jump

Part 4

Write the words into the correct sentences.

resolved	occasional	youth	courage
renew	setting	despite	remain

1 In case of an emergency, please _____ calm and call 911 immediately.

2 When spring arrives, the sun and rain _____ life in the flowers and trees.

3 It takes a lot of _____ to stand up and speak in front of a large audience.

4. We don't get much rain here, aside from the _____ thunderstorm in the summer.

5 The couple chose the perfect romantic _____ for their wedding.

6 Magazines about celebrities' private lives are popular with _____ .

7 Janice stayed at the office late, _____ feeling sick.

8 The group of high school girls _____ to keep in touch after graduation.

Practice 4

Part 1

Read the passage. Underline the words and word forms that also appear in the box.

traditional	aspect	attractive	in contrast to
daily	character	emotions	
mainly	appreciate	individual	

I recently took a class in ikebana, the traditional Japanese art of flower arranging. Ikebana is similar to Western-style flower arranging in that both styles use a variety of seasonal flowers and greens arranged in an attractive way. However, they differ in several important ways. First, in ikebana, the act of arranging the flowers should be peaceful and calming. The artist is completely silent while creating the arrangement. It is a time to remember our connection to the natural world and appreciate the beauty around us. For me, practicing ikebana has become a wonderful way to forget about the troubles of daily life. Second, in contrast to crowded Western-style arrangements, which use many types of flowers of different colors and can look "busy," ikebana features open, pleasing designs of mainly stems and leaves and just a few flowers or even none at all. Another important aspect of ikebana is the idea that the individual arranger should express his or her own character or emotions through the arrangement. In this way, the ikebana arrangement is more than flowers in a vase. It is a form of human communication. Although I still love making traditional Western bouquets, ikebana has given me a new way to relax and appreciate the beauty of nature.

Part 2

Read the text. Circle the letter of the correct answer.

I recently took a class in *ikebana*, the traditional Japanese art of flower arranging. Ikebana is similar to Western-style flower arranging in that both styles use a variety of seasonal flowers and greens arranged in an attractive way. However, they differ in several important ways. First, in ikebana, the act of arranging the flowers should be peaceful and calming. The artist is completely silent while creating the arrangement. It is a time to remember our connection to the natural world and appreciate the beauty around us. For me, practicing ikebana has become a wonderful way to forget about the troubles of daily life. Second, in contrast to crowded Western-style arrangements, which use many types of flowers of different colors and can look "busy," ikebana features open, pleasing designs of mainly stems and leaves and just a few flowers (or even none at all). Another important aspect of ikebana is the idea that the individual arranger should express his or her own character or emotions through the arrangement. In this way, the ikebana arrangement is more than flowers in a vase. It is a form of human communication. Although I still love making traditional Western bouquets, ikebana has given me a new way to relax and appreciate the beauty of nature.

1 The passage compares two styles of flower arranging.

   a true

   b false

2 The author has never tried Japanese flower arranging.

   a true

   b false

3 Japanese-style flower arrangers do not speak while they work.

   a true

   b false

4 Western-style flower arranging uses more flowers than leaves.

   a true

   b false

5 The author plans to stop doing Western-style flower arranging.

   a true

   b false

Part 3

Read each sentence. Circle the letter of the best meaning for the underlined word.

1 I recently took a class in ikebana, the <u>traditional</u> Japanese art of flower arranging.

   a unusual

   b excellent

   c established

   d casual

2 Ikebana is similar to Western-style flower arranging in that both styles use a variety of seasonal flowers and greens arranged in an <u>attractive</u> way.

   a wide

   b pretty

   c colorful

   d dark

3 It is a time to remember our connection to the natural world and <u>appreciate</u> the beauty around us.

   a enjoy

   b capture

   c sell

   d make

4 For me, practicing ikebana has become a wonderful way to forget about the troubles of <u>daily</u> life.

   a family

   b work

   c nighttime

   d everyday

5 Second, <u>in contrast</u> to crowded Western-style arrangements, which use many types of flowers of different colors and can look "busy," ikebana features open, pleasing designs of mainly stems and leaves and just a few flowers (or even none at all).

   a different from

   b related to

   c similar to

   d in addition to

6 Second, in contrast to crowded Western-style arrangements, which use many types of flowers of different colors and can look "busy," ikebana features open, pleasing designs of <u>mainly</u> stems and leaves and just a few flowers (or even none at all).

a somewhat

b mostly

c many

d only

7 Another important <u>aspect</u> of ikebana is the idea that the individual arranger should express his or her own character or emotions through the arrangement.

a opinion

b feature

c story

d meaning

8 Another important aspect of ikebana is the idea that the <u>individual</u> arranger should express his or her own character or emotions through the arrangement.

a single

b guest

c expert

d interesting

9 Another important aspect of ikebana is the idea that the individual arranger should express his or her own <u>character</u> or emotions through the arrangement.

a idea

b preference

c personality

d understanding

10 Another important aspect of ikebana is the idea that the individual arranger should express his or her own character or <u>emotions</u> through the arrangement.

a ideas

b feelings

c hopes

d questions

Part 4

Write the word to correctly complete each sentence.

attractive	appreciate	individual	mainly
aspect	traditional	character	
daily	In contrast to	emotions	

1 The newly designed office building is much brighter and more _____ than the old one.

2 University students _____ use online sources for their research projects.

3 The tango is a _____ dance from Argentina.

4 _____ past years, the weather has been very warm and mild this summer.

5 Alana went through several different _____ when she learned she would be president of the company.

6 I was tired this morning, so I decided to skip my _____ jog around the park.

7 Please hand out one sheet of paper and a pencil to each _____ student.

8 Tim is very similar to his father both in _____ and in appearance.

9 The only _____ of this movie I didn't like was the unrealistic ending.

10 It's important to take time to _____ your friends and family.

Practice 5

Part 1

Read the passage. Underline the words and word forms that also appear in the box.

as well as	convey	relationships	unlike
according to	tend to	generally	involves

The anthropologist Edward T. Hall first introduced the idea of "high-context" and "low-context" cultures to explain cultural differences in communication. According to Hall, high-context cultures are more common in Eastern countries such as Japan and China, whereas most Western countries are low-context cultures. Of course, communication is important in high-context as well as low-context cultures; it is just the communication style that differs.

According to Hall, both types of culture use nonverbal cues to communicate. However, unlike low-context conversation, high-context conversation involves greater use of nonverbal features such as voice, tone, and gestures. By contrast, people in low-context cultures, such as the United States and Germany, rely more on words to convey meaning. They tend to speak directly, but people from high-context cultures, such as Japan and China, often communicate indirectly.

Conversation is used to begin personal relationships in both high- and low-context cultures. People from high-context cultures share a lot of detailed personal information with friends and coworkers. By contrast, people in low-context cultures generally share only necessary information with smaller, select groups of people.

Part 2

Read the text. Circle the letter of the correct answer.

The anthropologist Edward T. Hall first introduced the idea of "high-context" and "low-context" cultures to explain cultural differences in communication. According to Hall, high-context cultures are more common in Eastern countries such as Japan and China, whereas most Western countries are low-context cultures. Of course, communication is important in high-context as well as low-context cultures; it is just the communication style that differs.

According to Hall, both types of culture use nonverbal cues to communicate. However, unlike low-context conversation, high-context conversation involves greater use of nonverbal features such as voice, tone, and gestures. By contrast, people in low-context cultures, such as the United States and Germany, rely more on words to convey meaning. They tend to speak directly, but people from high-context cultures, such as Japan or China, often communicate indirectly.

Conversation is used to begin personal relationships in both high- and low-context cultures. People from high-context cultures share a lot of detailed personal information with friends and coworkers. By contrast, people in low-context cultures generally share only necessary information with smaller, select groups of people.

1 Edward T. Hall is an expert on communication.

  a true

  b false

2 Both Eastern and Western cultures value communication.

  a true

  b false

3 People from low-context cultures probably speak more than those from high-context cultures.

  a true

  b false

4 High-context cultures do not use conversation to begin personal relationships.

  a true

  b false

5 People in high-context cultures communicate more often without using words.

  a true

  b false

Part 3

Read each sentence. Circle the letter of the best meaning for the underlined word.

1 Of course, communication is important in high-context <u>as well as</u> low-context cultures; it is just the communication style that differs.
   a in contrast to
   b as much as
   c in addition to
   d in front of

2 <u>According to</u> Hall, both types of culture use nonverbal cues to communicate.
   a In agreement with
   b As said by
   c As refused by
   d In addition to

3 By contrast, people in low-context cultures, such as the United States and Germany, rely more on words to <u>convey</u> meaning.
   a express
   b include
   c discuss
   d refuse

4 They <u>tend to</u> speak directly, but people from high-context cultures, such as Japan or China, often communicate indirectly.
   a are afraid to
   b find it hard to
   c do not like to
   d are likely to

5 Conversation is used to begin personal <u>relationships</u> in both high- and low-context cultures.
   a preferences
   b belongings
   c feelings
   d connections

6 By contrast, people in low-context cultures <u>generally</u> share only necessary information with smaller, select groups of people.
   a surprisingly
   b usually
   c happily
   d quickly

7 However, <u>unlike</u> low-context conversation, high-context conversation involves greater use of nonverbal features such as voice, tone, and gestures.
   a similar to
   b different from
   c related to
   d taken from

8 However, unlike low-context conversation, high-context conversation <u>involves</u> greater use of nonverbal features such as voice, tone, and gestures.

   a hates

   b uses

   c fails

   d interests

Part 4

Write the words into the correct sentences.

tend to	generally	relationship	unlike
involves	convey	according to	as well as

1 The research showed that people who live in warmer climates are _____ happier than those who live in colder areas.

2 Learning a language _____ using the language for real-life communication outside of a classroom.

3 People in the United States _____ take showers more often than baths.

4 When giving a presentation, you can use visual aids to _____ your ideas clearly.

5 A balanced diet and regular exercise are important for good physical health _____ a healthy mind.

6 Well, _____ the author of this book, children watch far too much TV.

7 Brianna and her sister have always had a difficult _____ . They fight all the time.

8 This dish is delicious. It's _____ anything I've ever tasted before.

APPENDICES

Appendix 1   Tips for Reading Tests

Tips for Reading Tests

All of the reading practice activities in My English Lab will help you improve your reading skills and lead to greater success on reading tests. Reading regularly in English, especially textbooks and academic texts, will help you build a strong vocabulary and increase your rate of comprehension.

Here are some additional useful tips and suggestions to help you succeed on reading comprehension tests.

General Suggestions

In most testing situations, your time will be limited. This can make you feel nervous and create pressure, making it hard to focus on what you are reading.

- Relax. Take a few deep breaths and clear your mind before you begin.
- Preview the entire test to see how many sections and points there are. Quickly calculate how much time you have to spend on each section.

Previewing Questions

- Read the test questions first. When you know what information you need, you can use time-saving strategies such as skimming and scanning to find it.
- Preview the title and the first and last few lines of each text. Then ask yourself questions about the details of the text. You can use the "five *W*s and an *H*" question words (*Who, What, Where, When, Why, How*) to guide your questions. For example, *Who are the people involved? What happened? What is the main point/author's purpose/author's opinion? Where did the events take place?*

Reading Strategies

- Always skim the whole passage quickly before you read carefully.
- Look for a pattern—sequence, comparison/contrast, cause and effect. Scan for transition words to help you.
- After skimming, read the passage carefully and highlight or mark the main idea and important supporting facts and ideas.
- Skip over words and phrases you don't understand, or use the context of the sentence or passage to guess their meanings.
- Make inferences and conclusions using your background knowledge about the topic.
- If there is time, use a chart or graphic organizer to write down the main points from the passage.

Appendix 2   Transition Words and Phrases

Transition Words and Phrases

Steps in a Process:
first, first of all, second, secondly, next, then, after, before, finally, once, when, now, while, during, at the same time, in the end

Order of Events:
Specific dates or time periods: *on January 3, on Thursday, last month, next week, in a year, before the war, in 2001, in recent years, in 1968, in the 1950s, several years ago, during World War II*
Time expressions: *when, now, during, soon, at that time*
Words and phrases that tell order: *in the beginning, at first, next, then, later, after that, finally, before, after*

Transitions for the Comparison/Contrast Pattern

	To compare	To contrast
Coordinating conjunctions and paired conjunctions	*and, as well as, both ... and ...*	*but, yet*
Transition signals	*similarly, too, also*	*by contrast, on the other hand, however, instead,*
Subordinators		*though, although, even though, while*
Others (adjectives, prepositions, verbs)	*be similar to, be like, be alike, be the same, have X in common*	*differ, be different from, be unlike, rather than*

Appendix 3 Reading Rate Table

Reading Rate Table

All of the passages are about 600 words long. To find your reading rate, find the reading time that is closest to yours. Then look across at the reading rate column.

Reading time (minutes)	Reading rate (words per minute)
1:00	600
1:15	480
1:30	400
1:45	343
2:00	300
2:15	267
2:30	240
2:45	218
3:00	200
3:15	184
3:30	171
3:45	160
4:00	150
4:15	141
4:30	133
4:45	126
5:00	120
5:15	114
5:30	109
5:45	104
6:00	100
6:15	96
6:30	92
6:45	89
7:00	85

Appendix 4   Reading Rate Log

Reading Rate Log

Under the Practice Activity number, write your comprehension score (number of correct answers). Then check (√) your reading rate. Write the date at the bottom of the chart.

Exercise	Intro	P1-R1	P1-R2	P1-R3	P2-R1	P2-R2	P2-R3	P3-R1	P3-R2	P3-R3
Comprehension Score										
Reading rate										
600										
480										
400										
343										
300										
267										
240										
218										
200										
184										
171										
160										
150										
141										
133										
126										
120										
114										
109										
104										
100										
96										
92										
89										
85										
Date										

Part 1 Comprehension Skills

Preview and skim the passage quickly. Then circle the letter of the best answer for each question.

To: Customers of Molly's Muffins
From: Darcy Lions, President
Date: April 12, 2014
Subject: New Policy Regarding Nutritional Information

At Molly's Muffins, our customers' satisfaction is our number one concern. As a result of our recent customer survey, we want to show our commitment to you by providing the healthiest, most nutritious products we can. Beginning on May 1, 2014, Molly's will begin publishing nutritional information on the packages of all of our baked goods. We agree with your feedback that customers should have access to this information to help them make healthy choices.

We believe that this new policy will help our customers feel confident in choosing Molly's Muffins. Molly's uses only the finest local, organic ingredients in our products, and we bake everything fresh each morning. Moreover, we offer a variety of low-calorie and vegetarian options without losing the wonderful flavor that has made us the most popular bakery in the area.

Nutritional information for all of our products will also be available on our website, www.mollysmuffins.pearson.net.

Thank you for choosing Molly's Muffins.

Sincerely,

Darcy Lions
President

1 This passage is from _____ .
   a a travel magazine
   b an economics textbook
   c a newspaper article
   d a business memo

2 The author of this passage intends to _____ .
   a inform people about something
   b give an opinion about something
   c teach people how to do something
   d persuade people to take some action

3 The purpose of this passage is to _____ .

   a warn employees about a safety issue

   b announce a new company policy

   c explain the history of the company

   d list job openings at the company

4 This passage gives information about all of the following topics EXCEPT _____ .

   a when the new policy will begin

   b what new products will be coming soon

   c what types of ingredients the company uses

   d why the company changed its policy

Part 2   Comprehension Skills

Read the scanning questions on p. 198. Then scan the text below for the correct answers.

To: Customers of Molly's Muffins
From: Darcy Lions, President
Date: April 12, 2014
Subject: New Policy Regarding Nutritional Information

At Molly's Muffins, our customers' satisfaction is our number one concern. As a result of our recent customer survey, we want to show our commitment to you by providing the healthiest, most nutritious products we can. Beginning on May 1, 2014, Molly's will begin publishing nutritional information on the packages of all of our baked goods. We agree with your feedback that customers should have access to this information to help them make healthy choices.

We believe that this new policy will help our customers feel confident in choosing Molly's Muffins. Molly's uses only the finest local, organic ingredients in our products, and we bake everything fresh each morning. Moreover, we offer a variety of low-calorie and vegetarian options without losing the wonderful flavor that has made us the most popular bakery in the area.

Nutritional information for all of our products will also be available on our website, www.mollysmuffins.pearson.net.

Thank you for choosing Molly's Muffins.

Sincerely,

Darcy Lions
President

1 Why is the company changing its policy?

    a Because it has a new president.

    b As a result of customer feedback.

    c It is changing some of its recipes.

    d Customers are choosing a more popular bakery.

2 When will the new policy begin?

    a April 1, 2014

    b April 12, 2014

    c May 1, 2014

    d May 12, 2014

3 What is the new policy?

    a using only local, organic ingredients

    b giving customers surveys

    c baking products fresh every morning

    d adding nutritional information to packages

4 Where can customers find nutritional information?

    a on packages for low-calorie and vegetarian options

    b on packages for baked goods only

    c on the company website only

    d on packages for baked goods and on the website

Part 3 Comprehension Skills

Read the passage and circle the letter of the correct response.

The periodical cicada is native to the eastern United States. It has one of the longest life spans of any insect in the world, but only a fraction of its life is spent above ground. Depending on the species, the insect's life cycle may be either thirteen or seventeen years long. Most of this time is spent underground, feeding on the fluid inside certain types of tree roots. After thirteen or seventeen years, the mature cicadas finally emerge from their underground existence. They are only active above ground for a period of approximately four to six weeks. During this time, groups of male cicadas gather in various locations and "sing" in order to attract females. This loud, metallic buzzing noise is one of the most unmistakable signs of summer in many places. A few weeks after mating, the female cicadas lay their eggs. Within two months, after only a short time spent out in the open air, the adults' life cycle is complete.

1 This passage is from _____ .

    a a fiction book

    b a textbook

    c a travel guide

    d an e-mail

2 What is the topic of this passage?

   a insects of the eastern United States

   b the life cycle of the cicada

   c mating habits of periodical cicadas

   d differences among cicada species

3 What is the main idea of this passage?

   a The periodical cicada lives a long life but only spends a short time above ground.

   b The male cicada uses a loud, metallic call in order to attract female mates.

   c The life cycle of male cicadas is different from that of female cicadas.

   d Many types of trees produce the fluid that cicadas eat.

Part 4 Comprehension Skills

Read the scanning questions. Then scan the text below for the answers.

The periodical cicada is native to the eastern United States. It has one of the longest life spans of any insect in the world, but only a fraction of its life is spent above ground. Depending on the species, the insect's life cycle may be either thirteen or seventeen years long. Most of this time is spent underground, feeding on the fluid inside certain types of tree roots. After thirteen or seventeen years, the mature cicadas finally emerge from their underground existence. They are only active above ground for a period of approximately four to six weeks. During this time, groups of male cicadas gather in various locations and "sing" in order to attract females. This loud, metallic buzzing noise is one of the most unmistakable signs of summer in many places. A few weeks after mating, the female cicadas lay their eggs. Within two months, after only a short time spent out in the open air, the adults' life cycle is complete.

1 What is a periodical cicada?

   a a type of bird

   b a type of insect

   c a type of fish

   d a type of tree

2 Where do periodical cicadas live?

   a in the United States

   b in the Middle East

   c all around the world

   d in various locations

3 How long do periodical cicadas live?

   a thirteen or seventeen years

   b four to six weeks

   c two months

   d a few days

4 What do periodical cicadas eat?

    a leaves of certain trees

    b fluid from tree roots

    c other insects' eggs

    d other insects

5 How do cicadas spend most of their time above ground?

    a searching for food

    b flying around

    c laying eggs

    d singing and mating

Part 5 Comprehension Skills

Read the passage and circle the letter of the correct response.

His gloved hands were clasped behind him, and he seemed to be lost in thought. Mrs. Hall noticed that the melted snow that still sprinkled his shoulders dripped upon her carpet.

"Can I take your hat and coat, sir," she said, "and give them a good dry in the kitchen?"

"No," he said without turning.

She was not sure she had heard him and was about to repeat her question.

He turned his head and looked at her over his shoulder. "I prefer to keep them on," he said with emphasis, and she noticed that he wore big blue spectacles with side-lights, and he had a bushy side-whisker over his coat collar that completely hid his cheeks and face.

"Very well, sir," she said. "As you like. In a bit the room will be warmer."

He made no answer and had turned his face away from her again, and Mrs. Hall, feeling that her conversational advances were ill-timed, laid the rest of the table things in a quick staccato and whisked out of the room. When she returned, he was still standing there, like a man of stone, his back hunched, his collar turned up, his dripping hat-brim turned down, hiding his face and ears completely. She put down the eggs and bacon with considerable emphasis and called rather than said to him, "Your lunch is served, sir."

"Thank you." he said at the same time and did not stir until she was closing the door.

1 What is the main purpose of this passage?

    a to describe the setting of the story

    b to describe the female character

    c to describe the male character

    d to describe an important event in the story

2 From this passage, we can infer that the two characters _____ .

    a work at the same place

    b are old friends

    c have never met before

    d are husband and wife

3 From this passage, we can infer that _____ .

    a Mrs. Hall owns an inn or restaurant

    b the man has several children

    c Mrs. Hall would like to marry the man

    d the man is from another country

Part 6 Comprehension Skills

Read the paragraph. Then circle the letter of the correct phrase to complete each sentence.

1 Karate and tae kwon do are both martial art forms from Asia. While the two sports are similar in some ways, there are also a number of important differences. Karate originated in Okinawa, Japan in the 5th century CE, while the earliest records of the beginnings of tae kwon do in Korea are dated several hundred years earlier, in 37 BCE. The name "karate" means "empty hand" in the Japanese language, meaning that practitioners perform the martial art with nothing—no weapons— in their hands. In Korean, "tae kwon do" translates to "the way of the foot and fist." While both art forms teach a variety of kicks, blocks, and punches, tae kwon do focuses somewhat more on the use of the feet and legs for kicking, while karate uses more upper body force. Both sports also emphasize mental training and character development and teach important principles such as respect, effort, self-discipline and control. Finally, both tae kwon do and judo are designated Olympic sports.

This paragraph describes _____ .

    a the steps in a process

    b a sequence of events over time

    c a comparison between two things

    d different causes and effects

2 A common problem among smartphone users is a broken front panel, the glass screen on the front of the phone. Breakage can occur as a result of an accidental drop or other impact to the front of the phone. It is possible to fix this problem without buying a new phone. Here's how. The first thing you need to do is purchase a front panel repair kit, available online for about $50. When you receive the kit, take all the items out of the box and place them on an even work surface. Next, use the small screwdriver from the kit to remove the two screws from the dock-connector end of the phone. Then place the suction cup from the repair kit firmly on the center of the broken front panel. Pull gently and carefully on the suction cup, and pull up on the panel slowly. Do not pull or cut the phone's cables. After you have successfully begun to separate the front panel from the phone, gently rotate the panel to about a 45 degree angle. Then pull straight up and the panel should release. Now you can set your new front panel from the kit into the phone's display assembly. Finally, tighten the screws to set it firmly in place.

This paragraph describes _____ .

    a the steps in a process

    b a sequence of events over time

    c a comparison between two things

    d different causes and effects

3 Sleet is a form of frozen precipitation like snow, hail, or freezing rain. Sleet is made up of tiny pellets of ice, each of which is only a few millimeters in size. Although they are small, these sleet pellets can create dangerously slippery conditions on roads and walkways. Sleet pellets are caused by certain special weather conditions. Temperatures on the ground must be near or below freezing. Cold temperatures high in the atmosphere create snow from the moisture in the clouds. As the snow falls, if there is a layer of warm air lower in the atmosphere, it causes the snowflakes to partially melt, but not completely. Then, as a result of the colder air closer to the ground, the partially melted snow refreezes and takes the round pellet shape of sleet.

This paragraph describes _____ .

   a the steps in a process
   b a sequence of events over time
   c a comparison between two things
   d different causes and effects

Part 7 Vocabulary Building

Read the list of words. Then circle the letter of the answer to each question.

1

connected	respectful	organized	honest

Which negative prefix can be added to all of adjectives?

   a ir
   b un
   c dis
   d il

2

enjoy	debate	believe	attain

Which suffix can be added to each verb on the list to make it an adjective?

   a tion
   b able
   c ful
   d ly

Part 8 Vocabulary Building

Circle the letter of the word form that correctly completes each sentence.

1 If the company is going to stay ahead of our competitors, we are going to need to _____ carefully.

   a strategy
   b strategize

2 I think you'll find the article about climate change very _____ for your research paper.

   a informative
   b information

3 The citizens wrote a letter saying that they _____ disagreed with the mayor's plan to decrease the school budget.

    a strengthen

    b strongly

Part 9   Vocabulary Building

Read the text with the missing words. Then circle the letter of the answer to each question.

April 12, 2014

Dear *Union Times* Editor,

    I am writing to express my ▓▓▓▓▓▓ with the town council's decision not to ▓▓▓▓▓▓ the school budget again this year. After attending last night's town meeting, it is ▓▓▓▓▓▓ to me that several of the council ▓▓▓▓▓▓ do not value our children's education ▓▓▓▓▓▓ enough. Those who voted down the proposal to increase the school budget by $90,000 in 2015, in my ▓▓▓▓▓▓, have essentially voted "no" to our children's future. The budget increase would have ▓▓▓▓▓▓ the school to provide music, ▓▓▓▓▓▓, and ▓▓▓▓▓▓ education two days a week ▓▓▓▓▓▓ of just one. These ▓▓▓▓▓▓ "special" subjects are important to providing students with a well-rounded education, creating ▓▓▓▓▓▓ habits and useful life skills, and ▓▓▓▓▓▓ students and keeping them interested in school. One ▓▓▓▓▓▓ a week is something, but it isn't nearly enough. I was ▓▓▓▓▓▓ when the increase did not pass last year but had hoped that this year things would be ▓▓▓▓▓▓.

Sincerely,

Brenda Jolie

1 What type of text is it?

    a an email to company employees

    b a letter to a newspaper editor

    c a university course description

    d a blog entry

2 What is the main purpose of the text?

    a to propose a new idea

    b to express an opinion

    c to request information

    d to express approval

3 Who is the author of the text?

    a a member of the town council

    b a concerned resident of the town

    c a high school student

    d the principal of the town school

4 What emotion is the author feeling?

    a fear

    b curiosity

    c disappointment

    d relief

Part 10 Vocabulary Building

Circle the letter of the preposition that correctly completes each sentence.

1 What time are you picking _____ your parents at the airport?

    a up

    b on

2 To avoid stress, try not to do too many things at once. It's not good for you to take _____ too much.

    a on

    b out

3 The store's alarm went _____ , but the thief had already broken the window and stolen a computer.

    a off

    b over

4 Will you be home this afternoon? I can stop _____ then and get today's class notes.

    a by

    b on

Part 11 Vocabulary Building

Underline the subject of the sentence.

1 Musicians Dick and Ted Nash are known around the world.

Part 12 Vocabulary Building

Underline the verb in the sentence.

1 For several hours, Karen and her whole family were held and questioned by the airport security officer.

Part 13 Vocabulary Building

Circle the letter of the correct signal word or phrase to complete the sentence.

1 Our train was delayed for several hours; _____ , they fixed the problem and we were able to continue our trip.

    a finally

    b in addition

    c however

    d moreover

2 _____ the Japanese martial arts of judo and tae kwon do are Olympic sports, kickboxing is not.

    a As well as

    b Although

    c Therefore

    d Finally

3 I feel that the length of the school day should be increased to give students more time to learn and do extracurricular activities. _____ , students should go to school one weekend day each week.

    a Moreover

    b As a result

    c Finally

    d Although

Part 14 Vocabulary Building

Circle the letter of the word that correctly completes the sentence.

1 Where is the newlywed couple? I have a special surprise for _____ .

    a their

    b they

    c them

    d they're

2 I'm sorry to hear the interview didn't go well. Please don't worry about _____ . There will be other opportunities, I'm sure.

    a its

    b it

    c it's

    d its'

3 We just got back from Disney World. It was the most wonderful vacation of _____ lives.

    a our

    b us

    c we

    d ours

4 Winona is beautiful, smart, talented, and funny. I really wish I could be more like _____ .

    a her

    b his

    c him

    d she

Part 15   Vocabulary Building

Circle the letter of the demonstrative pronoun or adjective that correctly completes each sentence.

1 Don't touch the red flowers on that bush. _____ are the ones that gave me a rash.

  a That

  b These

  c Those

  d This

2 Here's something I want to give you. My grandfather gave me _____ baseball when I was ten years old.

  a this

  b these

  c those

  d their

3 The teacher asked Amalia to leave class when she forgot her homework again. _____ was the last time Amalia forgot her homework.

  a This

  b That

  c Those

  d Then

Part 16   Vocabulary Building

For each group of sentences, circle the letter of the referent for the underlined phrase.

1 Cormorants, pelicans, and albatrosses are three different types of birds that live in areas close to the ocean. <u>These fascinating creatures</u> sometimes dive up to 15 feet below the surface to catch their food.

  a areas close to ocean waters

  b cormorants, pelicans, and albatrosses

  c three different types of birds

  d 15 feet below the surface

2 The X Games is a yearly event that features so-called extreme sports, such as snowboarding, skateboarding, and motocross. <u>This competition</u> features primarily young athletes performing gravity-defying tricks.

  a motocross

  b extreme sports

  c young athletes

  d the X Games

3 *Tā moko* is the art of facial tattooing that is practiced by the Maori people of New Zealand. <u>This traditional custom</u> began in the 1700s and was performed in order to mark the passage of young boys into adulthood.

  a New Zealand

  b Maori people

  c tā moko

  d adulthood

ANSWER KEY

PRE-TEST

Part 1   Comprehension Skills pp. 1–2

1. c, 2. a, 3. b, 4. d

Part 2 pp. 2–3

1. b, 2. b, 3. d, 4. a

Part 3 pp. 3–4

1. d, 2. b, 3. b

Part 4 pp. 4–5

1. c, 2. c, 3. b

Part 5 pp. 5–6

1. d, 2. c, 3. a

Part 6 p. 6

1. b

Part 7 pp. 6–7

1. c

Part 8 p. 7

1. d

Part 9   Vocabulary Building p. 7

1. c, 2. b

Part 10 p. 8

1. b, 2. a, 3. a

Part 11 pp. 8–9

1. b, 2. b, 3. b, 4. d

Part 12 p. 9

1. b, 2. a, 3. a, 4. b

Part 13 p. 9

1. My English professor

Part 14 p. 9

1. have been living

Part 15 pp. 9–10

1. d, 2. a, 3. b

Part 16 p. 10

1. a, 2. a, 3. b, 4. d

Part 17 pp. 10–11

1. a, 2. b, 3. a

Part 18 p. 11

1. b, 2. d, 3. c

Part 19   Vocabulary Building p. 11

1. b, 2. a

COMPREHENSION SKILLS

Previewing, Scanning, and Skimming

PREVIEWING

Practice 1 p. 12

Hundreds Left Homeless after Storm
1 What caused the damage to the homes?
9 Where are they people staying now?
12 Where did the dangerous weather happen?

Woman Wins Award for Charity Project
3 What kind of work did the woman do?
5 Whom did the woman help?
11 Who is giving the prize?

Operation Slows Down Athlete
2 What sport does the person play?
4 Why did the athlete need an operation?
10 When can the person play sports again?

Hunter's Dog Rescues Missing Hiker
6 How did the animal help the person?
7 How long was the person lost?
8 Where was the person hiking?

Practice 2 p. 13

1. 6   2. 1   3. 4   4. 3   5. 2

Practice 3 pp. 14–15

1. b, d   2. a, b   3. a, b   4. a, c

Practice 4 pp. 16–17

1. b, 2. c, 3. d, 4. a

SCANNING

Practice 1 pp. 18–19

1. 3

2. Carol Noonan

3. Monday and Wednesday

4. 7

5. Study Abroad Meeting

6. one

7. *Walking on Snow*

8. Brent Library

Practice 2 pp. 20–21

1. c, 2. b, 3. a, 4. b, 5. b, 6. c, 7. a, 8. b

Practice 3 pp. 22–23

1. kills	kill
kills	dangerous
dangerous diseases	diseases
2. insects	tree
problem	insects
insects	trees
insects	problems
trees	trees
insect	problem
trees	
3. bees	bees
bees	reason
disappeared	bees
bees	bees
bees	reasons
disappeared	

Practice 4 p. 23

(1) business

business

(2) principles

success

business

principles

business

success

(3) principle

success

business

business

(4) principle

success

(5) principle

(7) principles

success

SKIMMING

Practice 1 pp. 24–25

1. b, c, e

Practice 2 pp. 25–26

1. b, 2. a, 3. c

Practice 3 pp. 26–27

1. b, 2. c, 3. b

COMBINED SKILLS: PREVIEWING, SCANNING, AND SKIMMING

Practice 1 pp. 28–29

1. c, 2. b, 3. a, 4. c, 5. a

Understanding Paragraphs

UNDERSTANDING PARAGRAPHS

Practice 1 pp. 30–31

1. a, 2. b, 3. a, 4. b, 5. a

Practice 2 pp. 31–32

1. 2	2. 1	3. 9
4. 6	5. 5	

Practice 3 p. 32

1. The most common jobs for average Roman people were in agriculture and education, as well as in the military.

2. Small family farms have been declining for years because larger farms are taking over.

3. Most people looking for a job these days use Internet job boards to search for opportunities.

IDENTIFYING THE TOPIC OF A PARAGRAPH

Practice 1 pp. 33–34

1. b, 2. c, 3. b, 4. c

Practice 2 pp. 34–35

1. b, 2. a, 3. c, 4. a

IDENTIFYING THE MAIN IDEA

Practice 1 pp. 35–36

1. a, 2. b, 3. c

Practice 2 pp. 36–37

1. c, 2. b, 3. a

Practice 3 pp. 37–38

1. a, 2. a

IDENTIFYING SUPPORTING DETAILS AND INFORMATION

Practice 1 pp. 38–39

1. S, M, S, S

2. S, S, S, M

3. S, S, M, S

Practice 2 p. 39

1. a, b, d, e

2. a, c, d, e

3. a, c

Making Inferences

MAKING INFERENCES FROM DIALOGUE

Practice 1 p. 40

1. b, 2. a, 3. a, 4. b, 5. b

Practice 2 p. 41

1. b, 2. a, 3. a, 4. b, 5. a

Practice 3 p. 42

1. b, 2. a, 3. b, 4. b, 5. a

MAKING INFERENCES IN FICTION

Practice 1 p. 43

1. c, 2. a, 3. d, 4. b

Practice 2 p. 44

1. a, 2. b, 3. c, 4. a, 5. c

MAKING INFERENCES IN NONFICTION

Practice 1 p. 45

1. a, d, e, 2. b, c, d

Practice 2

Part 1 pp. 46–47

1. b, 2. a, 3. a, 4. b, 5. b

Part 2 pp. 47–48

1. a, 2. a, 3. b, 4. a, 5. b

FOLLOWING IDEAS IN PARAGRAPHS

Practice 1 pp. 48–49

1. a, 2. a, 3. a, 4. d, 5. b

Practice 2 pp. 49–50

1. c, 2. a, 3. a, 4. c, 5. a

Recognizing Patterns

SEQUENCE PATTERN

Practice 1 p. 51

1. First, Before, When, After that, Then, When, now, Once, Finally

2. before, First of all, Second, When, Once, Next, Now

Practice 2 pp. 52–53

1. 3, 4, 2, 1

2. 2, 1, 3

3. 3, 1, 4, 2, 5

4. 3, 1, 4, 2

5. 1, 3, 2

COMPARISON AND CONTRAST PATTERN

Practice 1 p. 54

Thai Food 1, 6, 9	Both Thai and Korean Food 2, 5, 8, 10

Korean Food 3, 4, 7	

Practice 2 p. 55

High-Context Cultures 1, 3, 9	Both High- and Low-Context Cultures 2, 5, 8

Low-Context Cultures 4, 6, 7	

CAUSE AND EFFECT PATTERN

Practice 1 p. 56

1. are caused, creates, a result of
2. result from, cause, responsible for, help, produce

Practice 2

Part 1 p. 57

1. a, 2. b, 3. a, 4. b, 5. a

Part 2 p. 57

1. a, 2. a, 3. a, 4. a

IDENTIFYING PATTERNS

Practice 1 pp. 58–59

1. b, 2. a, 3. a, 4. c, 5. a, 6. c

Comprehension Skills Practice Test

Part 1 p. 60

1. Scientists Hopeful for Cancer Cure
2. Fewer People Smoking at Work
3. Source of Strange Odor Still Unknown
4. Most Female Managers Want to Quit

Part 2 pp. 60–61

1. a, b, 2. a, b

Part 3 pp. 61–62

1. a, 2. c, 3. d

Part 4 pp. 62–63

1. 20
2. 35
3. 4
4. 7th Avenue
5. 50
6. 3
7. nothing

Part 5 pp. 63–64

1. a, c, d

Part 6 p. 64

1. c

Part 7 p. 64

1. a, 2. b

Part 8 p. 65

1. b, 2. a, 3. b

Part 9 p. 66

1. c, 2. b

Part 10 p. 66

S, S, M, S

Part 11 p. 67

1. a, 2. b, 3. a, 4. b

Part 12 pp. 67–68

1. a, 2. d, 3. b, 4. c

Part 13 pp. 68–69

1. a, d, e

Part 14 p. 69

1. no one knows the cause for sure
2. stay aware of the latest identity scams
3. our own immune systems

Part 15 p. 70

1. Because, As a result of, so, affect, A
2. on February 24, 1955, At the time, A short time later, When, C
3. Unlike, On the other hand, Although, Both, B

VOCABULARY BUILDING

Dictionary Work

PARTS OF SPEECH

Practice 1 p. 72

1. a, 2. c, 3. c, 4. c

Practice 2 p. 73

1. a, 2. b, 3. a, 4. c, 5. b

FINDING THE RIGHT MEANING

Practice 1 pp. 74–75

1.
    1 adj. a middle size or amount
    2 n. a way of communicating or expressing something
    3 n. the material an artist uses to create something
2.
    1 v. to make your clothes smooth using a flat, heated electrical appliance
    2 n. an object that is heated and that you push across a piece of clothing to make it smooth
    3 adj. made of iron (a metal)
3.
    1 n. the road or path that you follow to get to a particular place
    2 n. a manner or method of doing something
    3 adv. a large distance or amount of time

4.
    1 v. to decide to use money and time for a particular purpose
    2 v. to carry our or do something (usually wrong or illegal)
    3 v. to say that you will definitely do something

Practice 2 pp. 75–76

1. b, 2. b, 3. c, 4. c, 5. c

THE WAY WORDS ARE USED

Practice 1 p. 77

1. keep   4. at
2. short   5. walking
3. in   6. From

Practice 2 pp. 77–78

1. for   4. very
2. ago   5. any
3. that   6. For

Word Parts

ROOTS, PREFIXES, AND SUFFIXES

Practice 1 pp. 79–80

1. ance   6. ness
2. dis   7. re
3. un   8. in
4. al   9. im
5. less   10. able

Practice 2 pp. 80–81

1. loc, place   7. jec, throw
2. habit, live   8. port, carry
3. graph, written   9. lat, side
4. juven, young   10. dic, say
5. duc, lead   11. form, shape
6. meter, measure   12. dent, tooth

Practice 3 p. 82

dis-	im-
3, 6, 15	2, 14, 17

in-	il-
8, 20, 24	5, 9, 16

ir-	non-
4, 11, 22	7, 10, 18

mis-	un-
12, 19, 23	1, 13, 21

Practice 4 p. 83

1. antianxiety
2. supermarket
3. preassigned
4. postgraduate
5. unconscious
6. transaction
7. substandard
8. enable
9. overwork
10. biweekly
11. remind
12. extracurricular
13. autobiography
14. monorail
15. devalue

Practice 5 p. 85

adjective	hope	noun
adverb	bad	adjective
adjective	recycle	verb
adjective	impress	verb
adjective	interest	noun
noun	shy	adjective

Practice 6 pp. 85–86

1. reaction
2. resemblance
3. imaginable
4. truthful
5. childish
6. musician
7. popularity
8. capitalism
9. activist
10. annually
11. kindness
12. establishment
13. relationship
14. Reflexology
15. furious

WORD FORMS AND FAMILIES

Practice 1 p. 87

col 1 row 6: friend
col 1 row 7: strength
col 1 row 8: production
col 1 row 9: responsibility
col 2 row 3: strategize
col 2 row 4: inform
col 2 row 7: strengthen
col 2 row 10: energize
col 3 row 2: correct
col 3 row 3: strategic
col 3 row 4: informed
col 3 row 5: logical
col 3 row 8: productive
col 3 row 9: responsible
col 3 row 10: energetic
col 3 row 11: attractive
col 4 row 5: illogical
col 4 row 6: unfriendly
col 4 row 9: irresponsible
col 4 row 11: unattractive
col 5 row 2: correctly
col 5 row 4: informatively
col 5 row 7: strongly

Practice 2 pp. 87–88

1. b, 2. a, 3. b, 4. a, 5. a, 6. b, 7. b, 8. b, 9. a, 10. a

Practice 3 p. 88

1. settlers, settled, settlements
2. similarities, similar, similarly

3. developer, development, developed

4. confidence, confident, confidently

5. organizing, disorganized, organizer

Guessing Meaning from Context

WHAT IS CONTEXT?

Practice 1 pp. 89–90

1. b, 2. c, 3. a, 4. b

Practice 2 p. 90

1.	morning	7.	Sighing
2.	song	8.	repeated
3.	fragrance	9.	discouraged
4.	green	10.	tin
5.	bucket	11.	water
6.	brush		

GUESSING THE MEANING OF WORDS AND PHRASES

Practice 1 pp. 91–92

1. c, 2. a, 3. c, 4. a, 5. c

Practice 2 p. 92

1. b, 2. b, 3. a, 4. b, 5. b

GUESSING MEANING FROM A PASSAGE

Practice 1 p. 93

1. n. rain or snow

2. n. results of a particular action

3. v. warned of danger

4. v. stay

5. v. making planes unable to fly

6. adv. terribly, severely

7. adj. very cold, freezing

8. n. large mass of air

Practice 2 pp. 94–95

1. verb, look for

2. noun, feeling of being stressed or tense

3. verb, becoming more popular

4. noun, supporters

5. verb, fight against

6. adverb; very much, strongly

7. noun, the way something feels when you touch it

8. adjective, thinking about too many things at once

Practice 3 p. 95

1. hill

2. covered with small rocks

3. calmed, relaxed

4. confident, positive

5. crackling sound

6. tree branch

7. decided

8. strength, energy

Practice 4 p. 96

1. move from one place to another

2. warm and mild

3. plenty

4. baby whales

5. traveling

6. amazing accomplishments

7. natural sense or feeling

8. use

Phrases and Collocations

COMMON TYPES OF COLLOCATIONS

Practice 1 p. 98

1.	do	9.	office
2.	take	10.	cup
3.	have	11.	quickly
4.	get	12.	fluently
5.	make	13.	well
6.	heart	14.	carefully
7.	bowl	15.	early
8.	company		

Practice 2 p. 99

1. low
2. old
3. bad
4. good
5. difficult
6. under
7. in
8. during
9. at
10. on
11. take
12. keep
13. get
14. make
15. figure

PHRASAL VERBS

Practice 1 p. 100

1. wake up
2. goes off
3. take on
4. wash up
5. head out
6. stop by
7. pick up
8. give up

Practice 2 p. 101

1. do
2. made
3. Look
4. get
5. look
6. take
7. get
8. do
9. make

IDIOMS

Practice 1 pp. 101–102

1. help someone
2. quickly
3. try very hard
4. rest and relax
5. have no money
6. call or email someone
7. go to bed
8. be very familiar with something

Practice 2 p. 102

1. have enough money to pay the bills
2. give special permission
3. decide
4. give reasons for bad behavior
5. do something good for others
6. include something in your schedule or plans

Practice 3 p. 103

1. shoulder
2. heart
3. head
4. stomach
5. nose
6. leg
7. green
8. sweet
9. eyes

PHRASES IN CONTEXT

Practice 1 p. 104

1. a, 2. b, 3. b, 4. b, 5. a

Practice 2 p. 105

1. just in
2. hard
3. run out of
4. spare
5. on
6. spend
7. waste
8. take your

Practice 3 pp. 105–106

1. a, 2. b, 3. c, 4. a, 5. b

Practice 4 p. 106

1. do
2. make
3. do
4. make
5. make
6. do
7. make
8. do

Practice 5 p. 107

1. have
2. have
3. take
4. Take
5. have
6. has
7. have
8. have
9. take
10. take

Practice 6 p. 108

1. of
2. between
3. by
4. along
5. from
6. on
7. to
8. to
9. in
10. by
11. to
12. on
13. in
14. of
15. of
16. with

Following Ideas in Text

KEY PARTS OF SENTENCES

Practice 1

Part 1 p. 109

1. A lucky New Jersey man
2. he
3. Tom Fahner
4. He
5. the sun
6. I
7. Tom
8. I
9. the hiker
10. Tom
11. no one
12. he
13. It
14. I
15. Tom
16. It
17. It
18. The two
19. Rosco

Part 2 p. 110

1. was saved
2. was found
3. was hiking
4. reached
5. noticed
6. was setting
7. knew
8. had to hurry
9. said
10. took
11. found
12. was getting
13. looked
14. couldn't see
15. said
16. called
17. came
18. made
19. decided
20. was
21. tried
22. to stay warm
23. heard
24. running
25. stopped
26. started
27. was
28. were hunting
29. called
30. came
31. guided

Practice 2

Part 1 p. 110

1. Washington High School track star Crispin Matthews
2. he
3. Matthews
4. he
5. he
6. it
7. Matthews's ankle
8. The injury
9. Matthews
10. he
11. he
12. he
13. I
14. the doctors
15. he
16. I
17. Well-wishers

Part 2 p. 110

1. will have to sit out
2. recovers
3. says
4. is
5. understands
6. is
7. was injured
8. did not heal
9. required
10. to repair
11. had hoped
12. to join
13. will be
14. says
15. isn't
16. will do
17. tell
18. says
19. want
20. to start running
21. may send

SIGNAL WORDS AND PHRASES

Practice 1 pp. 111–112

1. b, 2. a, 3. a, 4. a, 5. b, 6. b

Practice 2 p. 112

1. in recent years
2. As a result of
3. such as
4. In the past
5. such as
6. At first
7. Furthermore
8. However

PERSONAL PRONOUNS AND POSSESSIVE ADJECTIVES

Practice 1

Part 1 pp. 113–114

A

1. he	9. me
2. he	10. I
3. he	11. it
4. he	12. you
5. him	13. me
6. you	14. I
7. I	15. me
8. you	16. me

B

17. it	19. he
18. I	20. him

C

21. you	32. him
22. I	33. we
23. he	34. he
24. I	35. us
25. him	36. I
26. you	37. you
27. I	38. him
28. it	39. you
29. you	40. him
30. us	41. he
31. him	

D

42. he	43. he

Part 2 p. 114

1. his	6. his
2. his	7. their
3. his	8. her
4. my	9. his
5. its	

Practice 2 pp. 115–116

1. a, 2. b, 3. c, 4. b, 5. a, 6. a, 7. b, 8. b, 9. a, 10. a, 11. a, 12. a

Practice 3 p. 116

1. b, 2. c, 3. a, 4. a, 5. c, 6. c, 7. b, 8. a, 9. b, 10. b, 11. a, 12. b

DEMONSTRATIVE PRONOUNS AND ADJECTIVES

Practice 1 pp. 117–118

1. b, 2. c, 3. a, 4. a, 5. c

Practice 2 p. 118

1 aurora borealis

2 solar wind

3 it hits Earth's magnetic field

4 electrical currents

5 size and appearance

6 auroras that occur at the southernmost tip of Earth

RELATIVE PRONOUNS

Practice 1 pp. 119–120

1. b, 2. a, 3. b, 4. b, 5. a

Practice 2 p. 120

1. television show

2. show

3. massive estate

4. their servants

5. The male head of the house, Lord Grantham

6. the couple

7. reasons

8. a task

9. dresses

10. actors

Vocabulary Building Practice Test

Part 1 p. 121

1. b, 2. c, 3. d, 4. a

Part 2 pp. 121–122

1. b, 2. b, 3. c

Part 3 p. 122

1. b, 2. a, 3. c, 4. d

Part 4 p. 123

1. ance
2. dis
3. un
4. al
5. less
6. ness
7. re
8. in
9. im
10. able

Part 5 pp. 123–124

1. loc, place
2. habit, live
3. mono, one
4. graph, written
5. juven, young
6. duc, lead
7. meter, measure
8. jec, throw
9. port, carry
10. auto, self
11. lat, side
12. dic, say
13. form, shape
14. dent, tooth

Part 6 p. 124

dis-	im-
2, 10	1, 8

in-	il-
11, 15	7, 9

ir-	non-
4, 16	6, 12

mis-	un-
3, 14	5, 13

Part 7 p. 125

1. anti
2. super
3. pre
4. post
5. semi
6. trans

Part 8 p. 125

adjective	joy	noun
adverb	warm	adjective
adjective	remove	verb
noun	locate	verb
adjective	disgust	verb
noun	fond	adjective

Part 9 p. 125

1. creation
2. correspondence
3. manageable
4. wonderful
5. brownish
6. historian

Part 10 p. 126

1. b, 2. a, 3. a, 4. a, 5. a

Part 11 pp. 126–127

1. a, 2. c, 3. a, 4. b, 5. b

Part 12 p. 127

1. c, 2. b, 3. c, 4. c

Part 13 p. 128

1. n. growth or development
2. adj. close together in one area
3. n. placement
4. v. working together
5. n. rules and laws

Part 14 p. 129

1. do, take, have
2. taxi, staff, cake
3. finally, completely, partly

Part 15 pp. 129–130

1. b, 2. c, 3. b, 4. b

Part 16 p. 130

1. b, 2. a, 3. b, 4. a

Part 17 p. 130

1. their
2. they
3. its
4. they
5. they
6. they
7. They
8. it
9. our

Part 18 p. 131

1. b, 2. c, 3. a

Part 19 p. 131

1. b, 2. b, 3. b

READING FASTER

Introduction Practice Questions

INTRODUCTION: PRACTICE QUESTIONS p. 134

1. c, 2. b, 3. b, 4. b, 5. a, 6. b, 7. b, 8. b

Timed Reading Practice

PRACTICE 1 STEVE JOBS: A PORTRAIT OF SUCCESS

Timed Reading 1 p. 137

1. b, 2. c, 3. a, 4. b, 5. a, 6. a, 7. b, 8. c

Timed Reading 2 pp. 139–140

1. b, 2. a, 3. b, 4. b, 5. a, 6. b, 7. a, 8. a

Timed Reading 3 pp. 141–142

1. c, 2. c, 3. a, 4. b, 5. a, 6. b, 7. a, 8. a

PRACTICE 2 WAYS OF LEARNING

Timed Reading 1 pp. 143–144

1. b, 2. b, 3. b, 4. a, 5. c, 6. b, 7. c, 8. c

Timed Reading 2 pp. 145–146

1. b, 2. b, 3. a, 4. a, 5. a, 6. b, 7. c, 8. b

Timed Reading 3 pp. 147–148

1. c, 2. b, 3. b, 4. c, 5. a, 6. a, 7. c, 8. c

PRACTICE 3 LANGUAGES AND CULTURES IN DANGER

Timed Reading 1 pp. 149–150

1. c, 2. a, 3. b, 4. a, 5. b, 6. b, 7. c

Timed Reading 2 pp. 151–152

1. c, 2. a, 3. a, 4. a, 5. b, 6. b, 7. a, 8. b

Timed Reading 3 p. 154

1. c, 2. c, 3. b, 4. c, 5. b, 6. a, 7. a, 8. a

STUDY SKILLS

Choosing Words to Learn

Practice 1 pp. 155–156

Answers will vary.

Practice 2 p. 157

Answers will vary.

Practice 3 p. 158

Answers will vary.

Practice 4 p. 159

Answers will vary.

Storing and Studying New Words

Practice 1 p. 161

Answers will vary.

Practice 2 p. 162

Answers will vary.

Practice 3 p. 164

Answers will vary.

Practice 4 p. 165

Answers will vary.

Practice 5 p. 167

Answers will vary.

Practice 6 p. 168

Answers will vary.

Reading for Study

Practice 1 p. 170

Answers will vary.

Practice 2

Part 1 pp. 170–172

Answers will vary.

Part 2 p. 173

Answers will vary.

Practice 3 p. 174
Answers will vary.

LANGUAGE IN CONTEXT

Practice 1
Part 1 p. 175
1. civilizations
2. army
3. throughout
4. took pride in
5. society
6. factor
7. crime
8. affected
9. agriculture
10. simply

Part 2 p. 176
1. b, 2. a, 3. b, 4. a, 5. b

Part 3 p. 177
1. c, 2. d, 3. a, 4. b, 5. a, 6. c, 7. b, 8. d, 9. c, 10. a

Part 4 p. 178
1. crime
2. affected
3. civilizations
4. agriculture
5. society
6. army
7. take pride in
8. throughout
9. simply
10. factor

Practice 2
Part 1 pp. 178–179
1. noticed
2. confirmed
3. debate
4. doubt
5. status
6. realized
7. planet
8. various

Part 2 pp. 179–180
1. b, 2. b, 3. a, 4. a, 5. b

Part 3 pp. 180–181
1. b, 2. b, 3. a, 4. c, 5. a, 6. c, 7. b, 8. d

Part 4 p. 181
1. debate
2. planet
3. doubt
4. status
5. realized
6. confirm
7. various
8. notice

Practice 3
Part 1 p. 182
1. youth
2. Despite
3. setting
4. renewed
5. occasional
6. courage
7. resolved
8. remain

Part 2 pp. 182–183
1. b, 2. b, 3. a, 4. b, 5. a

Part 3 pp. 183–184
1. c, 2. b, 3. a, 4. d, 5. a, 6. b, 7. b, 8. b

Part 4 p. 184
1. remain
2. renew
3. courage
4. occasional
5. setting
6. youth
7. despite
8. resolved

Practice 4
Part 1 p. 185

I recently took a class in ikebana, the traditional Japanese art of flower arranging. Ikebana is similar to Western-style flower arranging in that both styles use a variety of seasonal flowers and greens arranged in an attractive way. However, they differ in several important ways. First, in ikebana, the act of arranging the flowers should be peaceful and calming. The artist is completely silent while creating the arrangement. It is a time to remember our connection to the natural world and appreciate the beauty around us. For me, practicing ikebana has become a wonderful way to forget about the troubles of daily life. Second, in contrast to crowded Western-style arrangements, which use many types of flowers of different colors and can look "busy," ikebana features open, pleasing designs of mainly stems and leaves and just a few flowers or even none at all. Another important aspect of ikebana is the idea that the individual arranger should express his or her own character or emotions through the arrangement. In this way, the ikebana arrangement is more than flowers in a vase. It is a form of human communication. Although I still love making traditional Western bouquets, ikebana has given me a new way to relax and appreciate the beauty of nature.

Part 2 pp. 185–186

1. a, 2. b, 3. a, 4. a, 5. b

Part 3 pp. 186–187

1. c, 2. b, 3. a, 4. d, 5. a, 6. b, 7. b, 8. a, 9. c, 10. b

Part 4 pp. 187–88

1. attractive

2. mainly

3. traditional

4. In contrast to

5. emotions

6. daily

7. individual

8. character

9. aspect

10. appreciate

Practice 5

Part 1 p. 188

The anthropologist Edward T. Hall first introduced the idea of "high-context" and "low-context" cultures to explain cultural differences in communication. According to Hall, high-context cultures are more common in Eastern countries such as Japan and China, whereas most Western countries are low-context cultures. Of course, communication is important in high-context as well as low-context cultures; it is just the communication style that differs.

According to Hall, both types of culture use nonverbal cues to communicate. However, unlike low-context conversation, high-context conversation involves greater use of nonverbal features such as voice, tone, and gestures. By contrast, people in low-context cultures, such as the United States and Germany, rely more on words to convey meaning. They tend to speak directly, but people from high-context cultures, such as Japan and China, often communicate indirectly.

Conversation is used to begin personal relationships in both high- and low-context cultures. People from high-context cultures share a lot of detailed personal information with friends and coworkers. By contrast, people in low-context cultures generally share only necessary information with smaller, select groups of people.

Part 2 p. 189

1. a, 2. a, 3. a, 4. b, 5. a

Part 3 pp. 190–191

1. c, 2. b, 3. a, 4. d, 5. d, 6. b, 7. b, 8. b

Part 4 p. 191

1. generally

2. involves

3. tend to

4. convey

5. as well as

6. according to

7. relationship

8. unlike

POST-TEST

Part 1 pp. 196–197

1. d, 2. a, 3. b, 4. b

Part 2 pp. 197–198

1. b, 2. c, 3. d, 4. d

Part 3 pp. 198–199

1. b, 2. b, 3. a

Part 4 pp. 199–200

1. b, 2. a, 3. a, 4. b, 5. d

Part 5 pp. 200–201

1. c, 2. c, 3. a

Part 6 pp. 201–202

1. c, 2. a, 3. d

Part 7 p. 202

1. c, 2. b

Part 8 pp. 202–203

1. b, 2. a, 3. b

Part 9 pp. 203–204

1. b, 2. b, 3. b, 4. c

Part 10 p. 204

1. a, 2. b, 3. a, 4. a

Part 11 p. 204

1. Musicians Dick and Ted Nash

Part 12 p. 204

1. were held and questioned

Part 13 pp. 204–205

1. a, 2. b, 3. a

Part 14 p. 205

1. c, 2. b, 3. a, 4. a

Part 15 p. 206

1. c, 2. a, 3. b

Part 16 p. 206

1. b, 2. d, 3. c